DATE DUE

The Amerasia Papers:
Some Problems in the History
of US-China Relations

A publication of the
Center for Chinese Studies
University of California
Berkeley, California 94720

Cover Colophon by Shih-hsiang Chen

Center for Chinese Studies • CHINA RESEARCH MONOGRAPHS

UNIVERSITY OF CALIFORNIA, BERKELEY

/ N U M B E R   S E V E N

The Amerasia Papers: Some Problems in the History of US-China Relations

JOHN S. SERVICE

Although the Center for Chinese Studies is responsible for the selection and acceptance of monographs in this series, responsibility for the opinions expressed in them and for the accuracy of statements contained in them rests with their authors.

Contents

Foreword

Much of what has happened in Far Eastern politics since the end of World War II occurred because of some decisions taken (or, actually, avoided) by the United States Government during the last year of the war. In 1944 the successful Japanese offensives against the unprotected Chinese airfields that had been built on the initiative of Chiang Kai-shek and Claire Chennault had the effect of opening Allied eyes to the internal Chinese political situation. The failure of the Chinese armed forces to defend the airfields made it impossible any longer to deny that the Kuomintang was weak, afflicted with corruption, and divided internally against itself and that the Communists held most of north China. It was discovered that domestic political rivalries far outweighed in importance any further commitment on the part of Chiang or others to prosecute the war against Japan, and, in fact, that all major Chinese factions were preparing for the civil war that was expected to erupt after Japan surrendered. The United States had to reorient its policy to deal with—or at least accommodate itself to—this emerging situation, and it tried a number of things.

It sought first to place all of the various Chinese armed forces under the command of a single officer, General Joseph Stilwell. This failed because Chiang objected, and Stilwell was recalled. Then General Patrick Hurley attempted to mediate between the Nationalists and the Communists in what proved to be a poorly-informed, ill-advised, and unrealistic effort that also quickly failed. Hurley based his peace-making efforts on three more or less explicit assumptions, each of them false: (a) that Chiang Kai-shek was much stronger than the Communists; (b) that the Communists were not really "Communists"; and (c) that it was possible for either the Communists or the Kuomintang (or both) to surrender some of their power over their respective armed forces without at the same time joining in a genuine coalition government. When these mediating efforts collapsed, Hurley, by then the United States Ambassador to China, did two things that compounded the damage. One of them was a mistake; the other was a disgrace. First, he committed the United States to the exclusive support of Chiang Kai-shek as the sole leader of China; and second, he publicly blamed the failure of his mediating initiative on the entire staff of China specialists of the U.S. Foreign Service stationed in China, accusing them of betrayal when what they had actually done was to report accurately to their government why his mediation could not succeed. It was in this particular context that Yalta occurred, Roosevelt died, the war ended—and the Chinese civil war began.

Reflecting on American policy toward China in 1944 and 1945, Barbara Tuchman has recently concluded that "China was a problem for which there was no American solution. The American effort to sustain the status quo could not supply an outworn government with strength and stability or popular support. It could not hold up a husk nor long delay the cyclical passing of the mandate of heaven. In the end China went her own way as if the Americans had never come."* As much as I admire Barbara Tuchman's work, it seems to me that Americans cannot dismiss what happened in China twenty-five years ago as the working of some ineluctable "mandate of heaven." Nor is it true that the Chinese and the Americans went their own ways: instead they fought a war with each other on Korean soil and have remained hostile to each other ever since. There may not have been an American solution, but surely there was a better American policy than the one actually pursued.

Officers of the U.S. Foreign Service who were in China at the time, including the author of this study, recommended such a policy. It would have consisted of trying to prevent civil war in China (for example, by using U.S. influence to modify the Kuomintang's single party dictatorship) or, failing that, of not allowing the United States and the Soviet Union to be drawn into the Chinese civil war as the patrons, respectively, of the Kuomintang and the Communists. Instead, Ambassador Hurley's policies were the ones actually implemented, thereby hastening the civil war (by lifting the pressure on Chiang to reform) and driving the Chinese Communists into a decade-long alliance with Russia because of the United States' alliance with their enemy. One of the many ironies, not to say tragedies, of this history is that Hurley avoided being held responsible for his policies and, instead, managed to convince many Americans that his subordinates—men with several decades of experience in representing the United States in China—were the bunglers. When Senator Joseph McCarthy took up the search for scapegoats, these same members of the Foreign Service were vilified as virtual traitors. How the officers of the Foreign Service, all of them withdrawn from China by Hurley in April of 1945, are supposed to have caused the "loss of China" remains a McCarthyite mystery.

I first met John Service in 1962 when, having retired from the Foreign Service as American Consul at Liverpool, he enrolled at Berkeley to take an advanced degree in political science. Our first encounter came in a course on United States' Far Eastern policy which I, a freshly-minted assistant professor, was then teaching. After I had surveyed in my first lecture the topics to be discussed and had dwelt at some length on General Stilwell's mission to China, Service came up to me after class and in-

---

* *Stilwell and the American Experience in China, 1911–45* (New York: Macmillan, 1971), p. 531.

troduced himself. When I ascertained that he was none other than John S. Service, "our man in Yenan" during 1944 and 1945, I could only mumble, "Pleased to meet you. I think I'll go home and work on my lectures on Stilwell."

Born in 1909 in Chengtu, Szechwan, of missionary parents, John Service entered U.S. Government service in 1933 as a clerk in the consulate in Kunming. Speaking Chinese as virtually his native language, he was assigned successively to posts in Peiping, Shanghai, Chungking, and, in 1943, to the staff of the Commanding General, China-Burma-India Theater of War. As the State Department's liaison officer to the Army, he made two trips to the Communist capital at Yenan in 1944 and 1945. In April of 1945 he was "Hurleyed" out of China, and in June he was arrested as a suspect in the Amerasia case. His arrest was clearly a mistake: the initial Government raid on the offices of *Amerasia* magazine took place on March 11, 1945, and he did not arrive in the United States until April 12, 1945. Service's innocence in this affair was clearly attested by the Grand Jury's 20–0 vote to drop the charges against him. As I reread the Justice Department's account of this sensational incident, reprinted in this monograph, two thoughts came to mind: (1) if the State Department were half as smart as it thinks it is, one of its officers would have warned a man returning after many years in the field that the journalists of *Amerasia* were under investigation by the FBI; and (2) the sharp practices of the Justice Department in this case would themselves appear to have been worth a Congressional investigation. Of course the ultimate importance of the Amerasia case lay in Senator McCarthy's exploitation of it to intimidate some of the highest officials of the United States Government.

After having been cleared by the Grand Jury, John Service returned to work at the State Department, first as part of the State Department's advisory staff to General MacArthur in Tokyo and subsequently as deputy chief of mission in Wellington, New Zealand. On March 14, 1950, Senator McCarthy made his charges against Service in the Senate, and a year and a half later, despite a Congressional investigation clearing him, the State Department fired him. Between 1952 and 1957, Service worked in New York for a steam engineering firm—where he contributed to the invention of an improved steam trap (!)—and simultaneously fought his case to the Supreme Court. In June of 1957 the Court voted unanimously in his favor, and in September he returned to active duty in the State Department. In May 1962 he retired from the Foreign Service.

He did not, however, actually retire. At the University of California, Berkeley, Service obtained an M.A. degree in political science—I remember well his complaining about having to read Aristotle and Aquinas for the first time in thirty years—and went to work at the University's Center for Chinese Studies. At the Center he used his unmatchable knowledge of

China to help make the Center into one of the four or five leading research institutes in the United States committed to the scholarly study of modern China. Not the least of his activities were major efforts to build the Center's library of research materials on Communist China into one of the best in the world.

Throughout the period from 1952 to 1970 Service refrained from injecting his own commentary into the public and scholarly discussion of Chinese politics, despite numerous urgings from students of the Yenan period that he do so. His decision, in 1970, to break his silence will be of considerable importance to historians, although it is unfortunately occasioned by a renewal of the official attacks on him. Perhaps it is possible to find some excuses for the behavior in the early 1950's of certain members of the American Government, Congress, and citizenry toward the officials who served in China during the war. The Cold War was just entering one of its chillier phases, and people were confused and anxious. In searching for explanations for what had happened, Americans reenacted the ancient tragedy of the Persian generals who killed the messengers who brought bad news.

There is no excuse whatsoever for a repetition of these events in 1970. As the *New York Times* noted on February 15, 1970, the publication by the Senate's Internal Security Subcommittee of *The Amerasia Papers: A Clue to the Catastrophe of China* was nothing more than a crude attempt by the remnants of the "China Lobby" within the U.S. Government and on Taiwan to prevent any improvement in Sino-American relations—in this case, by interfering with the just-resuming ambassadorial talks between Washington and Peking at Warsaw. The method chosen for this lobbying—personal defamation—is similar to the campaign of vilification against Professor John K. Fairbank of Harvard that Taiwan has sponsored for the past few years.* The 113-page "Introduction" to the *Amerasia Papers* written by Dr. Anthony Kubek, Professor of History at the University of Dallas, is not simply a piece of disgraceful scholarship. It is so clearly propagandistically motivated that Dr. Kubek was given a "hero's welcome" in Taipei and the personal appreciation of Chiang Kai-shek (*New York Times*, March 31, 1970). The American taxpayers might have some legitimate questions about how the U.S. Senate came to serve as his publisher for this sort of effort.

Nevertheless, as Senator James O. Eastland notes in a foreword to the two-volume *Amerasia Papers*, "The primary importance of this publication probably lies in its value to historians as a basic sourcebook." Leaving aside Kubek's introduction, I am sure that the Senator is correct in that judgment. For many years to come historians will consult these reports of the U.S. Foreign Service, many of which were here published for

---

* cf. Leonard Gordon and Sidney Chang, "John K. Fairbank and His Critics in the Republic of China," *Journal of Asian Studies* XXX:1 (November, 1970), 137–49.

the first time. They constitute what is probably the single most important source in any language on the fateful decade of the 1940's in Chinese politics. The following monograph will be an indispensable guide to these reports, for the historian who wishes to study them, as well as for the student who is merely curious about their unusual title and odd publisher. Needless to point out, the author of this monograph and the author of a majority of the reports from Chungking and Yenan are the same man; and future generations of historians will benefit from both his foresight and his hindsight.

CHALMERS JOHNSON, *Chairman*
Center for Chinese Studies

Berkeley
April 1971

Author's Acknowledgements

My debt is great, and to many people. For willingness to share memories and contribute facts I thank numerous fellow veterans of the China wars, but especially John K. Emmerson, Fulton Freeman, John F. Melby, and Colonel David D. Barrett. For critical reading of the manuscript of Part Two, and the offering of thoughtful suggestions and important corrections, I am deeply grateful to a number of former State Department colleagues with first-hand knowledge of matters here referred to. They include O. Edmund Clubb, John P. Davies, Raymond P. Ludden, Edward E. Rice, Philip D. Sprouse, and John Carter Vincent. I was particularly fortunate in having similar assistance from Professors Chalmers A. Johnson at Berkeley and Lyman P. Van Slyke at Stanford. Reading the manuscript as scholars, rather than participants, their generous and painstaking comments were valuable for their competent objectivity and perspective. I must emphasize, however, that no person mentioned here is likely to agree with all that I have written. The interpretations, conclusions, and errors are my own.

Edgar Snow was kind in allowing me to quote from *Journey to the Beginning*. I am similarly indebted to Professor Tang Tsou and the University of Chicago Press for permission to quote from *America's Failure in China*. Georgianna Stevens allowed me to use the valuable papers of her late husband, Colonel Harley Stevens, a friend while he was OSS representative in Chungking during 1945. Miss Jane Kaneko went far beyond reasonable duty as a patient, cheerful, and expert typist. And, since no author can also satisfactorily be his own editor, the help of Mrs. Jo Pearson was invaluable. Finally, my gratitude to the Center for Chinese Studies at Berkeley is beyond adequate expression. It has made this monograph possible. But more, it has given me an opportunity in retirement of congenial, stimulating employment which, however distantly, has put me back into contact, after a long enforced absence, with the eternally absorbing and important subject of China. Dr. Kubek's criticism of this employment (*Amerasia Papers*, p. 70) is not the first that has failed to intimidate the Center, and the great University of which it is a part.

One additional debt should be noted. Although I dislike the packaging provided by Dr. Kubek and the Internal Security Subcommittee, I am glad to have my own reports now made available to me after twenty-five years. The reader of Part One will note that with official approval I once had a personal set of copies. After these were returned to me by the Department of Justice in 1945, and because my next assignment was to be Japan, I turned them over to the Office of Chinese Affairs. In my hearings in 1950 before the Loyalty Security Board and the Tydings Committee, my counsel and I considered that my best defense against some of the accusations would be the actual texts of my reports. But Chinese Affairs had by that time lost my copies, and it was never possible to reassemble anything like a complete set. Little did we suspect that the "evidence" needed for my defense was there all the time, locked up by the Department of Justice in the form of retained copies of my personal papers, eventually and imaginatively to be released as "a clue to the catastrophe of China."

On the day in December 1951 when every newspaper in Washington headlined my discharge as a Foreign Service Officer on grounds of doubtful loyalty, my wife and I suggested to our two older children in high school that a day or two of absence would be understandable. They declined the suggestion. One went on, not many months later, to be valedictorian of her senior class and recipient of an American Legion citizenship award. The other chose a career in the Foreign Service. All of which says something good about America. This book is for them, and also for the youngest who, having only been born on the day that the Grand Jury dealt favorably with my case, hardly had a chance to hear what it was all about.

PART ONE

The Amerasia Case

I
What Is an "Amerasia Paper?"

In February, 1970, the Internal Security Subcommittee, with the help of Dr. Anthony Kubek as editor, published a massive two-volume compendium entitled *The Amerasia Papers: A Clue to the Catastrophe of China*. The title itself provided a good clue to a hoary theme. Some scholars looking for documentary materials on the Yenan period noted a convenient source. Graduate students here and there, casting about for a topic for term papers or M.A. essays, pricked up their ears. Publicists in Taiwan expressed hopeful opinions running the gamut from "a turning point in history" to "a book of the century." But, on the whole, the book attracted little notice.

Then, on August 21, 1970, the Government Printing Office in its biweekly bulletin *Selected United States Government Publications* featured—for this normally austere and straitlaced sheet—a surprisingly flamboyant and imaginative notice.

THE AMERASIA PAPERS: A CLUE TO THE CATASTROPHE OF CHINA. These documents read like a spy thriller, but is all the more interesting because it is true. They contain hundreds of official documents, many hitherto unpublished, which reflect abundantly the tragic errors in the Far Eastern policy of the United States Government in the closing months of World War II. The story of what happened to China prior to, during, and immediately following World War II is the subject of a number of lengthy historical studies, one of which was the work of the author of these documents. That story, in brief, follows as Part I of this introduction. Part II treats the controversial case of *Amerasia* magazine, or "Case of the Six" as it was called in the newspapers in 1945 when six American citizens were suddenly arrested on charges of conspiring to commit espionage, and Part III presents an analysis of some of the documents, herein published in full text, which were written in 1943–1945 as official dispatches by one of the arrested six, John Stewart Service, then a young career diplomat on station in China.

39N.	Volume I. 1970. [1017] p. il.	
	Y 4.J 89/2:Am 3/v.1	$4.00
40N.	Volume II. 1970. [944] p.	
	Y 4.J 89/2:Am 3/v.2	$3.75

The GPO bulletin obviously has a very wide circulation: it claims 900,000. After its appearance, I began receiving inquires from far and

17

near, friendly and not so friendly. People asked and continue to ask: What is this all about? Is there new material on the case? Why is it being reopened after twenty-five years? It is understandable that questions are directed to me; I am the only person mentioned in the blurb.

SELECTING A TARGET

In this respect (but in very few others), the GPO advertisement is accurate. The book does, indeed, seem to concentrate on me as its main target. As Dr. Kubek puts it:

> His *central role* in *the strange case* of the *purloined Government papers* rests on the integral fact that *Service was the author of so many* of the documents *which turned up in the New York office* of an ardent Communist sympathizer in 1945. The content of these documents may prove, however, to be of even greater importance to the historical record than *the fact that they were stolen,* because herein the fall of China to Communism was anticipated *and espoused.* (Emphasis added.)[1]

Lest it be thought that I am immodestly jumping to conclusions, here—briefly—is what Dr. Kubek has done. He has carefully studied 923 "non-personal" documents turned over to the Subcommittee by the Justice Department. Of these, he has selected 315 ("more than a third") as significant enough to warrant publication. And of these 315, a "hundred-odd" (about a third of the total published) were originally written by me.

> Each has been chosen for at least one special reason—its source, its classification when known, its innate interest of content, or its diplomatic significance. The last reason is, of course, the most important. Among the 315 different documents to be published here, therefore, the hundred-odd items from the pen of John Stewart Service that were recovered in the Amerasia seizures are by far the most vital.[2]

Of course I was not the only officer reporting as an individual from China. There were several Foreign Service Officers attached, as I was, to the Army; others were scattered around the country by the Embassy to observe and report. From the mass of material available, Dr. Kubek has made the following selection:

E. E. Rice	8
E. F. Drumright	7
R. M. Service	5

---

[1] U. S. Senate, Committee on the Judiciary, Senate Internal Security Subcommittee, *The Amerasia Papers: A Clue to the Catastrophe of China* (Washington: Government Printing Office, 1970), p. 70 [hereafter cited as *Papers*].

[2] *Papers,* p. 71.

J. K. Penfield	5
R. S. Ward	5
J. K. Emmerson	3
P. D. Sprouse	2
R. P. Ludden	2
O. E. Clubb	2
J. P. Davies	1
A. R. Ringwalt	1
J. S. Service	101

This comes out to a total of 41 for eleven other experienced and capable Foreign Service reporters in China as against my 101. The Embassy at Chungking was a large and comprehensive reporting organization and certainly the principal source of information on China reaching the Department of State. Only 30 of its reports are included, only 6 from the important Consulate at Kunming, and only 12 documents from the whole State Department. It is preposterous to pretend either that I was that much more prolific or that my reports had that much more "interest of content" and "diplomatic significance." Some of Dr. Kubek's strains in building up my total will be discussed later.

To prepare the reader for the documents he has selected, Dr. Kubek has contributed a 113-page Introduction. This has three parts: a historical survey of Kuomintang-Communist relations, an account of the Amerasia case, and an analysis of the "Amerasia documents" published. The 30-page historical survey reaches John Davies, John Service, *et al.,* on page 22 and thereafter "Kuomintang-Communist relations" are largely ignored. I share the peroration with John Davies:

> . . . the hands at the control levers were those of a few young men on diplomatic duty in China. What John Paton Davies and John Stewart Service were writing in their official reports was of the greatest importance at the time. They were at the scene as expert observers, and their despatches from China contained opinion which was accepted as gospel in the Department of State. The slanted words of the career diplomats released the steam, therefore, to reverse the wheels at this juncture and change the direction of United States policy in the Far East.[3]

John Davies was not, of course, involved in the Amerasia case. So I clearly outshine him in Dr. Kubek's 40-page discussion of the case. In fact, I even outdo Jaffe, who pleaded guilty, and Larsen, who pleaded *nolo contendere.* Twelve pages seem to be devoted wholly to me, and I receive prominent mention on at least eight others.

Dr. Kubek turns next to an analysis of the Amerasia "collection as

---

[3] *Papers,* p. 30.

a whole." He warns his readers that I was not the only source of documents reaching the "mysterious network" of Amerasia.

> While it has been emphasized that the hundred-odd documents from the pen of John Stewart Service comprise the most significant segment of the 315 items published in these volumes, the reader will readily recognize many other documents to be highly important not only because of their source but because of their content as well.[4]

The 214 documents not credited to me are then dealt with in 5 pages, in which only 17 documents are specifically mentioned. By contrast, Dr. Kubek devotes 26 pages to my reports, with specific mention of 68 of them.

Actually, the point need not be made statistically: Dr. Kubek himself is quite direct—and insistent.

> . . . the one whose importance to these volumes is paramount. This person was John Stewart Service.[5]

> . . . the hundred-odd items from the pen of John Stewart Service . . . are by far the most vital.[6]

> . . . the hundred-odd documents from the pen of John Stewart Service comprise the most significant segment. . . .[7]

> His fifty-odd reports from the Communist base . . . are by far the most important documents in these volumes.[8]

For the busy reader, who has no time to wade through an unavoidably rather lengthy discussion, let me say, therefore, that there is in fact nothing new in this ponderous effort of Dr. Kubek and the Internal Security Subcommittee—except that my peripheral involvement in the Amerasia case has, after a lapse of twenty-five years, been miraculously metamorphosed into the "central role."

STOLEN PAPERS?

My "central role" in the Amerasia case, Dr. Kubek says, rests on "the integral fact" that I was the author of "so many" of the "purloined Government papers" seized in the possession of Amerasia. Dr. Kubek lays a foundation by insistently drumming into the head of his reader three points:

   a) that all the documents which he discusses and which are published in *The Amerasia Papers* were found by the FBI in the offices of Amerasia magazine;

---

[4] *Papers*, p. 74.
[5] *Ibid.*, p. 36.
[6] *Ibid.*, p. 71.
[7] *Ibid.*, p. 74.
[8] *Ibid.*, p. 86.

b) that they were all official government documents which had been stolen from the United States government; and

c) that a very large number—"a hundred-odd"—of these "pilfered . . . classified U.S. Government documents" were drafted by me.

Thus one reads:

> Dr. Kubek has examined some 1,700 Government documents seized on June 6, 1945, by the Federal Bureau of Investigation from the office of Amerasia.[9]

> More than 300 of these stolen wartime documents will be found in full text in the pages which follow.[10]

> Since all the documents published herein were recovered by the FBI at the time of the spectacular arrest, these volumes are entitled *The Amerasia Papers*.[11]

> In March of 1945—special agents of the Office of Strategic Services made a midnight raid on the headquarters of the little magazine. Here . . . were literally hundreds of classified U.S. Government documents . . . almost a hundred bore the signature of John Stewart Service . . . .[12]

> . . . the fact that they were stolen.[13]

> The preceding parts of the Introduction are to be regarded, therefore, as background for the reader's personal study of the recovered Amerasia papers themselves.[14]

> . . . the hundred-odd items from the pen of John Stewart Service that were recovered in the Amerasia seizures.[15]

> . . . the rich variety of materials that Amerasia editors received during World War II from their secret sources within the Federal Government.[16]

> In no way, of course, does the date of a document indicate just when the Amerasia people first saw it, but it may properly be assumed that the earliest were perhaps among the first to be pilfered.[17]

> The next documents from the pen of John Stewart Service to turn up in the Amerasia collection were his field reports . . . .[18]

---

[9] *Papers*, p. iii.
[10] *Ibid.*
[11] *Ibid.*, p. 2.
[12] *Ibid.*, p. 30.
[13] *Ibid.*, p. 70.
[14] *Ibid.*
[15] *Ibid.*, p. 71.
[16] *Ibid.*, p. 73.
[17] *Ibid.*
[18] *Ibid.*, p. 86.

Classification refers to the classification noted at the time the document was obtained from the Amerasia offices . . . .[19]

Dr. Kubek recognizes that in the case of one document, No. 315, he has a problem.

> Since Service was making comment here on an article appearing in the *New York Times* the day before, his memorandum could hardly have been either misdated or post-dated. It is possible, therefore, that this document was never in the actual possession of Amerasia, and that it ended up in the Department of Justice simply because it was among the papers confiscated by the FBI from Service's desk at the State Department at the time of his arrest.[20]

Only "skeptics," he goes on, could wish to consider that this might be the case with more than this single document. But to confuse even the skeptics, he concludes that it is "not really important . . . exactly how many documents Service passed—or how many documents comprised the total which Jaffe received from his network of sources" (which is hardly the point Dr. Kubek started out to discuss).

It so happens that the actual number of my reports of which copies were found in Amerasia has been no mystery since July, 1950. That is when the Tydings Subcommittee (of the Senate Foreign Relations Committee) published the entire transcript of my lengthy hearings before the Department of State Loyalty Security Board.[21] The actual number—a matter of public record for twenty years—was 41. Not "one hundred-odd."

While I am on the subject, testimony before the Loyalty Security Board, and in the Tydings Subcommittee hearings, established a number of facts about these reports:

a) None of them was in a form that could have come from me.

b) A number of them showed the fingerprints or bore the handwriting of E. S. Larsen—who was indicted and eventually pleaded *nolo contendere.*

c) All of the documents had been routed to the section in the State Department where Larsen was working.

d) Larsen had admitted giving some of the reports to Jaffe, and was an inconsistent and changeable witness regarding others—even concerning documents which he was known to have given to Jaffe.

---

[19] *Ibid.,* p. 115.

[20] *Papers,* p. 112.

[21] U. S. Senate, Committee on Foreign Relations, *State Department Employee Loyalty Investigation* [Hearings before a subcommittee of the Committee on Foreign Relations pursuant to S. Res. 231] (Washington: Government Printing Office, 1950), 2 volumes, 2509 pages [hereafter cited as *Tydings Transcript*]. My hearings before the State Department board are printed in Part 2, Appendix, pp. 1958–2509.

Dr. Kubek notes (correctly) that by official, "routine" approval of the U.S. Army headquarters in Chungking (for whom the reports were written), I had in my possession personal copies of the memoranda I had prepared during the Yenan period. He fails to note that I had also personally acquired and collected what was, at that time in the United States, probably a unique collection of recent research materials dealing with the Chinese Communist movement: publications, reports, speeches, notes of interviews, et cetera. There was, of course, nothing secret or improper about this attempt to find out all I could about the Chinese Communists: it had been my principal assigned official duty for a long time. All of these research materials were kept with the personal copies of my memoranda in my desk at the State Department. After my arrest, the entire contents of my desk — personal copies of memoranda, research materials, personal correspondence, address books, memos to myself—were taken by the FBI. It was not long, however, before the Department of Justice conceded that none of these materials were government property or taken from official files, and that they were all my personal and private papers. Accordingly, the Department of Justice very punctiliously returned them all to me—personally.

Fortunately, the Department of Justice was courteous enough to provide a list of these personal papers that were taken and then returned. Furthermore, so that I could be interrogated on them, the Loyalty Security Board provided a list of my reports of which copies were actually found in Amerasia. When these two lists are compared with Dr. Kubek's so-called "Amerasia papers," some quite interesting facts become apparent.

Sixty-nine of the documents which he selects to print were never anywhere near Amerasia. They are purely and simply (if those are the right words) lifted from my personal papers. The Department of Justice may have been proper and punctilious about returning the originals to me, but it appears that somebody thought it might come in handy to keep copies.

At one point in his Introduction, Dr. Kubek claims that the editors of Amerasia had obtained:

> . . . many translations of basic doctrinary pronouncements of the Chinese Communists. . . . In other words, the Amerasia editors were receiving grist of every sort, size, and texture for the mill they were operating in New York.[22]

This is a wonderfully graphic picture. Apparently to help drive home the point, Dr. Kubek prints a total of fifteen of these "doctrinary pronouncements"—which turn out mainly to be wartime writings by Mao Tse-tung and Liu Shao-ch'i. But it happens that all fifteen are among the sixty-nine documents just mentioned that were never near Amerasia. They all

---

[22] *Papers*, pp. 71–72.

come from my personal papers—in this case my research collection.

Some questions are suggested. Dr. Kubek tells us repeatedly that he is concerned with stolen government documents, of diplomatic and security significance. What, then, are these papers doing in here? Mao Tse-tung's well-known "Investigation of the Rural Village" and Liu Shao-ch'i's old standby "On Self-Cultivation" are not classified, not stolen, not U.S. government documents, and not reports of diplomatic significance. Even if they had been found in Amerasia (which in this case they were not), so what? Amerasia was a specialist magazine in Far Eastern affairs with a particular interest in China. What scholar of modern China would not be expected to have in his library these basic materials, and others such as Mao's *Selected Works*. Does not Dr. Kubek, himself, have these publications in his possession or readily available? It is hard, therefore, to see any reason for their inclusion here except to provide a suggestively prejudicial stage-setting. The reader apparently is intended to visualize a Communist magazine busily collecting Communist publications from a mysterious network of "pro-Communist" conspirators within the government. I suggest that the only thing mysterious here is the naiveté of Dr. Kubek, or his expectations of gullibility on the part of his audience.

I come next to a group of thirty-one documents among those selected by Dr. Kubek. As printed, all thirty-one are from my personal papers. But the material contained in each of them, though in somewhat different form, actually was found in the Amerasia office. The interesting question, of course, is the reason for this seemingly illogical choice. Why use a copy of a report from my personal file, when another copy of the same report was available from what may legitimately be called "Amerasia papers"? I have some thoughts on this, but they come more logically at a later point.

And then, finally, Dr. Kubek has printed fifteen of my reports which do *not* come from my own personal papers. These actually did come from among the "Amerasia papers."

To summarize, among the 315 documents published in *The Amerasia Papers,* a total of at least 115 are tied to me by authorship or were a part of my personal research collection. Of these 115 documents, 69 were from my personal papers and were not in Amerasia in any form; 31 were my personal copies although the same material was in Amerasia in a different form; 15 were from Amerasia. Thus, 100 documents as printed are from my personal papers. This makes Dr. Kubek's dismissal of "skeptics" seem perhaps a bit disingenuous—since the skeptics clearly win by a score of 100 to 15. Nor do I find it possible to agree with Dr. Kubek that the matter "is not really important."

DIPLOMATIC SIGNIFICANCE?

One thing that obviously is of importance to Dr. Kubek is to build up the number of my reports. This makes it difficult for him to adhere to his own standards for selection:

> Each [document published] has been chosen for at least one special reason—its source, its classification when known, its innate interest of content, or its diplomatic significance. The last reason is, of course, the most significant.[23]

So far as reports by me were concerned, diplomatic significance apparently included:

a request for travel orders,

an incomplete and abandoned draft of a memorandum,

very brief, sketchy outlines of contemplated but never written memoranda (5) [How did unwritten memoranda help to accomplish "the fall of China"?],

brief, routine transmission of texts of news broadcasts (3),

similar routine transmission of newspapers (at least 3).

Strangely, my systematic collection and forwarding of Yenan newspapers seems to have been one thing that particularly upsets Dr. Kubek:

> Service employed every device in the arsenal of propaganda . . . . One of his favorite methods was to deliver voluminous materials from the Yenan daily newspaper, the *Chieh Fang Jih Pao* . . . .[24]

The research and informational value of this type of material hardly needs emphasis to scholars. Personally, I was rather pleased with being able to obtain and forward the complete back file of this important and hitherto unavailable Party newspaper. And, as I pointed out in my first transmitting memorandum: "The *Chieh Fang Jih Pao* is probably of greatest value because it *is* a publicity and propaganda organ of the Communist Party." [25]

Indeed, it appears (with one exception) that every single piece of paper written by me, or attributable to me, that could be found either in Amerasia or among my personal papers, has been selected by Dr. Kubek for inclusion as an important and diplomatically significant document. If one could accept this evaluation with a straight face, it would seem that no field reporter has ever before had such a high batting average. It is an accolade which, under the circumstances, I decline.

The solitary exception—the only memorandum *not* selected by Dr. Kubek—was my memorandum No. 5, written from Chungking in Feb-

---

[23] *Papers*, p. 71.

[24] *Papers*, p. 98.

[25] *Papers*, p. 738; emphasis in the original.

ruary, 1945, entitled "Chinese Feelers Regarding Formosa." It reported the concern of some responsible non-Communist Chinese in Chungking that the National Government was not adequately prepared to take over the administration of Formosa (Taiwan) immediately after the Japanese surrender. In view of the record of events in Taiwan during the first two years of Nationalist administration, one wonders why this report was not considered to have some interest of content and diplomatic significance.[26]

One way that my total is increased is by duplicate printing of two of my memoranda. In each case, the basic memorandum (from my personal papers) is printed alone. Then it is reprinted as an enclosure to a transmitting Army report (from Amerasia). It seems reasonable to assume, however, that anything so bizarre is more likely to be the result of editorial oversight than conscious intent.

There is another way in which the total is given the appearance of being increased. Here is an example out of a group. In the *bona fide* "Amerasia papers" there was a copy of an Embassy despatch which transmitted and commented on a memorandum which I had prepared at Yenan. Among the personal papers from my desk, there was my file copy of that memorandum. For reasons not apparent, Dr. Kubek first prints the memorandum from my personal file and then, at a considerably later point, the transmitting Embassy despatch from Amerasia. Since the headings for both documents make prominent mention of "report from John S. Service," the unwary reader can hardly be blamed for feeling inundated by Service reports. But at least the editor does not—as in the paragraph above—reprint the memorandum itself for a second time.

To summarize, I have mentioned that Dr. Kubek lays a foundation for his allegation of my centrality in the Amerasia case by three much-repeated assertions: (1) that he is offering his readers only documents found in Amerasia; (2) that they were all documents stolen from the U.S. government; and (3) that a hundred-odd of these stolen official documents were drafted by me. It is now amply clear that the first assertion is false: so far as documents related to me are concerned, the overwhelming majority were never anywhere near Amerasia. The second assertion is likewise false: most of the papers he is talking about were not official documents, were never in any official file, and were not stolen— they were, in fact, my personal papers. Not much is left, by this point, of his third allegation. Dr. Kubek does indeed, by some remarkable exertions, put together one hundred pieces of paper originally drafted

[26] U. S. Department of State, *United States Relations with China with Special Reference to the Period 1944–1949* [*The China White Paper*] (Washington: Government Printing Office, 1949; reprinted with introduction by Lyman P. Van Slyke and index, Stanford University Press, 1967), pp. 307–310 and 923–938. For a more comprehensive treatment, see George H. Kerr, *Formosa Betrayed* (Boston: Houghton, Mifflin, 1965), *passim*.

by me; but the majority, being nothing more than my personal papers, were never in Amerasia and thus have no relation to the Amerasia case.

One would like to be able to conclude that Dr. Kubek had made a simple mistake in treating my personal papers and research materials as having been seized in the Amerasia office. But Dr. Kubek obviously knows the record; and he could hardly be that simple. The elaborate manner in which he has prepared and repeated these allegations makes it clear, instead, that *The Amerasia Papers* is a systematic attempt at fraudulent deception of the reader.

II
What Was the Amerasia Case?

One might leave the matter by noting that "the Amerasia Papers" do not contain many Amerasia papers—but Dr. Kubek does not. To buttress his allegation that I played a central role in the Amerasia case, he goes beyond the "these-are-all-stolen-government-documents" ploy in several important ways:

a) doubt is cast on the number of memoranda which I loaned to Jaffe;

b) it is then suggested that "many" documents were "delivered" by me to Jaffe; and finally,

c) the record is ignored and distorted to suggest non-existent mystery and official laxity in the prosecution of the case.

I have, of course, always acknowledged that I permitted Jaffe to read and to retain for a time in his possession eight to ten of my personal copies of descriptive reportorial memoranda which I had written in China.

> . . . I went through my personal copies of my Yenan memoranda and selected several—I think about 8 or 10—which were purely descriptive and did not contain discussion of American military or political policy. These I considered it would be appropriate to allow Jaffe, as a writer on China, to see . . .
>
> These personal copies I refer to, and from among which I allowed Jaffe to see selected ones of a descriptive nonpolicy nature, were some of my file copies of memoranda which I had written in China over my own signature, recording my own observations and conversations as a reporter. They did not represent, nor purport to represent, the views of the Embassy, the Army, or the Department of State. They bore only the unofficial classification which I placed on them when I wrote them, a classification which by this time was of no significance since the information contained in them had been extensively reported by American newspaper correspondents who had visited the Communist areas. They were not removed from any official files; they had never been in official files.
>
> It was not unusual to allow writers to have access to this type of factual material for background purposes, since reading the material or taking notes on it was always more satisfactory from the viewpoint of accuracy than merely relying on one's memory and oral recitation.[1]

---

[1] *Tydings Transcript*, pp. 1272–73. From my testimony before the Tydings Committee on June 22, 1950.

As already noted, I had official permission to retain these personal copies, and kept them in my desk at the State Department. They bore no official classification, were never part of the State Department or any other government files, and lending them to a journalist was not a violation of law (though admittedly—particularly with the benefit of hindsight—unwise and indiscreet). Furthermore, the papers were loaned: not "supplied," "delivered," or "passed." They were all returned by Jaffe to me, and no reproductions or copies were found in Amerasia. The record is more than amply clear on these points.

> Mr. HITCHCOCK. The personal copies which Service admitted lending to Jaffe never were part of the State Department files.[2]
>
> Senator TYDINGS. Now, if Service had given Jaffe his own personal copies, would he have violated any injunction of secrecy as to State Department documents?
> Mr. HITCHCOCK. To my knowledge he would have violated no law whatsoever or injunction the State Department may have had with reference to Service's personal copy . . . .[3]

> All documents found in his desk at the State Department were carbons of his reports which he [Service] was entitled to keep. As Mr. Service suggests, it is not logical that he should take official copies of his reports, that had become Government property, when he had carbon copies that he could freely lend without violating any law.[4]

> While not condoning it, we recognize that it was an accepted practice for State Department officials to impart some types of classified information to writers in order to give them background information for their articles. John S. Service was in an unusual position in China and, in accordance with General Stilwell's wishes, he maintained relations with the representatives in China of the American press in order to brief them on political and quasi-military developments in the China theater. He appears to have been allowed a greater freedom in contacts with the press than would an officer in a similar position in Washington. It should also be emphasized that both Mark Gayn and Philip Jaffe were considered reputable newsmen and writers by the public in the spring of 1945 when Service first met them.[5]

---

[2] *Tydings Transcript*, p. 1008. Mr. Robert M. Hitchcock was special assistant to the Attorney General in 1945 and in direct charge of the prosecution of the Amerasia case. The quotation is from his testimony before the Tydings Committee on May 26, 1950.

[3] *Ibid.*, p. 1007.

[4] U. S. Senate, Committee on Foreign Relations, *State Department Employee Loyalty Investigation* [Report of the Committee on Foreign Relations Pursuant to S. Res. 231] (Washington: Government Printing Office, 1950) 81st Cong. 2d sess. Report No. 2108, p. 93 [hereafter cited as *Tydings Report*].

[5] *Tydings Report*, p. 93.

Dr. Kubek, however, has it somewhat differently:

> According to a statement by Service in 1957 to the State Department security officer Otto Otepka, he passed only eighteen documents; and in his testimony E. S. Larsen admitted having shown to Jaffe some documents written by Service. It cannot be stated with certainty, therefore, exactly how many documents Service passed—or how many documents comprised the total which Jaffe received from his network of sources. The actual numbers, in both cases, are disputable and not really important.[6]

It is quite clear, I think, that to Dr. Kubek the actual number of documents that I "passed" to Jaffe is not really important. As I shall note presently, his next charge literally depends on this uncertainty.

A few points. I made no statement to Mr. Otepka, so far as I can remember, in 1957. I believe my first meeting with him was in the autumn of 1958 when I went through a lengthy "interrogation" (by a panel of three officers, not two as Dr. Kubek says) as a step toward my eventual security clearance.[7] This went on for more days and sessions than I can recall. Unfortunately, though a stenographer was present and busy, I have no transcript: the Federal loyalty security program had long since evolved beyond the stage of allowing the person most concerned to receive transcripts in proceedings such as this. I repeated my best recollection that the number of personal copies of my memoranda involved was eight to ten. It was then intimated (as it had been in even more vague terms in some of my previous hearings) that someone was supposed to have been heard to say to someone else that the number was eighteen. The implication—never made clear—was that this was a wiretap of a phone conversation between Jaffe and another person involved in the Amerasia case. There was never any identification of persons, never a recording, transcript, text, or even clear statement of just what was said. I could only reply that I believed (as I still do) that the number was eight to ten; but that since my recollection was not absolute, it would be difficult for me to prove otherwise if clear and positive evidence was presented that the number was eighteen. The panel made no attempt to present such evidence, and I have never seen or heard anything that could be considered evidence to show that my memory is incorrect. The panel was interrogating me, it might be noted, more than thirteen years after the event—which is now more than twenty-five years away. I should also mention here that it is likewise untrue that "Service told Otepka that his only motive in passing the papers to Jaffe was to discredit Ambassador Hurley."[8] I had no such motive; but even if I had, it is hard to see how

---

[6] *Papers*, p. 112.

[7] *Papers*, p. 67.

[8] *Papers*, p. 112, n. 252.

it would have been furthered by any such action—since none of the memoranda mentioned Hurley or dealt with his attempts to bring the Communists into a coalition government.

A Presumption of Guilt

Dr. Kubek is not really interested, however, in any such relatively modest number as eighteen. He is ready to go far beyond it.

> Because evidence to the contrary is lacking, it may be assumed that many of Service's documents found at Amerasia were delivered by Service himself in these few meetings with Jaffe and his associates.[9]

I understand that Dr. Kubek is not a lawyer: nor am I. Nonetheless, I find it rather startling to be told that if I cannot present complete and incontrovertible proof of innocence, then I am guilty. Innocence is not always easy to prove—though I have always thought that there was ample direct evidence in my own case. But if someone else is found to have done what you are accused of, is that not to be considered "evidence to the contrary?" The record, as in other aspects of the much investigated Amerasia case, is copious. A few examples:

> Senator TYDINGS. Let me ask you this: Was there any evidence gathered by the FBI that came to your knowledge that showed that Service was connected in any manner, shape, or form with the taking of documents from the State Department other than we have had described here in your memorandum?
> Mr. HITCHCOCK. No sir; other than the clearly identified eight State Department ozalid copies which were found in Jaffe's brief case which I assumed, up until the time Larsen had admitted giving them to Jaffe, might well have come from Service.
> Senator TYDINGS. Was he ever detected passing any document to anybody connected with this case or anybody on the outside?
> Mr. HITCHCOCK. No, sir, not to the best of my recollection.[10]
>
> Mr. HITCHCOCK. From my recollection—and I think it is pretty good on that point—Larsen was in a position to supply them.
> Mr. MORGAN. Any of the documents in the case?
> Mr. HITCHCOCK. Well, now as I said earlier this morning, my recollection is that virtually all of these documents, even those that had not originated from State, had been routed to State. Now all of these, from anything I know to the contrary, had to come from Larsen.[11]
>
> Mr. MORGAN. Is it proper to say, therefore, that from your handling of the situation, you were adequately satisfied on the basis

[9] *Papers*, p. 111.
[10] *Tydings Transcript*, p. 1008.
[11] *Tydings Transcript*, p. 1034.

of the documents and other Government material you had available to you, that the subjects who were being considered for prosecutive action were those who had a hand in obtaining these documents? Mr. HITCHCOCK. Yes; in this sense; that there was nobody else. Now, what I mean by that is—I am not trying to quibble. Larsen is the only person that I could ever attribute from the evidence submitted to us as having been able to do this, with the exception of Roth.[12]

In the first chapter, I mentioned a group of thirty-one documents printed by Dr. Kubek, where he had selected a copy from my personal papers although, in each case, the same basic material was among the documents actually found in Amerasia. This sort of thing might be regarded as an accident if it had happened once or twice; it cannot be an accident when, as here, it is done consistently. What, then, can be the explanation for this seemingly illogical choice?

Most of the copies of my reports that were in the possession of Amerasia had been forwarded to Washington under cover of Embassy despatches, Army or other official reports, or were ozalid copies prepared in—and hence clearly the property of—the State Department. As the record makes very clear, these various types of material were never available to me (since I never prepared the transmitting despatch or report). They were generally unknown to me, and were never in my possession. On the other hand, if it is alleged—as Dr. Kubek does repeatedly—that Amerasia had in its possession, not Embassy despatches, but my own file copies—which Dr. Kubek points out I had permission to retain—then the reader will be much more ready to believe Dr. Kubek when he "assumes" that "many of Service's documents found at Amerasia were delivered by Service himself. . . ."

An example may make this more clear. Document No. 275 is my report No. 13 from Yenan, dated March 15, 1945, giving a factual summary of "Chinese Communist Views in Regard to Sinkiang." The copy of this report which was actually in the possession of Amerasia was an ozalid facsimile reproduction of the signed original. It carried on its face State Department distribution symbols which linked it to the office in which E. S. Larsen worked. It was, in fact, one of the documents which Larsen had admitted giving to Jaffe. The personal copy of this report which was in my desk was a typed carbon copy. It could not have been very sharp and distinct, since it was the fourth copy, made on a small Hermes portable typewriter, at night in a cave in Yenan. But it carried my handwritten initials above my typed name on the last page. In the Foreign Service in those days (and perhaps also today), the drafter might sign the original but, of the duplicates, he initialed only the file copy.

---

[12] *Tydings Transcript,* p. 1035.

When we turn to Document No. 275 itself,[13] it will be seen from a thoughtfully added footnote that: "This is a carbon copy, but the initials JS are written above the typed signature." There is, therefore, no question whatever about the source of the document that Dr. Kubek has selected to print. Despite the facts that the copy actually in Amerasia was clearer and more legible, and carried markings which identified it indisputably as being government property, he has preferred the copy from my personal papers—which was never near Amerasia. The reader, particularly if he knows anything about State Department procedures, will naturally assume that Amerasia, where he is erroneously told it was found, could only have gotten this copy from me directly.

A STRANGE CASE?

Finally, Dr. Kubek persistently suggests that there was some mystery about the Amerasia case, and that it was mishandled and covered up.

> . . . reads like a spy thriller, but is all the more interesting because it is true.[14]

> . . . one of the strangest tales in recent American history.[15]

> The strange case of Amerasia, like many a fictional spy thriller . . .[16]

> . . . the strange circumstances. . . .[17]

> . . . perhaps the most bizarre of all its peculiar features.[18]

> . . . strange "arrangement" . . . a final peculiar piece of business. . . .[19]

> . . . strange case of the purloined Government papers. . . .[20]

> . . . secret sources within the Federal Government.[21]

> . . . through their mysterious network. . . .[22]

> . . . Service's role in the whole strange affair.[23]

---

[13] *Papers*, p. 1409.
[14] *Ibid*, p. iii.
[15] *Ibid.*, p. 30.
[16] *Ibid.*, p. 31.
[17] *Ibid.*, p. 35.
[18] *Ibid.*, p. 49.
[19] *Ibid.*, p. 51.
[20] *Ibid.*, p. 70.
[21] *Ibid.*, p. 73.
[22] *Ibid.*, p. 74.
[23] *Ibid.*, p. 111.

In no real sense was the Amerasia case tried; it was merely heard.[24]

. . . the annals of American jurisprudence contain few examples of misused legalism as shocking as this one.[25]

. . . the curtain was quietly drawn on the spectacular case of the purloined documents.[26]

Why, indeed, did the Criminal Division of the Department of Justice handle the whole case of Amerasia in so timid and apologetic a manner . . .?[27]

. . . the hitherto all-but-forgotten "Case of the Six" which had been so effectively buried. . . .[28]

Had the Amerasia case been prosecuted honestly and vigorously, as some had hoped . . . .[29]

One surprising aspect of this labored attempt to suggest dark mysteries, both in the background of the case itself and in the way in which it was prosecuted, is that Dr. Kubek is unable to offer any new facts whatsoever about the case that are not to be found in the transcript and report of the Tydings Committee. That transcript included testimony from the FBI and Department of Justice officials in charge of investigating and prosecuting the case. It also contained the report of the 1946 investigation by the Hobbs Committee of the House Committee on the Judiciary, the presentment of the New York grand jury in 1950, testimony by E. S. Larsen, and the full transcript of my own hearings before the State Department Loyalty Security Board as well as my testimony in three days of hearings before the Committee itself.

If there ever was a case which has been thoroughly investigated, and of which the full record has been opened to public scrutiny, it must be the Amerasia case. Unfortunately, the Tydings Committee finished its work twenty years ago, and its transcript and report total some 2,850 pages. From a record of this size (though the Tydings transcript is not entirely taken up with the Amerasia case), Dr. Kubek has been what can only charitably be described as "highly selective." It may be helpful to the reader, therefore, to insert here a factual summary of the case. This was prepared in 1950 by the Department of Justice for the Tydings Committee which, after its long investigation, concluded:

---

[24] *Ibid.*, p. 51.
[25] *Ibid.*, p. 52.
[26] *Ibid.*, p. 55.
[27] *Ibid.*, p. 59.
[28] *Ibid.*, p. 62.
[29] *Ibid.*, p. 113.

The facts set forth in the ensuing memorandum of the Department of Justice are in all respects consistent and in accord with the facts and evidence adduced before this subcommittee.[30]

* * * * *

MEMORANDUM OF THE DEPARTMENT OF JUSTICE ON THE AMERASIA CASE

INTRODUCTION

This report is a summary of the events relating to the prosecution in the Amerasia case. In addition to the salient facts, it sets forth the various prosecution problems encountered and the reasons for the decisions made at the various stages of the litigation. The legal conclusions expressed are documented by an analysis of the pertinent Supreme Court decisions, which is attached to this report as an appendix.

THE BACKGROUND OF THE CASE

"Amerasia" was a bimonthly magazine owned, edited, and published by Philip J. Jaffe in New York City. Kate Mitchell was an associate editor. The publication, in existence for some 8 years, had a small circulation, less than 2,000, and was devoted exclusively to political and economic matters in the Far East. Both its editorial position and the contents of its articles projected the pro-Communist viewpoint. Its chief appeal was to persons interested in a specialized study of pan-Pacific problems, events, and developments.

Since many avenues of communication between the Far East and the United States were closed during the war, persons interested in political, economic, and other developments in the Pacific area were cut off from the usual sources of public information and were largely dependent on information obtained through governmental sources, legally or illegally. Data of the character required could be obtained from censored dispatches, departmental releases and press relations offices, from on-the-record and off-the-record interviews with governmental officials, from monitored broadcasts, and from the Office of War Information. It appeared that classified documents were shown to writers and others for "background" purposes with the understanding that the article, story, etc. subsequently written would be submitted to censorship authorities. And, of course, in this case data of this character were also obtained by acquiring unauthorized access to actual Government documents and reports.

The Amerasia case investigation was commenced as a result of an instance in the latter category where the contents of a Government document, not authorized for publication, were found in an issue of the magazine Amerasia. An article, "The Case of Thailand," prepared by OSS, was reprinted in almost verbatim form at page 23 of the January 26, 1945, issue of Amerasia.

The Thailand article dated December 11, 1944, was part of a classified OSS document and in general pointed out the major differences of British and American viewpoints on Thailand, commenting

---

[30] *Tydings Report*, p. 122.

upon that country's political future. The document was a standard OSS report published periodically every 2 weeks. These reports were made up primarily for the use of OSS and State Department employees.

THE INITIAL SEARCH AND SEIZURE BY OSS

In February 1945 an official of the Office of Strategic Services, in examining the foregoing issue of the magazine Amerasia, noticed the Thailand article.

Since the unauthorized publication of the contents of a classified document would have been a violation of security regulations, the OSS official turned the document, together with the Amerasia article, over to Mr. Archibald Van Beuren, security officer of OSS, who, in turn, on February 28, 1945, took them to Mr. Frank B. Bielaski, Director of Investigation, OSS, in New York, N.Y. Mr. Bielaski was requested by Mr. Van Beuren to place under surveillance every person in Washington who had access to the document in an effort to determine who was supplying secret information to the editors of the Amerasia magazine. When Bielaski was informed that numerous persons had access to the document, he decided against surveillance of these individuals, and on his own initiative decided that the way to get the facts concerning the matter would be to go directly to the office of the Amerasia magazine.

The OSS approached the matter as being solely one of counter-security within that agency. It overlooked or disregarded the fact that there might be involved possible violations of Federal criminal laws and that they had no investigative jurisdiction whatever in respect to criminal offenses. Consequently, the OSS at this point should have referred the entire matter to the FBI, which has primary investigative jurisdiction of espionage cases and unlawful removal or concealment of Government documents.

Acting without the knowledge or approval of the Department of Justice, Bielaski proceeded to the office of the Amerasia magazine at 225 Fifth Avenue, New York City, and by subterfuge and without the knowledge or consent of Philip J. Jaffe, the sole owner and publisher of the Amerasia magazine, secured admission to the Amerasia premises around midnight on Sunday, March 11, 1945. For about 2½ hours thereafter Bielaski and 5 assistants thoroughly searched all the papers, records, and documents on the premises and, after examining in the neighborhood of 300 documents, Bielaski decided to take 20 or more of the documents to Washington as proof. After taking these documents, Bielaski and his assistants then replaced all the other documents so that there would be no evidence of their illegal search and seizure.

THE FBI INVESTIGATION

Immediately after this search and seizure of the documents in the premises of Amerasia, Bielaski came to Washington bringing with him the documents seized and reported to General Donovan, head of the OSS. Thereafter, the documents were shown to the Secretary of State. The latter immediately requested that future investigations be conducted by the Federal Bureau of Investigation and the documents were turned over to the Bureau at that time. With this information the Bureau immediately inaugurated an intensive and full-scale investigation beginning in the middle of March and continuing until after the arrests on June 6, 1945.

It is, therefore, clear the illegal search of the Amerasia premises and the illegal seizure of the documents by the OSS agents constituted the basic information which started the FBI investigation in motion. Until the FBI received these documents in March 1945 it had no knowledge of the activities of the OSS agents and was not then conducting an independent investigation of this matter.

The investigation launched by the FBI, consisting largely of continuous physical surveillance, established that Jaffe, in the spring of 1945, made several trips to Washington on which he contacted Emmanuel S. Larsen, a China specialist, employed by the State Department. Jaffe also contacted Andrew Roth, an ONI lieutenant who was a Far East specialist and a one-time employee of Amerasia. John S. Service, a State Department Foreign Service employee on duty in China, returned to the United States on about April 15, 1945, and was observed in the company of Jaffe on several occasions between that time and the time of his arrest on June 6, 1945. On some occasions, these persons were observed studying papers together or passing papers to each other, but since both Jaffe and Roth were writing books at the time and all of the persons were interested in a common subject, no significant or guilty connotations could be drawn from such conduct without some admissible evidence of identification of the papers as official documents. However, there was no evidence of the contents or nature of the papers which were passed between these persons.

Insofar as criminal prosecution was concerned, the carefully observed actions of the suspects in this respect were as consistent with innocence as with guilt. As was later found by the House subcommittee which made a painstaking examination of the case, "No Government items were ever seen to be passed from one subject to another, although all of them were under constant surveillance for some time." (Report of Subcommittee IV of the Committee on the Judiciary, House of Representatives, 79th Cong., 2d sess., pursuant to H. R. 430.)

While in New York City, Jaffe was, of course, in daily association with Kate Mitchell, his office associate. He was also in frequent contact with Mark Gayn, a correspondent and magazine writer who also specialized in far eastern subjects. Once during the investigation, Gayn while riding on a bus was observed reading what appeared to be a copy of an official report. This report, it was later ascertained, had to do with common gossip about the marital relations between Generalissimo Chiang Kai-shek and his wife. Generally speaking, the results of the physical surveillances of the subjects while in New York were of a neutral or negative character except as proof of association. The surveillance failed to establish the actual theft or unauthorized removal of a single official document by any one of the subjects and no evidence was adduced which indicated that any official document or other paper was ever passed or delivered by any of the suspects to a known or suspected espionage agent. In this connection, the House subcommittee which later reviewed this case found: "although the various parties were frequently observed in the company of one another by trained investigators, no one of them was ever seen to deliver any Government items to another."

The investigation of the FBI, in addition to establishing association between the various subjects, also established that there were numerous classified documents or copies of such documents on the premises of Amerasia, at Larsen's home and in Gayn's home. The possession of these documents was established by means of unauthorized and illegal entries upon the premises of the subjects and the information and evidence so obtained could not, of course, be legally used in a criminal prosecution. In fact, in the event of a subsequent trial or even pre-trial hearings, in which the evidence was challenged, the Department would have been required to concede the facts as to the illegal trespasses, searches, and seizures.

The offices of Amerasia were entered without search warrants on March 20, 1945, March 26, 1945, March 27, 1945, April 23, 1945, April 24, 1945, and May 14, 1945, and the documents found therein inventoried and photographed.

The apartment of Philip Jacob Jaffe was entered without search warrants on April 2, 1945, and April 6, 1945. No material of interest was located.

The apartment of Emmanuel Sigurd Larsen was entered without a search warrant on April 6, 1945, and some of the documents found were photographed.

The apartment of Mark Julius Gayn was entered without a search warrant on April 6, 1945, and April 27, 1945. Photographs were made of the documents found.

The apartment of Kate Louise Mitchell was entered without a search warrant on March 31, 1945. Nothing material was found.

Of course, a criminal prosecution in any case, and particularly in this case, would be the greatest of deterrents. But even absent the possibility of a successful prosecution (because of the necessary methods by which the evidence in this case was secured), the steps taken by the FBI were more than justified, not only to put a stop to the loose handling of Government documents, but also to protect the internal security of the country.

SUBMISSION OF CASE TO CRIMINAL DIVISION

Until May 29, 1945, the Criminal Division of the Department had no knowledge of the facts hereinbefore set forth or of the investigation conducted by the OSS or the FBI. On that date the First Assistant of the Criminal Division was given a memorandum dated May 29, 1945, which had just been received from the FBI. This memorandum briefly summarized the salient facts developed by the FBI investigation. The First Assistant was instructed to study this memorandum and make an immediate decision with respect to prosecution. The FBI memorandum itself solicited a decision within 24 hours as to the arrest of the subjects.

The First Assistant reviewed the FBI memorandum and then conferred with the FBI officials who had the case in charge. After this conference and after a review of the memorandum of May

29, 1945, he came to two conclusions. The first conclusion was that the Department did not then have the necessary legal evidence available to convict the individuals involved. An attachment to the memorandum of May 29, 1945, under the heading "Evidence" pointed out the warning that—"Most of the foregoing information regarding the contacts made by the various principals and the documents which were exchanged were obtained through highly confidential means and sources of information *which cannot be used in evidence.*" [Tydings Committee emphasis.]

The Criminal Division, of course, recognized the obstacles inherent in the case. Nevertheless, it was concluded that, with the usual "break" which attends the apprehension of Federal law violators, sufficient evidence might be obtained to establish a case. This conclusion was based on two factors: One, that more than 80 percent of Federal law violators confess their offense after their arrest, and two, by confronting the suspects with the incriminatory documents expected to be found on their arrest, damaging admissions might be obtained.

It was decided to authorize the issuance of a complaint for three reasons:

First, we were then at war and the indications were that the suspects were engaged in what might be dangerous espionage activities. Their arrest would at least put a stop to these activities and unearth their ramifications. The Bureau "anticipated that a considerable amount of additional evidence will, of course, be developed" against contacts and associates of the defendants after their arrests.

Second, it was hoped that sufficient legal proof might be acquired by admissions upon their arrest and otherwise.

Third, there existed the possibility that timely motions to suppress any documents which might be seized at the time of the arrest might not be made.

The Criminal Division authorized the filing of a complaint on June 5, 1945, against Philip J. Jaffe, Emmanuel Sigurd Larsen, Andrew Roth, and John Stewart Service as suggested by the Bureau. In addition, the Criminal Division authorized the arrest of Kate Louise Mitchell and Mark Julius Gayn. The complaint charged all six with a conspiracy to violate title 50, section 31 of the Espionage Act, having to do with the unauthorized removal and possession of documents relating to the national defense.

On June 6, 1945, all the defendants were arrested in New York City or in Washington, D.C., and in each case where a defendant was found on his premises, the premises were thoroughly searched and the documents found removed by the arresting officers. No "consent to search" authorizations were obtained from any of the defendants.

The results of the arrests, the searches and the interviews were, on the whole, disappointing and did not provide the prosecution, except in the case of Larsen and Jaffe, with the evidence hoped for as to when, where, how, and by whom the official papers were removed and received by the defendants. No documents were found on Roth or Service at their premises. Jaffe, Mitchell, and Roth declined to sign statements. Only a small percentage of the documents seized by the FBI related to the national defense.

After the arrests, the prosecution of the case was, on June 13, 1945, assigned to Robert M. Hitchcock, a Special Assistant to the Attorney General, one of the most able, experienced, and conscientious trial attorneys in the Department. Designated to assist him was Donald B. Anderson, a former Federal Bureau of Investigation special agent, State judge, and prosecutor.

All of the defendants were separately represented by counsel and all indications were that the case would be vigorously defended. Defense counsel requested conferences with representatives of the Criminal Division, and demanded early hearings in New York and Washington. Since preliminary hearings before a United States Commissioner would not have been in the interests of the Government because they would prematurely expose the prosecution evidence, an immediate indictment was sought to make such hearings unnecessary. An indictment would eliminate the defendants' right to a preliminary hearing at which evidence of probable cause would have to be adduced. This was particularly important for the additional reason that it would require considerable time to process in the FBI laboratory hundreds of seized documents for fingerprinting, handwriting, and typing and to trace them to their official sources, etc.

From the very beginning, counsel for some of the defendants advised that motions would be made attacking the arrests and the seizure of the documents and that application would be made to the court seeking to suppress the evidence so obtained.

As a matter of fact, as early as June 11, 1945, Larsen had ascertained from the building superintendent that he had permitted agents to enter Larsen's apartment without a search warrant. This did not become known to the prosecutors until September 28, 1945, when Larsen filed a motion to suppress.

In view of the fact that the Government's knowledge of the existence of the seized documents was obtained by prior illegal entries and searches, it was inevitable that a court would suppress all of the evidence seized at the time of the arrests with the result that the Government would be without a provable case. For the Supreme Court has held that where information has been obtained by the Government through a previous unconstitutional search and seizure "not merely the evidence so acquired shall not be used before the court but that it shall not be used at all" (*Silverthorne Lumber Co.* v. *United States*, 251 U. S. 385, 389). This quoted language has been construed by the Supreme Court as making inadmissible not only the evidence illegally obtained, but also all evidence derived from leads or clues, because they are "fruits of the poisonous tree" (*Nardone* v. *United States*, 308 U. S. 338, 340–341).

It is appropriate to note here that, somewhat analogous to the question of unlawful search and seizure, certain information was in the possession of the Criminal Division which had been furnished by the FBI with the admonition that such "information regarding the contacts made by the various principals and the documents which were exchanged were obtained through highly confidential means and sources of information *which cannot be used in evidence.*" [Tydings Committee emphasis.] This information was obtained by the Bureau through the medium of technical surveillance, which included the recording of conversations between some of the defendants.

One such conversation between Jaffe and Service, occurring in the former's room at the Statler Hotel, Washington, D.C., on May 8, 1945, has been widely publicized recently due to the fact that a single sentence thereof found its way into the record of an executive session of the Senate committee. In order that this single sentence might be viewed in its setting, rather than out of context, the Department of Justice on June 26, 1950, made available to the committee the transcript of the conversation relating to this particular statement.

Information of this type of course could have no bearing on the question of prosecution. It was furnished by the FBI with the explicit admonition that it was obtained through highly confidential means and sources of information and could not be used in evidence. Moreover, evidence obtained by wire tapping or through leads or clues therefrom is inadmissible in court (*Nardone* v. *United States,* 302 U. S. 379, *Nardone* v. *United States,* 308 U. S. 338, and *Weiss* v. *United States* 308 U. S. 321), and evidence obtained by planting microphones on a defendant's premises cannot be used when a trespass accompanies its installation. (See *Goldman* v. *United States,* 316 U. S. 129; compare *United States* v. *Coplon,* 88 F. Supp. 921 (SDNY).) Hence, information of this type could not be considered in weighing the possibility of successful prosecution in this case.

THE GRAND JURY PRESENTATION

As previously indicated, in order to forestall preliminary hearings during which the Government's evidence would be needlessly divulged while the defendants could remain silent, an early presentation to a grand jury was decided upon. This early presentation was planned even though the case was not yet ready for presentation and the analysis and tracing of the documents had been barely begun.

While the matter was being presented to the grand jury, some of the defendants requested a conference with the Assistant Attorney General in charge of the Criminal Division. These requests were received on June 21, 1945, the first day of the grand jury presentation and on the days immediately following. It was suggested to counsel for the defendants that if they would agree to a postponement of the preliminary hearings the Government would afford the defendants an opportunity to confer with the Criminal Division. Defense counsel agreed to a postponement of the preliminary hearings, requesting an opportunity for a further discussion of the case.

Thus the necessity of an early indictment was averted, since the Government was no longer faced with revealing its evidence in a preliminary hearing. The FBI was, of course, still engaged in the laborious task of processing the hundreds of documents that had been seized.

A conference was held on June 27, 1945. Counsel for the defendants Mitchell and Gayn represented that their clients were not guilty of a criminal offense and that what they did was being done by every newspaper reporter, columnist, correspondent, and writer in New York and Washington.

During this conference, it was brought out that the current grand jury would go out of existence in a few days and a discussion was had as to whether the Government would apply to the court to extend the term of the grand jury then in session or re-present the matter to the new grand jury. The Criminal Division representatives stated that they were inclined to extend the grand jury for another month but that they would review the whole case subsequent to the conference.

Immediately after the conference was concluded, Kate Mitchell's attorney offered to have her appear before the grand jury, waive immunity, and answer every question put to her. This offer was particularly favorable to the Government. For, in addition to enabling the Government to make out a stronger case against defendants than could be otherwise established, the defendants' defensive evidence is obtained and the witness leaves himself open to a charge of perjury in the event he makes a false statement in his sworn testimony before the grand jury.

Thereafter, the attorneys for Jaffe, Gayn, and Service also made this same unusual offer in writing although Jaffe later failed to appear and testify. The Government agreed to the appearance of the defendants before the grand jury and coupled the acceptance with a demand that such defendants also submit themselves to examination by the Government prosecutors prior to their appearance before the grand jury. Another condition imposed by the Government was that the New York defendants, in the event of their indictment, would not contest their removal from New York to Washington. These conditions were agreed to by the defendants.

With the case in the position outlined, it was decided, subject to the grand jurors' consent, to withdraw the case from the expiring grand jury which had only heard 1 day's testimony and re-present the evidence to a new grand jury. This decision was based on the following considerations and no others:

1. The evidence and, in particular, the documents seized, hundreds in number, were not ready for presentation to the grand jury.

2. The offer of the defendants to be examined by Government counsel and appear before the grand jury without immunity or counsel necessitated a more deliberate and time-consuming approach, preparation, and grand jury presentation.

The grand jury which heard 1 day's testimony on June 21, 1945, and which was expiring on July 2, 1945, was informed of the above considerations. They were also informed that if they desired to retain jurisdiction in the matter it would be necessary for the Government to get an order extending their term for a month or 6 weeks. The grand jurors agreed without any objection to have the case withdrawn from their consideration.

The preparation of the case was continued on an intensive scale during the month of July 1945. Starting on July 23, 1945, the Government prosecutors started the pre-grand jury examination of those defendants who had offered to waive immunity. They were cross-examined and confronted with the documents, and every effort was made to establish their possible complicity. As the preparation and exposition of the case developed it became increasingly clear that Jaffe and Larsen were the main culprits. Jaffe, Larsen, and Roth did not submit to examination by the Government prosecutors or appear before the grand jury.

The presentation of the case to the grand jury was commenced on July 30, 1945, and sessions were held on July 30, 31, August 1, 3, 6, and 7, 1945. Three of the defendants (Service, Mitchell, and Gayn) and 24 Government witnesses including 16 FBI agents testified before the grand jury. It must be emphasized that each witness who had testified on June 21, 1945, before the previous grand jury was again called and testified before this grand jury and all pertinent evidence, documentary or otherwise, supplied to the Criminal Division was presented to or made available to the grand jury for its consideration.

On August 10, 1945, an indictment was returned against Jaffe, Larsen, and Roth charging them, in substance, with conspiracy to embezzle and remove official documents without permission. The grand jury refused to indict Service, Gayn, and Mitchell after listening to their own testimony and the Government's testimony and evidence with respect to them.

The grand jury, in voting for or against indictments, voted as follows:

	For indictment	Against indictment
Jaffe	14	6
Larsen	14	6
Roth	13	7
Gayn	5	15
Mitchell	2	18
Service	0	20

Twelve grand jurors must, of course, concur before a valid indictment can be returned. The vote of the grand jury was particularly significant since the proceedings were ex parte and only the Government's evidence was presented except for such explanations as were made by the defendants who testified without the aid of counsel.

Many of the grand jurors who voted for no bills, after listening to the testimony, adopted the position that the loose method of handling, filing, controlling, and releasing official papers almost invited the form of activity in which the defendants were engaged. They also took the position that many other newspapermen and writers, besides the defendants, were obtaining access to classified material for background purposes and that the remedy lay within the departments and agencies rather than in prosecution.

Not only was the attitude of the grand jurors indicative of what might be expected of petit jurors, but it should be borne in mind in considering the question of the disposition of the case that the remaining defendants would be represented by counsel on their trial, and would have their own witnesses and an opportunity to testify themselves. It is also worthy of note, in view of the grand jury vote, that after a 3- or 4-month trial, only one petit juror would be required to prevent the conviction of the defendants.

And, finally, whereas a grand jury may indict merely upon a showing that there is probable cause for believing an offense has been committed, the petit jury cannot convict unless it is satisfied beyond a reasonable doubt that a defendant is guilty.

In this type of case it is important that the Government's evidence be clear and convincing. To lose a case of this kind is bad not only for the prosecution, but it could have an adverse effect on public opinion as to the real danger involved in cases of this nature. In other words, the country would tend to depreciate the case and the seriousness of the conspiracy. In this connection it is interesting to note that the Department of Justice, with one exception, has not lost a single case where Communist activity was a feature of the case. It might be added there that in one case, now pending, the Government has been unable to date to institute prosecution because the evidence obtained would not be admissible in a trial of the case.

As stated previously, the indictments returned charged Jaffe, Larsen, and Roth in substance with conspiracy to embezzle and remove official documents without permission. The Government had abandoned the doubtful premise that any considerable part of the documents related to the national defense. One factor to be considered in evaluating this decision then reached by the prosecutors is that none of the documents seized by the OSS were known or available to the prosecutors at that time.

Specific documents which appeared to relate to the national defense were made the object of special study by Department attorneys and FBI representatives with a view to making out possible substantive charges of espionage against one or more of the defendants. However, this study revealed in each instance that proof of some vital element was lacking. In addition, an indictment, charging bribery was prepared with respect to Larsen and Jaffe, but an analysis of the facts available established that such a charge could not be sustained because the money paid by Jaffe to Larsen's wife was ostensibly for typing copies of Larsen's personal records and not for the purpose of influencing the official conduct or action of Larsen.

The indictment, as drawn, did not require the Government to prove that the documents related to the national defense—only that they were official documents. The indictment returned was based on the same conspiracy section of the Criminal Code as the complaint. Thus it is clear that the defendants were subject to the same punishment on either theory. The only result in the change between what the complaint charged and what the indictment charged was to lessen the burden of proof for the Government.

In this connection, it is interesting to note that the House subcommittee which later reviewed this case stated, after examining all the documents, "Few, if any, of the identifiable classified documents involved in this case had any real importance in our national defense or our war effort."

In addition, the subcommittee also made the following observations with respect to the nature and contents of the documents involved:

(1) Many had already been given wide publicity.

(2) Many of the identifiable documents might have had their evidential value destroyed by reason of the court's sustaining the defendants' motions attacking the warrants of arrest.

(3) Most of the "classified" items in question were copies. There were few, if any, original documents.

(4) The bulk of the documents were not of recent date. Some were dated as early as 1936, were innocuous in content, and were and could have been generally known to anyone interested in the information they contained.

(5) Most of the items seized at Jaffe's offices were typewritten copies. Some of such copies were proved to have been typed in one of the Government departments. It may be fairly inferred that the originals of such copies were never removed but that copies were made at the department or agency where the originals reposed.

(6) Most of the items dealt with personalities or political aspects in countries of the Far East.

(7) * * * there was no evidence that any of the documents or copies were ever put to any use harmful to the war effort.

(8) Many "classified" Government documents or copies were found in the possession of some of them, the greater part of the documents pertaining to political matters in Japan, China, India, and Asia.

After the return of the indictment, Jaffe, Roth, and Larsen pleaded not guilty and attorneys for Larsen and Roth indicated that they would contest the case very vigorously and would not plead guilty. On the other hand, Jaffe's counsel indicated the possibility of a plea in the event that no sentence of imprisonment were imposed.

Since Jaffe, Roth, and Larsen were charged together in a single indictment as codefendants, the normal and desirable procedure would be a joint trial of all three. It was for this reason that the Government did not at first regard these overtures favorably.

ATTACK UPON THE GOVERNMENT'S PROOF

While the case was in this status in the last week of September 1945, several things happened which threatened to destroy the Government's case.

It developed that sometime shortly after Larsen was released on bond following his arrest he contacted E. R. Sager, the manager of his apartment house in which he lived, and told him that he, Larsen, knew that someone had been in his apartment. He inquired whether Sager had let the persons into his apartment. It appears that Sager admitted that he had given the FBI agents the keys to Larsen's apartment.

Thereafter, and on September 24, 1945, Larsen telephoned Sager and stated, "you remember you told me you let those men into my apartment." To this Sager replied "Yes." Larsen thereupon informed Mr. Sager that his attorney was desirous of obtaining an affidavit from Sager, setting forth the facts of the situation.

The facts were that the agents had previously entered the apartment of Larsen twice without a search warrant, once on April 6, 1945, to inventory and photostat the documents on the premises and to take typewriting specimens and once to install a microphone in an apartment in the same building into which Larsen was to move on June 1, 1945.

On September 28, 1945, the Criminal Division was informed that Larsen's attorney was about to file a demurrer, motion to quash the indictment and an application to suppress the evidence obtained from the search of Larsen's apartment.

Representatives of the Criminal Division conferred with FBI officials on the morning of September 28, 1945, and it was generally agreed that the case was in serious jeopardy. A number of suggestions were made and discarded. The possibility of offering to suppress voluntarily all of the documents seized from Larsen at the time of his arrest, and then attempt to establish the case against Larsen on the basis of documents found in the possession of Jaffe, was discussed. However, the most serious problem was that Jaffe would learn of Larsen's motion and file a similar motion, in which event the entire case would be destroyed. And if Jaffe's motion to suppress were granted, the suppressed evidence not only would not be admissible against Jaffe, but would also be inadmissible against Larsen and Roth on a joint trial of all three. See *Goldstein v. United States* (316 U. S. 114, 119–120); *McDonald* v. *United States* (335 U. S. 451, 456, 457, 461). In view of the imminence of Larsen's motion, time was of the essence and immediate action had to be taken, if the prosecution of Jaffe was to be salvaged.

The first assistant thereupon called Jaffe's counsel and discussed his previous suggestions with respect to a plea of guilty and a conference was arranged for the early afternoon, that same day, September 28, 1945.

While waiting for Jaffe's Washington counsel to appear, Larsen's motion to quash the indictment and suppress the evidence was served upon the Department.

Immediately after the motion papers were served, Jaffe's attorney appeared for the conference. Before admitting him, inquiry was made of the clerk of the district court as to whether Mr. Larsen's attorney had filed the motion to quash. The clerk stated that the motion had just been filed and had already been reviewed by the press.

The motion as filed alleged briefly that the evidence obtained by the Government had been obtained by illegal searches and seizures, by wire tapping and by the illegal detention of the defendant. Larsen supported the application by a detailed 13-page affidavit in which he swore that at the time of his arrest at his apartment the agents betrayed a prior knowledge and familiarity with his personal effects which they could not have acquired by legal means. He also set forth the building manager's admission that he had permitted the agents to have access to his apartment in the absence of Larsen and prior to his arrest.

It was realized that when Jaffe's lawyer concluded his conference with the Department, he would learn of Larsen's motion from the newspaper accounts, and would thereafter in all probability initiate a similar motion on behalf of his own client. It was thought imperative to do whatever possible to salvage the case against Jaffe. To this end an effort was made to obtain an immediate and firm commitment from Jaffe's attorney that Jaffe would plead guilty.

During the discussions the parties to the conference speculated on the nature of the sentence which the court would be likely to impose. The Criminal Division advised Jaffe's attorney that the judges of the District of Columbia did not ordinarily ask for or request any recommendation and that we were not in a position to make any commitment with respect to sentence. After some discussion, it was finally agreed that Jaffe would plead guilty and the Government would, if permitted, recommend the imposition of a substantial fine. The maximum fine was $10,000 and it was understood that such a fine would be paid by Jaffe in the event it was imposed. However, Jaffe's counsel conditioned his commitment upon the premise that the court would consent to hear a recommendation from the Government. After Jaffe's counsel was firmly committed to pleading his client guilty, inquiry was made as to the earliest time in which the plea of guilty could be entered. Jaffe's counsel stated that the plea would be entered whenever the Government could arrange for it.

This conference took place on Friday afternoon, September 28.

The Criminal Division was anxious to dispose of Jaffe's case before he would reconsider (as he had done before) or file a motion to suppress the evidence obtained from his premises. Upon inquiry it was learned that Judge Proctor would be holding court on Saturday morning, September 29, 1945. Judge Proctor was asked to take Jaffe's plea and agreed to do so. Judge Proctor also advised that he would consent to hear the recommendation of Government and defense counsel as to sentence after a plea of guilty was entered by Jaffe.

On Saturday morning, September 29, 1945, Jaffe pleaded guilty to the felony charge. Judge Proctor heard the views of Jaffe's counsel and Government counsel. Government counsel recommended that a substantial fine be imposed. After hearing counsel for both parties, Judge Proctor imposed a fine of $2,500, which was paid. There had not been any presentence conference or consultation of any kind with the court before the case came on for plea and sentence.

With the case of Jaffe safely disposed of in what was considered a manner satisfactory under the circumstances, the Department was still confronted with the motion to suppress filed by Larsen. A number of conferences were held with the attorneys for Larsen and

47

Roth in an effort to obtain pleas of guilty but without success. Larsen's attorney at first took the position he would not consider a plea until his motion to suppress was decided.

The time for filing the Government's response to the motion to suppress was deferred. In response to the motion, the Government would have been obliged to admit the illegality of the search and seizure. However, the necessity for making this admission was averted when Larsen's counsel finally offered to plead his client nolo contendere if he could receive some assurance that only a moderate fine would be imposed. He pointed out that Larsen had been imposed upon by Jaffe, that he had lost his Government position which he had held for 10 years, that he was unemployed and penniless, and that he had a wife and family dependent upon him.

The Government was aware of these facts and finally agreed, if consulted by the court, to recommend a fine of $500. This position was taken largely because of the above factors but also because we realized that Jaffe was the main culprit, that he had corrupted Larsen and was responsible for his plight, and that it would be manifestly unjust for Larsen to receive a sentence greater or even equal to that imposed upon Jaffe. Larsen entered a plea of nolo contendere on November 2, 1945 and was fined $500, as recommended by the Government.

Only the case against Roth now remained. This case was very weak and depended on several pages of handwriting and typewriting (identified as Roth's) of what appeared to be official documents.

. . . .

In view of the state of evidence above outlined, the decision was reached that the case against Roth could not be successfully prosecuted. After several postponements of hearings on motions brought by Roth's attorneys, and after an unsuccessful effort was made to place it on the pending inactive docket, the Government was forced to nolle prosse the case against him on February 15, 1946.

This report is not intended to qualify the seriousness or gravity of this case. The FBI's prompt and vigorous action in face of a situation already tainted with illegality was of inestimable service to this country. This report only deals with the difficulties of successful prosecution and the bases for the decisions made.[31]

*   *   *   *   *

Among the various investigations of the Amerasia case, I have mentioned the Federal grand jury in New York. This was a "runaway" grand jury. Following Senator McCarthy's much-publicized charges, this grand jury, "acting on its own authority" and utilizing its subpoena power, made an independent investigation. If Dr. Kubek would like to suggest bias on

---

[31] *Tydings Report,* pp. 123–133. The memorandum is printed in full except for one omission—before the penultimate paragraph—of details of the evidence against Roth, against whom charges were dropped. The appendix which followed this memorandum is a technical legal discussion of precedents and Supreme Court decisions, under the fourth and fifth amendments, which the Department of Justice believed to be controlling. For reasons of space, it is not reproduced. It can be found in *Tydings Report,* pp. 133–136.

the part of the Democratic majority of the Tydings Committee (Senators Tydings, McMahon, and Green), he can hardly level such an accusation against the grand jury. It is interesting, therefore, to note that its presentment, dated June 15, 1950, included the following conclusions:

> The grand jury also found no evidence to indicate that the Department of Justice was remiss in its prosecution of the case.

> The grand jury believes that the American people have been poorly served by the compounding of confusion through disclosures of half-truths, contradictory statements, etc., in this and similar cases.[32]

There is then, no great mystery about the way the case was handled. "The tainted nature of the original search by OSS agents infected the entire investigatory process which followed." The illegal entries having become known to one of the defendants (Larsen), the prosecution moved quickly to salvage what it could of the case by accepting a guilty plea from Jaffe with a moderate fine and no demand for a jail sentence. Similarly, it was agreed that Larsen would plead *nolo contendere* and pay a fine of $500. The Tydings Committee came to the conclusion:

> The fact that some of the defendants did not receive the punishment which we today feel they deserved or which we would like to have seen them receive is the result of certain incidents of the case which have been heretofore discussed and not the result of dereliction on the part of the prosecuting officials. Under all of the circumstances of the case, we are constrained to suggest that the Department was fortunate in securing the punishment that was meted out.[33]

> Our inquiry has been thorough and designed to develop every logical source through which information of relevance to the case might be obtained.
> This case has now been considered (1) by the Hobbs Committee of the House of Representatives in 1946; (2) by a special grand jury in New York in 1950; and (3) by this subcommittee. In each instance the conclusion is the same—indeed, the only conclusion which the facts will support—that no agency of our government was derelict in any way in the handling of the Amerasia case.[34]

Parenthetically, this matter of illegal entry and search did not enter into and could not have affected the grand jury consideration of my case and its decision against an indictment. In any event, there was no illegal entry of my temporary residence, and I had no government documents in my possession.

---

[32] *Tydings Report,* pp. 136–137.
[33] *Tydings Report,* p. 140.
[34] *Tydings Report,* p. 144.

Since Dr. Kubek has some 44 footnote references to the Tydings transcript, one must assume that he is familiar with this record. If he is not, he certainly should be. But in his effort to convince his readers that my role in the "strange" case was "central," there is much that he chooses to omit. He notes, for instance, that the grand jury voted 20-0 against my indictment (one seems to feel that this in itself is meant to be evidence that there was something strange about the case: it has, as a matter of fact, already been so considered by at least one writer in Taiwan). But he fails to mention that I waived immunity and appeared voluntarily before the grand jury. He repeats (without source) the statement (made by Senator Joseph McCarthy) that the FBI gave assurances that the evidence was "airtight." But he ignores the letter in the record from the Department of Justice denying that such assurance was ever given.[35] He repeats (without source) the accusation (again from Senator McCarthy) that Undersecretary of State Grew was forced to resign as a result of my clearance. But he fails to see the clear evidence — including a letter from Mr. Grew — that this was not true.[36]

He refers to the OSS raid on Amerasia on March 11, 1945, and the finding there of "hundreds" of classified government documents, but fails to note that this clearly indicated that Amerasia's source of government documents was already fully developed before I arrived in the United States on April 12, 1945.[37] Likewise, he fails to note the record that the FBI indicated to the Departments of State and Navy on April 18—before I had ever met Jaffe, Larsen, Mitchell, or Gayn—that it was ready to present the case for prosecutive action.[38] In other words, even before I was first sought out by the Amerasia group, the FBI was satisfied that the source of Amerasia's documents was known and the case solved.

Dr. Kubek also chooses to ignore some very direct refutations of his allegation that I had a central role in the Amerasia case:

> Mr. McINERNEY. The evidence on Service was thin. They said there was in Jaffe's office, as I recall it, copies of his confidential reports. When we arrested, or made the searches, we found copies of his report. We interviewed Larsen, and Larsen admitted that he had given Service's copies to Jaffe, and Service had not given them. Service was very surprised that Jaffe had that report. It was on that thin allegation that we authorized on Service. . . .[39]

---

[35] *Tydings Transcript,* p. 2310.
[36] *Tydings Transcript,* p. 1277.
[37] *Tydings Report,* p. 91.
[38] *Ibid.*
[39]*Tydings Transcript,* p. 2289. Testimony of Mr. James McInerney, Assistant Attorney General in charge of the Criminal Division, Department of Justice, before the Hobbs committee in 1946.

Mr. MORGAN. You saw all the evidence I assume, available in connection with John Service.

Mr. McINERNEY. Yes, sir. You mean—

Mr. MORGAN. At that time.

Mr. McINERNEY. I, personally?

Mr. MORGAN. I mean, at the time of the prosecution, were you cognizant and familiar with the evidence against Mr. Service?

Mr. McINERNEY. Yes, sir.

Mr. MORGAN. And, on the basis of your knowledge of such evidence, did you feel that prosecution of him was warranted?

Mr. McINERNEY. No, sir.[40]

To summarize. After laying a foundation of assertion that a hundred-odd stolen government documents written by me were found in Amerasia, Dr. Kubek goes on to "assume" that many of these documents were delivered by me to Jaffe, and that I had a central role in a strange case which was not prosecuted honestly and vigorously, but instead effectively buried. I submit that, by any definition, this is clear and serious defamation.

The Amerasia case, after all, involved the criminal charge of "conspiracy to embezzle, steal, and purloin property, records, and valuable things of the records and property of the United States." To this charge, one man pleaded guilty and another, *nolo contendere.* Punishable crimes, against the United States and during a time of war, were obviously therefore committed. For Dr. Kubek to say that I had a "central role" in such a case cannot be anything other than saying that I, too, was guilty.

In other words, Dr. Kubek, without being able to offer the slightest scintilla of new evidence or information, blandly denies the validity (good faith? honesty?) of a whole series of decisions conscientiously reached over the years by numbers of boards, grand juries, committees, and individuals, who had before them the whole record:

a) the grand jury, which voted unanimously against my indictment,

b) the State Department, under Secretary Byrnes, which cleared me and returned me to duty in August, 1945,

c) the Loyalty Security Board, under General Snow, and the responsible security and personnel officers of the Department of State, under Secretaries Marshall and Acheson, who cleared me in some seven investigations and hearings between 1946 and 1951,

d) the Tydings Subcommittee, including Senator Lodge, which found Senator McCarthy's charges—similar to those here revived by Dr. Kubek—to be unfounded,

e) the State Department, under Secretary Dulles, which accepted my return to duty (after the Supreme Court had ruled unanimously

---

[40] *Tydings Transcript,* p. 998. Testimony of Mr. McInerney before the Tydings Committee on May 4, 1950.

that my discharge was illegal) and which, under Secretary Herter, restored my security clearance in 1959 after another full investigation.

There is much more that might, but need not, be said about Dr. Kubek's rewriting of the Amerasia case. His failings are not limited to astigmatism; there are also many plain errors of fact. But my chief concern here is to point out the fraudulent representation that a hundred-odd reports of mine were found in Amerasia, and the defamation in the statements that I delivered many documents to Jaffe and had a central role in the Amerasia case. As to why I, personally, should have been picked as the prime target of Dr. Kubek's massive work, I can only fall back on one of his own favorite words: I find it very "strange."

PART TWO

American Policy in China: 1944 and 1945

Introduction to Part Two

Extremely important are two facts which can no longer be disputed: . . . (2) the official policy of the United States Government in support of Chiang Kai-shek's Nationalist regime in China was actively opposed and subverted during World War II by a few junior American career diplomats on station in China, John Stewart Service conspicuous among them.[1]

Before one can intelligently discuss this "non-disputable" main conclusion of Dr. Kubek, it is necessary to examine American policy in China in a little more detail than Dr. Kubek provides. It is quite clear that Dr. Kubek's mind is fixed on the period while Hurley was in China and on Hurley's own exposition of that policy. The situation that led to Hurley's mission to China developed in the early summer of 1944, and he resigned as ambassador in November 1945. My own reports which Dr. Kubek (and Hurley) have found most "subversive" were also made during the same general period. The two years 1944 and 1945 will therefore be the focus of the summary discussion of American policy in China that takes up the following five chapters.

For specifics on this policy, Dr. Kubek is not very helpful. As often seems to be the case when he is on unfirm ground, he relies on reiteration:

The Ambassador [Hurley] had received an implicit directive from the President of the United States to uphold the National Government of Chiang Kai-shek and to work for the unification of all the military forces of China under the Generalissimo's command.[2]

The basic American wartime policy toward China, as expressed repeatedly by the President and the Secretary of State and clearly understood in Washington and throughout the nation, was *to uphold in all possible ways* the central government of Generalissimo Chiang Kai-shek and to support his armies in the field against Japan.[3]

Service, the Ambassador charged, was working to undercut *the first objective of the American mission* as defined by the President, i.e., to uphold the Chinese Central Government under Chiang Kai-shek.[4]

American policy had shifted away [by late 1945] . . . from its earlier position of *unilateral support* of Chiang Kai-shek's regime.[5]

---

[1] *Papers*, p. 112.
[2] *Papers*, p. 104.
[3] *Ibid.*, p. 79; emphasis added.
[4] *Ibid.*, p. 109; emphasis added.
[5] *Ibid.*, p. 25; emphasis added. By "unilateral support" I assume Dr. Kubek means support only of Chiang Kai-shek's regime, as opposed to the more usual

This narrowly limited conception of American policy in China as being the personalized support of Chiang Kai-shek is one that developed gradually in General Hurley's mind. It became strengthened over the passage of time as Hurley found himself mired down in the intransigent realities of Chinese politics, and was crystallized in his angry resignation and the postwar debates over who "lost China."[6] Understandably, it has become a basic myth of the China lobby. There is good reason, however, why Dr. Kubek does not try to document these assertions: the documentation does not exist. On the other hand, there is a great deal of documentation to the contrary.

---

sense of support without consideration of any reciprocation or action from the other party.

[6] See Don Lohbeck, *Patrick J. Hurley* (Chicago: Regnery, 1956), pp. 279–281 and *passim*.

III
Chinese Unity Through American Command

When Cordell Hull, who had been Secretary of State from 1933 to near the end of 1944, came to write his *Memoirs* he looked back retrospectively on American wartime policy in China:

> Toward China we had two objectives. The first was an effective joint prosecution of the war. The second was the recognition and building up of China as a major power entitled to equal rank with the three big Western allies, Russia, Britain, and the United States, during and after the war, both for the preparation of a postwar organization and for the establishment of stability and prosperity in the Orient.[1]

From Pearl Harbor through 1942 had been a time of defeat and disappointment. By 1943, though the CBI (China-Burma-India) Theater had a priority far behind Europe and even the Pacific, the resources of the Allies were beginning to be brought into play. Tonnage of supplies to China over the "Hump" was slowly being increased in the face of great difficulties. Several Chinese divisions were flown to India, trained there, and beginning to prove themselves in a slow, laborious, "shoe-string" campaign—pushed almost literally by General Stilwell each step of the way—to open a road from Assam through North Burma and eventually to reach China. In Yunnan province within China, another 30-division Chinese force was gradually assembled (with many delays on the Chinese side) to be trained by American officers and equipped with new American arms, so as to be in readiness to drive west and coordinate with the campaign in North Burma.[2]

Stilwell and the War Department in Washington were convinced that this opening of a road into China was vital to making China an effective factor in the war. Without the road, it would be impossible to arm and supply a reformed Chinese army. Without such an army, it would be im-

---

[1] Cordell Hull, *The Memoirs of Cordell Hull* (New York: Macmillan Co., 1948), II, p. 1583. Cited in Tang Tsou, *America's Failure in China 1941–50* (Chicago: University of Chicago Press, 1963), p. 33.

[2] Charles F. Romanus and Riley Sunderland, *Stilwell's Mission to China* (Washington: Department of the Army, 1953), chapters VI and VII. This is the first of three volumes in the official War Department history of the CBI Theater; Dr. Kubek's failure to use this invaluable, authoritative source is only one of the more startling omissions in his cited materials.

possible to use China as a base for the attack on Japan, or even to defend the American air fields already being built in China.[3] Chennault and Chiang Kai-shek believed there was an easier way: the use of air power alone. With a tiny air force of 105 fighters, 30 medium bombers, and 12 heavy bombers, Chennault insisted that he would "destroy the effectiveness of the Japanese Air Force, probably within six months, within one year at the outside" and thus "accomplish the downfall of Japan."[4]

Roosevelt overruled the unanimous opinion of all his own military advisers and decided, in the spring of 1943, to back the Generalissimo and Chennault. In his explanation to Marshall, the President explicitly rejected the bargaining or *quid pro quo* way of working with the Chinese.

> All of us must remember that the Generalissimo came up the hard way to become the undisputed leader of four hundred million people—an enormously difficult job to attain any kind of unity from a diverse group of all kinds of leaders—military men, educators, scientists, public health people, engineers, all of them struggling for power and mastery, local or national, and to create in a very short time throughout China what it took us a couple of centuries to attain.
>
> Besides that the Generalissimo finds it necessary to maintain his position of supremacy. You and I would do the same under the circumstances. He is the Chief Executive as well as the Commander-in-Chief, and one cannot speak sternly to a man like that or exact commitments from him the way we might do from the Sultan of Morocco.[5]

On the political side, the effort to have China recognized as a major power seemed to make more encouraging headway during 1943. In January, China signed treaties with America and Britain that ended a century of extraterritoriality. In October, the Moscow Declaration formally recognized China as a member of the Big Four.[6] In November at Cairo, Chiang and his military advisers were invited, for the first time, to participate in an Allied conference. And, in the Declaration of Cairo that followed the meeting, China was solemnly promised the return of all ter-

---

[3] Romanus and Sunderland, *Stilwell's Mission,* p. 269, summarizes the American military view at the beginning of 1943: "The Joint Chiefs of Staff were now firmly behind operations to break the blockade of China, and so an offensive in Burma was high on the agenda of the next great Anglo-American conference, that of Casablanca, 14–23 January 1943. In preparing to take part in the conference, the JCS listed among desirable operations for 1943 one in Burma to reopen the line of communications to China in order to obtain 'bases essential to eventual offensive operations against Japan proper.' Here was stated the strategic goal: staging areas and airfields in north China."

[4] Romanus and Sunderland, *Stilwell's Mission,* pp. 252–253.

[5] *Ibid.,* p. 279.

[6] Tang Tsou, *America's Failure,* p. 39, notes: "The Moscow Declaration vividly revealed America's faith in the capability of general principles couched in ambiguous language to exorcise the conflicts among nations. . . ."

ritories (including, of course, Taiwan) lost to Japan since 1895. In December, the American Congress also repealed the Chinese Exclusion Acts. It seemed quite fitting that President Roosevelt should say, in his Christmas Eve message to the Nation: "Today we and the Republic of China are closer together than ever before in deep friendship and in unity of purpose."[7]

Roosevelt's words may have had some validity as he spoke, but they were already fading in meaning. The Cairo Conference, it quickly developed, was the high water mark of Roosevelt's efforts to eschew the use of pressure on Chiang, and to treat China as an equal among the great powers. Hard facts soon began to impinge on the illusions. After Cairo, Roosevelt moved sharply and unmistakably toward the Stilwell-Marshall approach of conditional support of China.[8] One problem for the future would be that disillusionment does not automatically release the bonds formed during a period of illusion.

A number of factors undoubtedly lay behind this shift in Roosevelt's attitude. One of these must certainly have been the cumulative effect of Chiang's own tactics "of making exorbitant demands and counterdemands, of attaching nullifying conditions and high prices to American proposals, of making hints and threats of separation."[9] At Cairo it had been difficult to obtain his assent, in spite of generous political concessions, to the Allied proposal to retake North Burma. After Cairo, and the withdrawal of the Allied commitment to a large-scale amphibious operation in the Bay of Bengal, his demands for "compensation" of a billion dollars (plus a doubling of aircraft for the 14th Air Force and the Chinese Air Force and immediate quadrupling of Hump tonnage) impressed Washington as only a slightly veiled form of blackmail.

A second factor, it can be assumed, was that about this time American military planners in Washington were revising their thinking about the best and quickest way to attack Japan. On the day that Stilwell arrived in Cairo, American Marines had landed successfully on the Gilbert Islands. The main attack on Japan, it soon developed, would be through the Pacific. The military importance of China rapidly diminished.

Another factor must have been the encouraging intimations from Stalin. At Teheran, Stalin reiterated his earlier statement to Hull in October that Russia would join the war against Japan after the defeat of Germany. Barbara Tuchman sums it up admirably: "Coming on top of the discouraging encounter with the Chinese, it raised the possibility of a substitute for China both as wartime partner and afterward. . . . In the cordial mood

---

[7] *China White Paper*, p. 37.

[8] It is for this reason that Romanus and Sunderland title their chapter on the Cairo Conference (*Stilwell's Command Problems*, Ch. II): "Sextant: The Watershed."

[9] Tang Tsou, *America's Failure*, p. 109.

of a historic meeting he [Roosevelt] formed the conclusion that Stalin was 'getatable' and could be drawn into postwar cooperation for common aims."[10]

And finally, there was the fact that Chennault's air campaign in China, despite receiving the support he claimed sufficient, was not proving anywhere near as effective as he had promised. By contrast, Stilwell's North Burma campaign was getting slowly under way.

Roosevelt's adoption of a policy of conditional support was made clear very soon in 1944. Chiang's demand for the billion-dollar loan was refused, since it could serve no clearly useful purpose in the Chinese war effort. The Chinese insistence that American military activities in China be financed at the official rate of 20 to 1 was met by a statement that American expenditures would be limited to $25,000,000 a month. Inflation had reached the point where the open-market rate was already 230 to 1 and rising steadily; a $25,000,000 limit applied at the official rate would ultimately force American withdrawal from China. The Chinese dropped the issue.[11]

The next problem to arise was the Chinese refusal to have the Y-Force (the 30 American-trained and equipped Chinese divisions in Yunnan) commence the drive westward across the Salween for which it had been created. The immediate crisis was that not only Stilwell's campaign in North Burma but the whole Allied position in Assam and India was being endangered by a desperate Japanese drive on Imphal. After several exchanges of messages, Roosevelt, in a message of April 3 to the Generalissimo, laid it on the line:

> ... A shell of a division opposes you on the Salween. Your advance to the west cannot help but succeed. To take advantage of just such an opportunity, we have, during the past year, been equipping and training your YOKE Forces. If they are not to be used in the common cause, our most strenuous and extensive efforts to fly in equipment and to furnish instructual personnel have not been justified.[12]

With no action forthcoming from the Chinese, Marshall instructed CBI Headquarters on April 10 that unless the Y-Force moved, lend-lease shipments for it should end. On April 14, General Ho Ying-chin, the Chinese Minister of War and Chief of Staff, issued the order for the Sal-

---

[10] Barbara Tuchman, *Stilwell and the American Experience in China, 1911–1945* (New York: Macmillan Co., 1971), p. 407.

[11] Romanus and Sunderland, *Stilwell's Command Problems,* pp. 298–301.

[12] *Ibid.,* p. 310. This message was handed by General Hearn in Chungking to Madame Chiang (because the Generalissimo was ill). Subsequent comments by Madame Chiang to General Hearn—that the tone of the message might jeopardize rather than improve the chances of moving the Y-Force—led to the conclusion that the message had not yet been delivered. "The President immediately ordered that future messages from him to the Generalissimo were to be delivered in person to the Generalissimo by the senior U.S. Army officer present in Chungking."

ween crossing. The Generalissimo never replied to Roosevelt's message of April 3. Instead, General Ho addressed a message to Marshall which included the statement: "Decision to move part of YOKE Force across Salween was made on initiative of Chinese without influence of outside pressure, and was based on realization that China must contribute its share to common war effort."[13] But the Chinese did move; and General Hearn restored the Y-Force tonnage allocations. It was with this background of an effective *quid pro quo* policy that Hurley was sent to China.

During the spring of 1944 another major military crisis was developing within China. Without heavy commitment of their already thinning forces, the Japanese were opening up the rail route from Peking to Canton, mopping up the advanced operating bases of General Chennault's Fourteenth Air Force, and causing concern that their drive might carry as far as Chungking or—even more critically for American aid—to the "Hump" terminus of Kunming. In the face of this potential disaster for China, Chiang Kai-shek was unwilling to commit his own "Whampoa" units; unwilling to withdraw and utilize the large forces (300,000 to 500,000 men) engaged in blockading the Communists in the north (which of course meant that the Communists also had to immobilize a large part of their own forces for protection); unwilling to permit the Americans to give desperately needed supplies to Nationalist commanders (such as Hsueh Yueh)[14] who were bearing the brunt of the Japanese advance; and even refusing the relatively few replacements urgently required for the Y-Force to complete the last stage of reopening the Burma Road.

In Washington, the American Joint Chiefs of Staff agreed that the situation called for new measures:

> The time has come, in our opinion, when all the military power and resources remaining to China must be entrusted to one individual capable of directing that effort in a fruitful way against the Japanese. There is no one in the Chinese Government or armed forces capable of coordinating the Chinese military effort in such a way as to meet the Japanese threat. During this war, there has been only one man who has been able to get Chinese forces to fight against the Japanese in an effective way. That man is General Stilwell.[15]

President Roosevelt accepted the JCS recommendation. The result was his message of July 6, 1944, to the Generalissimo, which may be worth quoting in full.

> The extremely serious situation which results from Japanese advances in Central China, which threaten not only your Government

---

[13] *Ibid.*, pp. 312–314.

[14] For an excellent analysis of this incident involving General Hsueh Yueh, see Warren I. Cohen, "Who Fought the Japanese in Hunan? Some Views of China's War Effort," *Journal of Asian Studies*, 18:1 (November 1967), pp. 111–115.

[15] Romanus and Sunderland, *Stilwell's Command Problems*, p. 382.

but all that the U.S. Army has been building up in China, leads me to the conclusion that drastic measures must be taken immediately if the situation is to be saved. The critical situation which now exists, in my opinion calls for the delegation to one individual of the power to coordinate all the Allied military resources in China, including the Communist forces.

I think I am fully aware of your feelings regarding General Stilwell, nevertheless I think he has now clearly demonstrated his far-sighted judgment, his skill in organization and training and, above all, in fighting your Chinese forces. I know of no other man who has the ability, the force, and the determination to offset the disaster which now threatens China and our over-all plans for the conquest of Japan. I am promoting Stilwell to the rank of full general and I recommend for your most urgent consideration that you recall him from Burma and place him directly under you in command of all Chinese and American forces, and that you charge him with the full responsibility and authority for the coordination and direction of the operations required to stem the tide of the enemy's advances. I feel that the case of China is so desperate that if radical and properly applied remedies are not immediately effected, our common cause will suffer a disastrous set-back.

I sincerely trust that you will not be offended at the frankness of my statements and I assure you that there is no intent on my part to dictate to you in matters concerning China; however, the future of all Asia is at stake along with the tremendous effort which America has expended in that region. Therefore I have reason for a profound interest in the matter.

Please have in mind that it has been clearly demonstrated in Italy, in France, and in the Pacific that air power alone cannot stop a determined enemy.

Matter of fact, the Germans have successfully conducted defensive actions and launched determined counter-attacks though overwhelmingly outnumbered in the air.

Should you agree to giving Stilwell such assignment as I now propose, I would recommend that General Sultan, a very fine officer who is now his deputy, be placed in command of the Chinese-American force in Burma, but under Stilwell's direction.[16]

This was indeed, as the President put it, a "radical" remedy. Parenthetically, it was not one that originated with General Stilwell. Nor had I yet visited Yenan or made any such suggestion for the use of the Communist forces. This could be regarded as "unilateral support," though probably not in the sense intended by Dr. Kubek. At any rate, Chiang's reception of it was frigid.[17]

---

[16] *Ibid.*, pp. 383–384.

[17] Because standing orders required personal delivery of such messages to the Generalissimo, I was called upon to serve as interpreter for General Ferris. For my future career, it was probably an unfortunate assignment (but not the only one during this period). Despite what seems to have been a continuing Chinese (and American) assumption that I had something to do with the content of the message, I was in fact as completely surprised as the recipient.

The Generalissimo temporized, and asked the President to send a special representative to China to discuss details of the arrangements for Stilwell's command. For this particular mission, General Hurley was selected. His orders from the President, as he communicated them at the time to the State Department, were brief and to the point:

> You are designated as my personal representative with General Chiang Kai-shek. You will report directly to me. Your mission will be to promote harmonious relations between General Chiang and General Stilwell and to facilitate the latter's exercise of command over the Chinese armies placed under his direction.
>
> You will be charged with additional specific duties. (General Hurley explained in this connection that the additional duties would pertain to supplies and that the directive therefor would come from the War Department.)
>
> In carrying out your mission you are to maintain intimate contact with Ambassador Gauss at Chungking and to keep him advised of your activities.[18]

The scope and nature of Hurley's directive from the President was subsequently to become the subject of much confusion and controversy. This was generated largely by Hurley's own vague, contradictory, and increasingly self-serving statements as his actions and policies came under criticism. It is worth noting, therefore, that Hurley's own contemporaneous account indicates that Roosevelt's instructions were limited and specific: to improve relations between Chiang and Stilwell, and to "facilitate" Stilwell's command of the Chinese armies.

FRUITS OF FAILURE

The details of the negotiations that led finally to the recall of General Stilwell have been exhaustively studied by others.[19] The question of chief concern here is whether Roosevelt's action in recalling Stilwell constituted abandonment of the policy of conditional support of Chiang and his government. The answer is not wholly clear. Tang Tsou concludes: "What the recall of Stilwell signified above all was the defeat of the United States in her application of the tactics of pressure, due to a failure of judgment and will rather than the objective weakness of her political position."[20] It is certainly clear that the American policy was defeated *in this particular instance.* It also seems clear that Roosevelt, after this experience, made

---

[18] *Foreign Relations 1944,* pp. 250–251. Inexplicably (in view of the clear record), Dr. Kubek states (*Papers,* p. 24) that Hurley was sent to China in response to a suggestion by Chiang, supported and transmitted by Vice President Wallace, that the President "send a personal representative to China to serve as a liaison between the central government at Chungking and the Communists at Yenan."

[19] The fullest account, with texts of most of the relevant messages, is Romanus and Sunderland, *Stilwell's Command Problems,* Chapters XI and XII. A comprehensive summary account is Tang Tsou, *America's Failure,* pp. 109–124.

[20] Tang Tsou, *America's Failure,* p. 122.

no further attempt to pressure Chiang Kai-shek in such a drastic manner. I suggest, however, that the history of this incident, and the developments that followed, show that the basic policy of conditional support continued to be followed. Furthermore, American support of Chiang and China came to be more limited as China's role diminished.

In August, before Hurley's departure from Washington, Chiang had raised three conditions: one of these was that China must control lend-lease and the United States must give generous financial aid.[21] Roosevelt brushed these conditions aside. Hurley arrived in Chungking on September 6. It soon became apparent that the Americans and Chinese were far apart in their conception of Stilwell's duties and authority as commander of the Chinese armies. Hurley felt that progress was being made toward resolving these problems: other, more objective sources, find no such evidence.[22]

The impasse was broken by the intrusion of another issue. On September 15, the Generalissimo—alarmed over Japanese advances in Kwangsi—proposed the withdrawal of the Y-Force from the Burma border (where it had just taken Tengchung and only needed to take Lungling to control the entire trace of the Burma Road) in order to protect Kunming. Stilwell's report of this alarming news was relayed to Marshall at Quebec, where Roosevelt and Churchill were meeting with the Combined Chiefs of Staff. Here the American and British leaders, military and civilian, were all—for the first time—in hearty agreement. It was apparent that the Japanese were being routed in Burma; a full scale amphibious assault on Rangoon to complete the recovery of all of Burma had just been approved on September 14. The threatened Chinese withdrawal of support would upset this plan. A stinging reply to Chiang was promptly prepared, approved and signed by Roosevelt, and despatched by the War Department to Stilwell for delivery.[23]

This message, and Stilwell's personal delivery of it (which may under the circumstances have been impolitic but was in accordance with existing orders), was utilized by Chiang as the pretext he had been hoping for to repudiate his earlier promise to place Stilwell in command. His first, "insubstantial" ground was that "Stilwell's delivery of the message in person made him Stilwell's subordinate."[24] Chiang (and Hurley as well) were apparently convinced that Stilwell himself had drafted the message.

21 Romanus and Sunderland, *Stilwell's Command Problems*, p. 414.

22 For example, Tang Tsou, *America's Failure*, p. 113: ". . . contrary to Hurley's subsequent account, there was no agreement from beginning to end of the negotiations on Stilwell's authority. . . ."

23 The text of the message appears in Romanus and Sunderland, *Stilwell's Command Problems*, pp. 445–446. Although perhaps not meriting the common description as an "ultimatum," it was unquestionably blunt and harsh. Why it was sent through Stilwell, instead of Hurley as the President's Special Representative, does not appear from the record.

24 Tang Tsou, *America's Failure*, p. 114.

Chiang next threatened (in a "confidential" talk to the Kuomintang's Central Executive Committee that soon leaked) to fight on, if necessary, without American aid. Hurley supported Chiang: "There is no issue between you [Roosevelt] and Chiang Kai-shek except Stilwell. . . . My opinion is that if you sustain Stilwell in this controversy, you will lose Chiang Kai-shek and possibly you will lose China with him."[25] Of some, but intangible, weight is also the fact that Stilwell's own acid, cantankerous temperament was well known to Roosevelt and had been the cause of recurrent complaints—and not from Chiang alone. Basically, the issue resolved itself to Chiang's insistence on his prerogative as chief of state. And this was a basis which Roosevelt found difficult to reject.[26]

Stilwell, then, was recalled. On this point, Chiang won. But it was not a very sweeping victory. The CBI Theater was split, and General Wedemeyer assigned to command the new China Theater. Lend-lease, which had been a bone of contention, remained in Wedemeyer's hands. The Y-Force stayed where it was, continued its drive on Lungling, and shortly joined up with the forces in North Burma to reopen the Road. Although Chiang specifically offered Stilwell's successor the command of Chinese troops, this was categorically declined: "As stated in my October 6 message, I do not feel that an American should in the present situation assume responsibility in a command position for the operations of Chinese forces in China."[27] And Wedemeyer's orders as Theater Commander indicated a mission much more restricted than that assigned to Stilwell.[28] He was given no orders "to increase the effectiveness of United States assistance . . . and to assist in improving the combat efficiency of the Chinese Army." There was, however, one new proviso pregnant with significance for the future: "You will not employ United States resources for suppression of civil strife except insofar as necessary to protect United States lives and property."

The policy significance of the Stilwell recall may be debatable. But there can hardly be any doubt that it marked another downward step in U.S.-China relations. To be sure, not all the participants realized this. The Generalissimo, on one hand, was apparently and quite understandably "confirmed in his belief that the United States was so dependent on him to protect her Far Eastern interests and so lacking in firmness of purpose in the pursuit of her policy that she would finally yield to his insistent demands and accept his views, no matter what he did or refused to do."[29]

---

25 *Ibid.*, p. 117.

26 See, for instance, Roosevelt's statements to Marshall in March 1943; footnote 5, above.

27 Roosevelt message of October 18 to Chiang; Romanus and Sunderland, *Stilwell's Command Problems,* pp. 468–469.

28 For Stilwell's orders, Romanus and Sunderland, *Stilwell's Mission to China,* p. 74. For Wedemeyer's orders, *Foreign Relations 1944,* pp. 178–179.

29 Tang Tsou, *America's Failure,* p. 122.

Hurley, it would seem, also came to the conclusion (though the record shows no basis in messages from the President) that the tactics of pressure had been unwise and were being abandoned. In any event, he showed no discouragement over what might to most people have appeared to be the failure of his mission.

On the American side, there was a legacy of frustration and bitterness. It was to be the Generalissimo's last diplomatic victory for many years. "Moreover," as Romanus and Sunderland point out, "the President's answers to the Generalissimo, progressively colder and less accommodating, suggest a corresponding alteration of attitude on Mr. Roosevelt's part toward the Generalissimo and China."[30] It seems clear that the defeat was accepted at least in part because of the general realization in Washington by this time that China's importance was drastically reduced. Militarily, it was no longer planned or expected that China would play a significant role in the war against Japan: the landings in the Philippines were already impending. Politically, Roosevelt's long and fervently held hope that China would become a great power in the near future now was seen as an illusion. Instead, he turned more actively to the exploration of the possibility of wartime and postwar cooperation with the Soviet Union as a basis for stability in the Far East.

---

[30] Romanus and Sunderland, *Stilwell's Command Problems,* p. 469.

IV
Ambassador Gauss Offers Neutral Advice

The Joint Chiefs of Staff memorandum to President Roosevelt recommending that the Gordian knot in China be cut by putting both Nationalist and Communist forces under the command of General Stilwell was dated July 4, 1944.[1] Coincidentally, on the same day (but obviously without knowledge of Washington developments), Ambassador Gauss in Chungking launched another, more friendly, attempt to use American influence in resolving the China impasse. As would be expected of this professional diplomat with long experience in China, it was a reasonable, carefully thought-out proposal; and it was given a preliminary test before commitment. The exploratory occasion was a long private conversation between Counselor of Embassy George Atcheson and Sun Fo.

> Atcheson then put forward an idea I had mentioned in our discussions in the Embassy by "wondering" whether it would be helpful for the Generalissimo to call all factions (including the Communists) and himself into a military council or high command and appeal to them to accept with him joint responsibility for effective military operations to save what remains of the country, giving them the fullest assurances that he wished to eliminate from the military scene all internal political maneuvers and calling upon them to participate with him in working out and carrying out a plan of joint operations, at same time appealing to people for revival of resistance and a united front. Atcheson said that he thought this would be a statesmanlike step for the Generalissimo to take and one which could not help but enhance his prestige at home and abroad as China's leader. Sun received this suggestion with apparent enthusiasm.[2]

It will be noted that this suggestion assumed, and was not unflattering to, the leadership of the Generalissimo; and that it was completely devoid of any threat or suggestion of American power to give or withhold. It has been criticized as being vague and ill-defined.[3] But this was precisely, and

---

[1] Romanus and Sunderland, *Stilwell's Command Problems*, p. 382.

[2] Telegram 1159, Gauss to Secstate, July 4, 1944 (*Foreign Relations 1944,* pp. 116–117). Sun Fo, the son of Sun Yat-sen, was then President of the Legislative Yuan. George Atcheson was a highly competent, senior member of the China corps of Foreign Service officers; he was later (like many others) to incur the overflowing antipathy of General Hurley.

[3] See, for instance, Herbert Feis, *The China Tangle* (Princeton: Princeton University Press, 1953), p. 174: "No version of this proposal that I have read tells

intentionally, one of its merits. It did not unrealistically hope to resolve, at one stroke, the bitterness and rivalries that had built up over the years.[4] Rather, it sought a minimum and flexible means (with the details to be worked out by the Chinese groups involved) of making a start toward bridging the chasms that were dividing the country. If successful, it could have brought about some revitalization of China's stagnant war effort. But more importantly, it could have provided a foundation for progress toward meeting the crisis, by now foreseen by all, that would face China if still un-unified when the Soviet Union entered the war and—with even more force—on the day that Japan was defeated.[5]

Parenthetically, I find it hard to resist pointing out that this proposal, like that of the Joint Chiefs, was also made several weeks before I reached Yenan and submitted the first of those reports that Dr. Kubek finds so lethal.

WASHINGTON PUSHES

The normally slow-moving State Department reacted to this cautious initiative with alacrity and enthusiasm.[6] Gauss was encouraged to persist and escalate. Two conversations with T. V. Soong, then Minister of Foreign Affairs, were only mildly encouraging. These were supposed to involve Tai Chi-t'ao, President of the Examination Yuan, and "one of the Generalissimo's oldest and closest friends" (who was living at the time with Soong).[7] Meanwhile, Gauss transmitted a new message from President Roosevelt, dated July 14, to Chiang Kai-shek as part of the effort to promote cooperation between the Chinese factions. Though referring to Chiang's recent conversations with Vice President Wallace, rather than specifically to the Gauss proposal for a "war council," this message urged a "working arrangement" with the Chinese Communists, particularly as a prelude to Chiang's hope for better relations with the Soviet Union.[8] Finally, there was a check-back with Sun Fo, with whom the matter had first been broached. This time he was less hopeful: "Dr. Sun expressed strong concurrence, but added with a shrug: 'The civil and military power in the Government is centered in one man.' "[9]

---

clearly just how this council would function, or how the differences would be adjusted."

[4] The plan was, of course, intended to bring in not only the Communists but also other important and disaffected groups in the country: provincial military leaders, intellectuals, and others excluded from the Generalissimo's narrow nexus of power. It was not, however, a full-fledged "coalition government."

[5] See, for example, despatch 2932 from Gauss to Secstate, September 4, 1944 (*Foreign Relations 1944*, p. 545).

[6] Telegram 931, Secstate to Gauss, July 8, 1944 (*Foreign Relations 1944*, p. 120).

[7] Telegram 1205, Gauss to Secstate, July 12, 1944 (*Foreign Relations 1944*, pp. 124–126); telegram 1288, Gauss to Secstate, July 25, 1944 (*Foreign Relations 1944*, p. 132).

[8] *Foreign Relations 1944*, p. 245.

[9] Telegram 1373, Gauss to Secstate, August 9, 1944 (*Foreign Relations 1944*, pp. 139–140).

It was not until August 31 that the Ambassador had his chance for a face-to-face talk with Chiang Kai-shek. The result was not encouraging: "While saying that it might at least be worth study, the Generalissimo did not appear to be more than politely responsive to the suggestion."[10] Washington, however, was unwilling to let the matter drop. Its response was a first-person message from Secretary of State Hull to the Ambassador in Chungking:

> The *President and I* have given careful consideration to your telegrams 1159, 1205 and 1480 [see footnotes 2, 7, and 10, above]. We agree with you that a positive, frank and friendly approach to Chiang on the subject of governmental and related military conditions in China should be made at this time.
> . . . It is requested that you inform Chiang that the *President and I* feel that your suggestion is practical and timely and deserving of careful consideration; that we are concerned, not only regarding non-settlement with the Chinese communists, but also with regard to reports of discontent and dissidence in other parts of the country among non-communist Chinese; that we are not interested in Chinese communists or other dissident elements as such, but that we are anxious on our own behalf and on the United Nations' behalf, as well as on behalf of China, that the Chinese people develop and utilize, under the leadership of a strong but representative and tolerant government, the physical and spiritual resources at their command in carrying on the war and in establishing a durable democratic peace; and that to this end factional differences can and should be merged and settled by intelligent conciliation and cooperation. We feel that a council or some body representative of all influential elements in the country and with full powers under Chiang's leadership would be a most effective organ for achieving this end. . . . You may, in addition, utilize *as from us* such portions of the cogent argumentation set forth in your reference telegrams as you choose, and also the views well expressed by Atcheson in his conversation with Sun Fo (your 1373) on August 9. . . .[11]

Since Atcheson's statements in his second talk with Sun Fo had now been specifically elevated as being the views of President Roosevelt and Secretary Hull, it is pertinent to examine them:

> . . . Atcheson went on to say that, in his opinion, Chinese Government now has greatest opportunity of hundred years of close contact with West to lead China to her rightful place as one of the great democratic nations of the world by bringing all elements together to

---

[10] The Ambassador's radio summary, telegram 1480, is in *China White Paper*, pp. 561–563; his fuller report by mail despatch is in *Foreign Relations 1944*, pp. 544–551.

[11] Emphasis added. A full and close paraphrase of this message is in *China White Paper*, pp. 563–564; the original text is in *Foreign Relations 1944*, pp. 567–569. The minor differences are almost entirely in word order. This is the only instance I know of where the editors of *Foreign Relations 1944* considered it necessary or desirable to repeat material already published in full in the earlier *China White Paper*.

form solidly united front against enemy and to lay firm foundations for China's future role in peace. He said United States not only wanted strong and united China—this had always been cardinal principle of American policy—but, as Dr. Sun was aware, United States Government had been striving vigorously in China's behalf to build up China as one of the Big Four so that as such China could, in actuality, be a great nation and exert effective influence in Far East for peace, postwar stability and political and economic collaboration with United States and other nations for benefit of all countries which were looking to new era of economic and political security based on liberal principles of cooperation and mutual good-will. Atcheson said United States could not do this alone; it was not merely question of giving military aid to China and supporting China diplomatically in world councils and affairs, but China must actively help herself. He pointed out that China was not doing so and was seemingly allowing the prospects for a great national and international future to be jeopardized by the deterioration which was not only progressing in the military field, but in the internal and, in some respects, in the international political scenes.[12]

CHIANG REFUSES

The Generalissimo received Ambassador Gauss, accompanied by Counselor Atcheson, for an hour and a half of "friendly conversation" on September 15. For a talk of this importance and length, Gauss's radio report was—even for this man of few wasted words—unusually terse. The Ambassador had, indeed, run into a stone wall; and he made no attempt to conceal his deep disappointment.

> . . . As regards question of coalition war council or similar arrangement, Chiang said he was already considering steps looking to that end but changed immediately to a dissertation on the People's Political Council now in session. Upon my mentioning that People's Political Council was purely advisory body he said he assumed that our suggestion did not contemplate change in government structure, something which should not be attempted at this time. I replied that I looked upon participation of minority parties in government as desirable; that a national government is frequently resorted to in times of crisis; but my suggestion did not contemplate immediate reorganization of government but rather setting up of a war council on which civilian and military leaders of other parties or groups would participate to face the problems of the present situation, and to share responsibility. I hoped that in this manner the distrust now so evident between KMT and Communists could gradually be dissipated and from there on the unification of China could go on to a more satisfactory basis in due course, but the council should in my opinion have both authority and responsibility, responsibility being the sobering element in a council of factions established to meet a crisis. Chiang said again that he was "considering steps" and expressed

---

[12] See footnote 9, above. It was to these statements that Dr. Sun expressed "strong concurrence." The reader will remember that this was a telegram; hence the omission of articles and other unessential words.

hope that "time would come" when representatives of parties other than Kuomintang could be taken into the Government . . .[13]

At this point, Washington gave up. A memorandum from Cordell Hull to the President concluded:

> . . . The impression which Ambassador Gauss received of Chiang's reaction to our approach is not encouraging. However, it is believed that the approach was worth while. It put on record with Chiang our feeling with regard to the political situation in China. At the same time it may serve to influence him to make changes which by conviction he would never make, but which he may nevertheless make as a matter of expediency in response to advice from us. . . . a firm and consistent exertion of influence upon Chiang may be effective in at least bringing about an amelioration of unsatisfactory conditions in China. While no early and general improvement is anticipated, it may be possible to arrest further deterioration and prepare for more effective Chinese cooperation in future American operations in China and for cooperation between China and the USSR in the event of Soviet military action against Japan.[14]

Secretary Hull's memorandum was certainly right in its conclusion that Chiang would never make changes "by conviction"; but the logic that "he may nevertheless make [such changes] as a matter of expediency in response to advice from us" seems based on little more than what seemed reasonable to outsiders. We are indebted to Professor Tang Tsou for pointing to an entry in Chiang Kai-shek's diary during this period (August, 1944):

> So long as I am alive and healthy, the nation will have a future. Although the Communist party has an international background and mysterious plots, one day it will ultimately come to a dead end. There is no need to be unduly anxious, if only I can bear the abuses and wait for the opportune moment. If the time comes when there is no other alternative, then the only way to deal with the situation is to cut the entangled hemp with a sharp knife. At this time, all sacrifices will not be begrudged, even if there is the danger of destroying the nation and ruining the family.[15]

One other note may be relevant. Professor Tsou seems to suggest that this American approach to Chiang was known to the Communists and

---

[13] Telegram 1567, from Gauss "for the Secretary and the President," September 16, 1944 (*Foreign Relations 1944*, pp. 573–574). The Ambassador undoubtedly, as was his invariable and meticulous habit, forwarded a much fuller report by mail pouch; this does not appear in the *Foreign Relations* volume.

[14] Memorandum, Hull to Roosevelt, September 25, 1944 (*Foreign Relations 1944*, p. 594).

[15] Tang Tsou, *America's Failure*, p. 173, citing Chiang Ching-kuo, *Wo-ti fu-ch'in*, (*My Father*), chap. 3, pp. 4–5. Professor Tsou points out that "to cut the entangled hemp with a sharp knife" is a general equivalent to "cutting the Gordian knot." Apparently there is no English translation of Chiang Ching-kuo's book about his famous father.

thus influenced the raising of their political price for a settlement, specifically their formal demand, on October 13, for the establishment of a coalition government. I believe that this was not the case. Ambassador Gauss was deeply imbued with a long background of American policy of non-interference in the internal affairs of China. He regarded this proposal as a matter of great delicacy and gravity (justified by the seriousness of the situation developing in China) and treated it with the highest confidence. There was some consideration during his talks with the Generalissimo, and in the interchange of messages with the State Department, that he might make a generally similar approach to the Communists. Gauss was instructed that he could express "the views of the American Government in general in regard to the need of Chinese unity"—which meant that he was not to put himself in the position of supporting Chiang's political aims. Chiang, on the other hand, wished the Ambassador to "impress Lin [Lin Tsu-han, the Communist representative then in Chungking] that the Chinese Communists must submit unconditionally to the principle of unified military command under the Generalissimo and to the political control of the National Government."[16] When Chiang learned of the restrictions placed on the Ambassador, he dropped the subject. There was thus no contact by the American Embassy in Chungking with the Communists in regard to this matter. So far as I was concerned, although I was in Chungking when the proposal was first advanced, I knew nothing of it until my return from Yenan on October 23 (when I was told in confidence and detail by Ambassador Gauss himself). The Communists may have had sources within the National Government; but the only persons there who may be assumed to have known of it were Sun Fo, Tai Chi-t'ao, T. V. Soong, and Chiang Kai-shek himself. There is a more natural explanation for the Communists raising their ante; as both Ambassador Gauss and Professor Tsou point out, time was working in favor of the Communists as they consolidated their hold in the rural areas of North China and the crisis deepened in the rest of China.

MORE FRUITS OF FAILURE

I have described this non-productive episode in U.S.-China relations in some detail for several reasons. For one thing, it has tended to be overlooked or minimized. Perhaps this is natural since it was intentionally put forward in a quiet, "face-saving" way by a discreet, almost self-effacing diplomat. Also, it was submerged by the high drama of events that accompanied and immediately followed it: the Stilwell recall, and the Hurley negotiations with the Communists. But since we have heard a great deal over the years about the United States trying to "force Chiang Kai-shek as the price of our assistance to bring Chinese Communists into his gov-

---

[16] See documents referred to in footnotes 10, 11, and 13, above.

ernment to form a coalition,"[17] it may be well to recall that a serious attempt was made, in a friendly manner with no suggestion of threats or a *quid pro quo,* to persuade Chiang that unity was a serious problem—not only for the immediate prosecution of the war but also for China's role in the peace—and that we offered no hard-and-fast solution because we considered it a Chinese problem which the Chinese themselves should solve.[18]

Finally, non-productive though it seemed at the time, it inevitably had an effect in setting the stage for the ensuing scenes. On the Chinese side, Chiang had rebuffed another attempted American "intervention"—mild and well-intentioned though that intervention was. On the American side, frustration and alarm over the looming war-end crisis was increased. The U.S. Army had, in effect, written off the China Theater. President Roosevelt had become discouraged that China could play a major postwar role. Now the State Department (as we shall see in more detail at a later point) was to become steadily more pessimistic about the prospects for Chiang's regime, and more anxious to avoid unconditional American commitment to that regime.

Part of this new stage setting was a change in the American actors. General Stilwell had already gone. Now suddenly, only a few days later on November 1, Ambassador Gauss resigned. For the record, he was tired and not in good health. It is true that he had served as ambassador in Chungking for three and a half years in uncomfortable and difficult conditions. The fatigue, though, was largely of the spirit. He had been patient with more than a reasonable share of special Presidential envoys: White House assistant Lauchlin Currie (several times), Wendell Willkie, and Vice President Wallace, to name the more prominent. But until Hurley burst in upon Chungking (on September 6), none had seemed so actively to try to demonstrate to the government to which he was accredited that the American ambassador was a superfluity. Indeed, Hurley's first and most flagrant violation of his Presidential instructions had been of their third paragraph: "In carrying out your mission you are to maintain intimate contact with Ambassador Gauss at Chungking and to keep him advised of your activities."[19] However, Gauss had a soldier's sense of

---

[17] For instance, *Papers,* pp. 27 and 29 (the latter quoting John F. Kennedy in 1948).

[18] See particularly the report of Ambassador Gauss's first interview with Chiang (*Foreign Relations 1944,* p. 548). It should also be remembered that the attempt to impress Chiang with the desirability of Chinese unity has been a major subject of discussion during the recent (June, 1944) visit to Chungking of Vice President Wallace; see, for instance, *Foreign Relations 1944,* p. 234, and *China White Paper,* pp. 549, 552–554, 555–556, 559, and 560.

[19] The fact that the Ambassador was, for instance, completely uninformed of the talks leading up to the Stilwell recall is graphically illustrated by his letter of September 28, 1944, to the Secretary of State (*Foreign Relations 1944,* pp. 256–258).

duty and he was not burdened with an overweening pride. What dominated his long private conversation with me on the night of October 23—when I was just in from Yenan and on the eve of my departure for Washington—was the long and serious thought that he had devoted to developing his proposal to Chiang, his disappointment at the blunt, almost out-of-hand way it had been dismissed by the Generalissimo, and his deep discouragement about these implications for the future of China and American interests involved there. It was with this background that he asked me to carry a personal message to responsible officers in the State Department: that he would be submitting his resignation formally within the next few days, and they were to understand that this was not a pro forma resignation normally submitted at the end of a presidential term but one that he seriously wished to have accepted.[20]

---

[20] Roosevelt's third term was just ending. I delivered the Ambassador's oral message on October 30 to Assistant Secretary Grew. The White House then announced his resignation before he had actually submitted it (*Foreign Relations 1944*, pp. 185–186, 188–189).

V
General Hurley Sustains Chiang

China, though perhaps not Chiang Kai-shek, had lost two sincere and experienced friends. She had gained a new one; it remained to be seen whether his enthusiasm and ambition would make up for his lack of knowledge and experience. Washington hesitated briefly over the appointment of a new ambassador. Hurley was already on the spot, and obviously eager.[1] Furthermore, within a week after the Stilwell recall (which should, by Hurley's original directive, have terminated his mission to China), the Generalissimo, in a personal message to President Roosevelt had requested his assignment "on a more permanent basis":

> You were good enough to indicate in your message of October 6th [5th] that although there would not be, in the present situation, an American officer in command of Chinese ground forces in China, you are willing to continue General Hurley as your personal representative regarding military affairs in China, although your original directive to General Hurley of August 18th seems to limit the subjects on which he is authorized to cooperate with me.
>
> I do hope that General Hurley's assignment as your personal representative will be on a more permanent basis, and that he will be given a directive broad enough that he could cooperate with me on many vital questions involving our military relationship with U.S.A. For instance, I am relying upon him for assistance in negotiation with the Chinese Communists with whom he is already conferring. It is my purpose to increase the Communist troops in the regular forces of the National Army, and this now constitutes one of the most vital requisites in our war against Japan. General Hurley has my complete confidence. Because of his rare knowledge of human nature, and his approach to the problem, he seems to get on well with the Communist leaders. As your personal representative, possessing my full confidence, his contribution in solving this hitherto insoluble problem would be of the greatest value to our war effort.
>
> I am sending this message through the present channel because it affects General Hurley personally.[2]

---

[1] Hurley tried hard to give the impression that he scorned diplomatic assignments, and anything connected with the State Department (see, for instance, Lohbeck, *Hurley,* pp. 278–279, and 308–309); the fact, however, is that he sought the appointment as ambassador when he was first approached in August about going to China as the President's special representative (*Foreign Relations 1944,* pp. 247–248).

[2] The full text is in *Foreign Relations 1944,* p. 170, with the explanation (n. 87): "Undated telegram sent by T. V. Soong to Harry L. Hopkins, with the following introductory sentence: 'Generalissimo asked me to request you to transmit the following personal message to the President.' Copy obtained from the Franklin

Had the State Department had knowledge of this out-of-channels message, it might have noted several things about it.[3] First, it was a thinly-veiled request that the regularly appointed ambassador (Gauss) be replaced by Hurley; the kind of broad mission that Chiang envisaged would leave the ambassadorship—if not occupied by Hurley—only a ceremonial shell. Second, it was a clear recognition by Chiang—and, I suggest, also by Hurley—that Hurley's original directive was in fact the negotiation of Stilwell's command of Chinese troops. Third, it indicated that Hurley had already, without authorization or consultation with Washington, entered into negotiations with the Chinese Communists. But, and more important, his services as mediator were being undertaken, at least in Chiang's mind ("I am relying upon him for assistance in negotiation"), almost as a spokesman for the Generalissimo. This was very different from the limited and strictly neutral approach which Secretary Hull (in his "The President and I" instruction of September 9) had authorized Gauss to make to the Communists, and which the Generalissimo had dropped as soon as he learned that it would be limited to putting forward American concerns rather than presenting the Kuomintang terms.[4]

A NEW AMBASSADOR

Whatever, and in what circles, consideration was given in Washington to these matters, Hurley was appointed ambassador by Roosevelt on No-

---

D. Roosevelt Library, Hyde Park, N.Y." A partial text (substantially all of the second paragraph) appears in Lohbeck, *Hurley,* pp. 308–309, where the date is given as October 25, 1944. This seems consistent with the contents. Since the Hyde Park copy is undated, and since Lohbeck's book gives no indication of having utilized the Roosevelt papers, it seems logical to assume that Hurley received a copy at the time from either Chiang or T. V. Soong. There is one variation in the two texts, just above the middle of the second paragraph. The Hyde Park version: "It is my purpose to increase the Communist troops in the regular forces." The Lohbeck/Hurley version: "It is my purpose to incorporate the Communist troops in the regular forces." Several statements seem a little surprising. "This now constitutes one of the most vital requisites in our war against Japan." This was a constant theme of Hurley; but as recently as June 22, the Generalissimo had insisted to Vice President Wallace: "Please understand that the Communists are not good for the war effort against Japan" (*China White Paper,* p. 554). Or, "he [Hurley] seems to get on well with the Communist leaders"—something that Chiang was hardly in a position to know at first-hand (and Hurley had not yet been to Yenan where the real leaders were). If Hurley was not a party to the drafting, one would guess that he was not far removed.

[3] The Chinese cannot, of course, be blamed for seeking to develop and utilize any channels into the center of power in Washington that seemed best able to further their own purposes. The fact is that they became extremely adept at and prone to use these roundabout and not strictly official channels. Hurley himself, as the record abundantly shows, also considered himself little bound by normal channels.

[4] For Hull's instruction see Chapter IV, note 11. For the report by Gauss of the Generalissimo's obvious lack of interest in the kind of approach he was authorized to make, see Chapter IV, note 13.

vember 17.[5] And the attempt to bring about a settlement between the National Government and the Communists did, in fact, become Hurley's primary—one could reasonably say, all-absorbing—concern for most of the next year. In his biography of Hurley, Don Lohbeck states that Hurley received a "new directive" which, "as Chiang had requested," was broad.[6] Neither Lohbeck nor any other scholar has, however, found the text of such a directive; nor could such a directive have come from the President orally, since Hurley was not in Washington between August 1944 and March 1945. What Lohbeck does cite is Hurley's own formulation of his "understanding [of] the policy of the United States in China" which he put together much later, and after much water had flowed under the bridge, at a time when the State Department was beginning to question the implications of some of the commitments that Hurley seemed to be making.[7]

The manner in which Hurley first became involved in the Kuomintang-Communist negotiations seems to be indicated by an enigmatic document which, through somewhat mysterious channels, did not become known to the State Department until several years later in 1949.

October 17, 1944.

Suggestions

1. We suggest that General Hurley hold a talk with Messrs. Lin Tzu-han and Tung Pi-wu, the Communist members of the P. P. C.

---

[5] In view of Dr. Kubek's remarkable estimate of my influence on policy ("the hands at the control levers were those of a few young men . . . John Paton Davies and John Stewart Service": *Papers*, p. 30), perhaps a personal reminiscence may be permitted. I was actually in Washington during this period, and was called by Harry Hopkins for a discussion of the situation in China. At its conclusion, Mr. Hopkins asked whether I thought that Hurley might be a good appointment as ambassador. My reply, for several stated reasons, was that it would be "a disaster." It was not many days later that I read that the appointment had been made. History has not altered my opinion.

[6] Lohbeck, *Hurley,* p. 310. The reference is obviously to the Chiang Kai-shek letter of October 25 to Roosevelt—which seems to amount to the rather unusual suggestion that directives to American ambassadors are based, not on American interests, but the wishes of the receiving country. There is no published reference to any reply by Roosevelt to this letter from Chiang; but, as Romanus and Sunderland point out (*Stilwell's Command Problems,* p. 469), it was a period when Roosevelt's correspondence with the Generalissimo was becoming "progressively colder and less accommodating, suggest[ing] a corresponding alteration of attitude on Mr. Roosevelt's part." As we shall see, the Roosevelt messages also became less frequent.

[7] *Foreign Relations 1944,* p. 745. The State Department had not, up to this date, heard anything officially of what the Ambassador was doing; his own preference was to report only to the President—but even then chaotically, sporadically, and only through non-State Department (Army or Navy) channels. Secretary Stettinius's rather diffident request for a report is in *Foreign Relations 1944,* p. 744. There are innumerable additional, variant versions of Hurley's conception of his "instructions," "directive," "mission," or "understanding of policy" (see, for instance, *Foreign Relations 1945,* pp. 107–114, 172–177, 555–557, and 722–726), but he never quotes a specific document and usually avoids terms as definite as "directive."

now in Chungking. Such talk is of course of a private and confidential character; Lin and Tung should be made to understand that they must not give it any publicity without the General's approval.

2. It is hoped that when the aforesaid talk takes place, the General will state the attitude of the American and Russian governments concerning the Chinese Communist Party, and stress the necessity of the Communists to come to an immediate agreement with the Chinese government. A question may be put, we think, to Lin and Tung whether the Communists desire the General's good-office for bringing about a settlement with the government. It may be indicated to them that if Yenan is willing to accept the General's good-office, he will put forward a proposal of settlement, provided he can obtain a previous assurance from the Chinese government that the latter would not object to his making such a move.

The press and radio at Yenan is conducting a very violent anti-government propaganda which benefits nobody except our enemy and the puppet government at Nanking. This propaganda handicaps our negotiations seriously. It will do well if the General can persuade the Communists to stop it.

Some arrangement for a personal contact between the Generalissimo and Mr. Mao Tze-tung, leader of the Communists, appears to be necessary if a speedy and real settlement is sought. We should like the General to give Lin and Tung a hint on this point.

3. Should Yenan react favorably toward the General's suggestion, he will, we submit, proceed to draft a proposal of settlement and hand it over to both the Chinese government and the Communists. Before the drafting we should like to give the General a full account of what the government has conceded and may possibly concede regarding the various points of dispute. We hope that the General's proposal will not go beyond what we may possibly persuade the government to accept.[8]

Not knowing what to make of this unsigned and unidentified paper, the puzzled editors of *Foreign Relations 1944* label it vaguely as: "Document Prepared in the Embassy in China." It does not require much imagination or even, I suggest, a close reading, to realize that the "we" who prepared the document were not Americans at all: they could only be representatives of the Kuomintang side in the dispute with the Communists. Since General Hurley never mentioned the paper, there is no way of knowing his attitude toward it. But within the next four days after the paper was dated, he had had two conversations with the Communist delegates in

[8] *Foreign Relations 1944,* pp. 650–651. A footnote (no. 33) explains: "All documents on this file number 893.00/1–1049—were taken from a microfilm roll received by the Department in January 1949 from the Embassy in China, at Nanking." I am indebted to Professor John F. Melby, who served in the Embassy at Nanking and subsequently was a member of the group engaged in the Department in putting together and editing the *China White Paper,* for some additional information (personal letter of January 19, 1971):

Some several weeks after the *China White Paper* appeared in August 1949 I chanced across Harry Hinderer who had been the Chief Administrative Officer in Nanking. He told me that after the Embassy files had suddenly

Chungking (Lin Tsu-han and Tung Pi-wu); he saw them again on October 23;[9] and on November 7 he flew to Yenan carrying a draft agreement "corrected by Wang Shih-chieh and General Chang Chih-chung" (the Kuomintang negotiating team). And though to more conventional mediators it might seem to qualify his "good-office," it does appear to reflect the

been shipped out of China in the late fall of 1948 to avoid their being seized by someone during the ensuing chaotic period, he had found a wad of papers wedged into the back of a filing drawer. All the papers dated back to Chungking days. Rather than taking a chance on shipping any more papers or entrusting them to be hand carried by people already overburdened with the last dregs of civil war, he microfilmed them and brought the roll back to Washington, having then burned the papers.

A cursory check of the 1944 and 1945 volumes of *Foreign Relations* indicates that at least 46 documents, considered by the editors to be of significance sufficient to merit inclusion in these collections, are known to the State Department (and to historians) only by their having been preserved and forwarded in this unusual and much delayed manner. All the documents relate to Kuomintang-Communist relations in late 1944 and to General Hurley's mediation effort. Since they did not reach Washington until 1949, it should be appreciated that while the negotiations were proceeding (in 1944 and 1945), the State Department and other interested agencies in Washington (including the White House) were substantially uninformed—except for General Hurley's own brief and usually incomplete reports.

[9] The fact that Hurley had seen the Communist delegates twice is shown by a letter from them to Hurley dated October 21, 1945; see *Foreign Relations 1944*, p. 655. The publication of this letter, and the document referred to in note 8, clears up a minor mystery that has puzzled me at least for many years. Theodore H. White and Annalee Jacoby recount the following episode in their valuable, contemporary account of this period, *Thunder Out of China* (p. 250):

Even before Stilwell had been relieved, Hurley confided to one of the authors of this book that he had been negotiating with Chiang Kai-shek and Chungking's two leading Communists. This was vital information; it meant that for the first time America was taking active steps to avert a Chinese civil war. The author questioned the ambassador; Hurley could not pronounce the Communists' names, but he listened to descriptions of the Communist emissaries and agreed that yes, those were the two men with whom he had worked, and he was hopeful of a solution. Thereupon both authors hastened to the Communists to verify the story and to learn their views as to the possibility of a settlement and what they thought of Mr. Hurley? The Communists flatly denied that they had ever met the ambassador. They asserted that they had invited him to dinner but that he had never replied, and they had no idea when they might be asked to participate in the start of negotiations. The correspondents returned to Hurley and told him what the Communists had said, asking for a clarification of the story, but beyond repeating that he had been presiding over negotiations, the ambassador was unable to account for the confusion.

The two men whom the ambassador had taken for the Communist emissaries were never positively identified. Hurley had noticed their presence in the course of a routine meeting, but that was all. One thing is certain. They were not the accredited representatives of the Yenan government.

Hurley, following the strict injunction in the first paragraph of the "Suggestions," had been more successful in sealing the lips of the Communist delegates than in restraining his own expansive inclination to impress correspondents with the progress that he was making in "saving China." For background on why the "Sugges-

assumptions and spirit with which Hurley embarked on his ambitious endeavor.

A NEW APPROACH

One of these assumptions was that he was not to "pressure" Chiang Kai-shek. One can only suggest that Hurley's memory was short. The proposal to place General Stilwell in command of all Chinese troops, specifically including the Communists, was after all a very strong and direct attempt to "pressure" the Generalissimo.[10] And it was precisely to apply pressure, on the spot and in a personal (even if persuasive) way, that President Roosevelt had sent Hurley to China only a few weeks before. It is true that the pressure had failed. But there is nothing in the tone or phraseology of President Roosevelt's two replies to Chiang of October 5 and 18 that indicate or imply that he had changed his basic attitude.[11]

A second major assumption was that Hurley's principal mission was to "sustain" Chiang Kai-shek. Of course, China was our ally; we recognized the National Government; and Chiang Kai-shek was the head of that government. We also recognized Chiang as the commander in chief of the China Theater of the war. Diplomatic relations are normally between recognized governments, rather than linked to specified leaders.[12] In the case of Great Britain, for instance, it would have seemed strange during the war to insist that we were committed to the leadership of Winston Churchill; when power shifted to the Labor Party and Clement Attlee, it made no difference in our relations and support. To change the example a bit, one wonders if Hurley would have argued that because the USSR was our ally we were also committed to support the Russian Communist Party and specifically to sustain the leadership of Stalin.[13] In other words,

---

tions" were so insistent on confidentiality, one can refer to Chiang Kai-shek's second meeting with Ambassador Gauss on September 15 (see *Foreign Relations 1944*, p. 573): "The Generalissimo later raised question whether if proposed conversation with Lin should take place, Communists might not publicize it for their own purposes, perhaps to indicate that American Government was countenancing or supporting them or at least was mediating between them and the National Government."

[10] Romanus and Sunderland, *Stilwell's Command Problems*, pp. 383–384.

[11] *Ibid.*, pp. 459 and 468–469.

[12] There has, however, been a historical tendency of Western nations (including the United States) in their dealings with non-Western or less developed countries to put their support behind the hopefully effective, "strong-man" type of leader. Examples in China have been Western support of Yuan Shih-k'ai and various subsequent warlord figures to the neglect of other political forces within the country. In his narrow fixation on "sustaining" the Generalissimo, Hurley was thus in one sense (though one that was hardly complimentary to China) being traditional.

[13] Perhaps one should not be too confident of Hurley's reactions, even in the case of Stalin. For a brief period in 1942, Hurley had served as the first American diplomatic representative in New Zealand. When I served in that country in 1946–1948, the memories of his stay were still vivid. One of the most common related to a national election. The incumbent Prime Minister, seeking reelection, was Peter Fraser, the astute leader of the Labor Party. He and Hurley soon—and quite

"support China" was not necessarily the same thing as "sustain the Generalissimo." This was a distinction that General Hurley never seemed able to make.

A third general consideration seems to have been in Hurley's mind, at least when he entered into the negotiations. This was apparently what Hurley considered to have been an oral commitment by Chiang to make some (and presumably, in Hurley's mind, substantial) concessions in order to reach a political settlement with the Communists. Hurley mentioned this agreement in conversations at the time, but seems to have been reluctant to include anything but vague mention of it in his reports; I have found no record of the agreement having been defined or put into writing. He referred to it, for instance, in a conversation with John Davies on November 13: "One of the conditions which he and the Generalissimo agreed to in connection with the removal of General Stilwell, General Hurley stated, was that the Generalissimo would undertake to reach an agreement with the Communists."[14]

There is no need to recount in detail the story of General Hurley's negotiations. It has been told by Hurley himself, by the State Department, by Professors Feis and Tsou, and if one has the patience to pursue the scattered documents it can be traced in the 1944 and 1945 volumes of *Foreign Relations*.[15] Very briefly, Hurley took with him to Yenan a rather bland set of five points that had been drawn up by him and approved by the KMT negotiators.[16] The Communist leaders prepared their own five points, calling for a coalition government, which Hurley with helpful enthusiasm then reworked and improved (and signed along with Mao Tse-

---

properly—became good friends. Fraser recognized Hurley's penchant for oratory and began making it a habit to invite Hurley to accompany him to meetings during the campaign. The American Minister would at some point be introduced as an honored guest and asked to make a few remarks. These would invariably start out as a rip-snorting, flag-waving talk about the war (then at a low ebb, especially so far as New Zealand was concerned) but end up as a strong endorsement of his "old friend, staunch ally, and great leader of the country"—Prime Minister Fraser. The reactions to this story of the American Republican boosting the socialist New Zealander varied, of course, according to the party affiliation of the teller, though all could agree that Hurley was a most unusual diplomat. Fraser (and Hurley) won.

[14] John Davies, memorandum of November 14, 1944, "Conversation with General Hurley" (*Foreign Relations 1944*, pp. 692–693). Mr. Davies was a Foreign Service Officer attached to the staff of General Wedemeyer—as he had been previously to the staff of General Stilwell. One can only speculate about Hurley's seeming reticence regarding this "understanding" with the Generalissimo. At the time he thought he reached it, Hurley was keenly sensitive to American criticism in China that he had "sold out" Stilwell. By the time that Chiang's willingness to make concessions later proved to be something less than Hurley had assumed, Hurley had thoroughly committed himself to Chiang. Bringing the agreement into the open would also do nothing to add to Hurleys' self-image as a negotiator.

[15] Lohbeck, *Hurley*, pp. 307–387; *China White Paper*, pp. 73–110; Feis, *China Tangle*, pp. 208–225, 255–303; Tang Tsou, *America's Failure*, pp. 288–345.

[16] For Hurley's original draft: *Foreign Relations 1944*, p. 659. For the draft as corrected by the KMT delegates: *ibid.*, p. 666.

tung).[17] Hurley's elation at getting Communist agreement to what he considered an eminently reasonable settlement was dashed when he returned to Chungking and found it totally unacceptable to Chiang Kai-shek.[18] The Kuomintang side then prepared several versions of a three-point counter-draft, omitting reference to a coalition government, which was equally unsatisfactory to the Communists.[19] Despite energetic efforts by Hurley to keep the negotiations alive, they ground to a halt and it was obvious by mid-February 1945 that an impasse had been reached. At this point, Hurley went to Washington. After his return in April, via the Soviet Union, an unproductive attempt was made to resume discussions. It was not until August 1945, after the Japanese surrender and the signing of the Sino-Soviet Treaty, that real negotiations recommenced with the visit of Mao Tse-tung to Chungking. These talks again proved unsuccessful. Hurley returned to the United States in late September and resigned on November 26, 1945, blaming their failure on "professional foreign service men . . . and the imperialist bloc of nations."[20] The Marshall Mission tried to pick up the pieces.

One of the sad aspects of this whole exercise in futility is that there is no indication that Hurley ever had a clear understanding of the difficulty of the problems or the nature of the issues that were involved. At the beginning, this was certainly not his fault. He had no background of experience or knowledge of Chinese affairs; and he had been sent out hurriedly with the sketchiest of briefings and no adequate staff.[21] But after his ar-

---

[17] *Ibid.*, pp. 687–688. The principal Communist contribution was: "The present National Government is to be reorganized into a Coalition National Government embracing representatives of all anti-Japanese parties and non-partisan bodies. . . . At the same time the National Military Council is to be reorganized into the United National Military Council consisting of representatives of all anti-Japanese armies." Hurley's main contribution was a full Bill of Rights, including such specific details as Habeas Corpus and "those two rights defined as freedom from fear and freedom from want." Interesting details of this episode are provided by David D. Barrett, *Dixie Mission: The United States Army Observer Group in Yenan, 1944* (Berkeley: Center for Chinese Studies, 1970), pp. 56–76. One value of Colonel Barrett's account is that this was the only occasion, so far as I know, during all these lengthy negotiations that Hurley was accompanied by any American other than an interpreter and/or stenographer. Since the Chinese accounts have not been published, Colonel Barrett's eyewitness report is the only one—limited to this one incident though it is—that does not come from Hurley himself.

[18] Hurley apparently never was convinced that the Communist "five points," which he freely conceded owed much to his drafting, were anything but fair; see, for instance, *Foreign Relations 1944*, pp. 696, 699, 734.

[19] *Ibid.*, pp. 697–698, 703–704, and 706–707. An interesting sidelight on the tactics involved is that T. V. Soong sought to have the KMT counterdraft—incompatible in every point with the draft agreement which Hurley had signed in Yenan—put forward as Hurley's own proposal. Hurley refused.

[20] *Foreign Relations 1945*, pp. 722–726.

[21] Hurley had made a three-day visit to Chungking in November 1943 in connection with possible Chinese participation in the Teheran Conference. His briefing for his mission in August 1944 apparently consisted of one conversation with President Roosevelt and one talk with members of the State Department. His staff

rival, for reasons—some of personality—which do not need elaboration here, he clung to several basic misconceptions. And, as difficulties appeared and success continued to elude him, he developed a new (and sometimes conflicting) rationale to buttress them. The reader in 1971 may well say that the perspective of history and the recent publication of pertinent documents have made things clearer now than they were in 1944 and 1945. To some extent, of course, this is true. But I think that the record (including Dr. Kubek's selected compilation, but more particularly the far more inclusive and representative volumes of the *Foreign Relations* series for 1944 and 1945) will show that a great many Americans (including those both in the State Department and in the field) did see these problems at the time and did try to call attention to them.[22]

The first of these misconceptions was that the primary importance of Chinese unity was to increase the military effort against Japan. As late as January 31, 1945, he was insisting:

> We are fighting a relentless enemy. That, in my opinion, justifies our action in attempting to unify the forces of China to help us defeat the enemy. A unification of the military forces of the Communist Party and National Government would have a battle effect, equal at least, to one fully equipped American Army. The result of unification of the Chinese military forces is worthy of much more consideration than it has heretofore received from America.[23]

It is true that when Hurley was sent to China in August 1944, there was a Japanese drive that threatened to end or make even less effective the Chinese war effort. But this drive—Japan's last-gasp military effort in China—had reached its high-water mark in December. By the time that Hurley was reporting, the Japanese were pulling back; and, as we have seen, the results of Teheran had made it unnecessary that China would play any very significant role in the war against Japan. What was uppermost in the minds of both parties (and of most American observers except Hurley) was the situation that would prevail in China on the day of Japan's defeat.

It should be acknowledged here that this point has been obscured by the fact that others besides Hurley who were involved in China policy during this period were also invoking short-term military desirability (i.e., the more effective prosecution of the war) as the most feasible means of

---

consisted of one Army officer (Colonel Edward J. McNally) as aide and one sergeant-stenographer. It was (mistakenly) assumed that in Chungking he would work closely with General Stilwell and Ambassador Gauss.

[22] One of the more incredible aspects of Dr. Kubek's documentation of his historical introduction is that he has only one reference (*Papers*, p. 24, n. 39) to *Foreign Relations 1944* and no reference at all to *Foreign Relations China 1945* (published in 1969).

[23] Telegram 141, Hurley to Secstate, January 31, 1945 (*Foreign Relations 1945*, p. 192).

achieving important—but quite different—long-range political objectives (i.e., to ward off civil war, to avoid driving the Communists into dependence on the USSR, and to bring about postwar unity and stability). The explanation, I think, is that we were all imbued (rightly or wrongly) with the conviction that American policy in the prosecution of the war was based primarily on military considerations. We therefore assumed that our recommendations had little chance of being heard at policy-making levels in Washington, let alone acted upon, unless they could be shown as being related directly to the war.

A second Hurley misconception was that a political settlement between the two parties should not be difficult to achieve because their aims and objectives were not basically dissimilar. This was a favorite theme of Hurley, and his statements of it are numerous. One example will suffice:

> . . . [T]wo fundamental facts are emerging: (1) the Communists are not in fact Communists, they are striving for democratic principles; and . . . (2) the one party, one man personal government of the Kuomintang is not in fact Fascist, it is striving for democratic principles.[24]

Here again, this is not the newly-arrived Hurley reporting; he had been in China for five full months, of which he had spent most of the past four in negotiations with the two parties.[25] As an American lawyer and politician, steeped in American political traditions of legal safeguards, constitutionalism, and democracy, it seemed natural to him—as he showed near the outset in his drafting of the five-point agreement in Yenan (which he continued to consider a "fair" basis for a settlement)—that the problem could be solved by a dose of American legal formulae and political principles: government of the people, by the people and for the people, a Bill of Rights, Habeas Corpus, and so on. What was necessary, and what he unfortunately lacked, was an elementary knowledge of the geography of the particular swamp into which he had plunged. More specifically it would have been helpful if he had had some understanding of at least:

---

[24] Telegram 180, Hurley to Secstate, February 7, 1945 (*Foreign Relations 1945*, p. 211). This is the second of a four-part message which constituted Hurley's first effort—three and a half months after they had commenced—to give Washington a chronological and more or less comprehensive report of the negotiations. The report, in fact, was made only after long efforts by the staff of the Embassy in Chungking to convince him that such reporting was desirable (*ibid.*, pp. 732–734).

[25] Hurley was neither a reader nor a very good listener. He was bothered by his eyes, and one assignment of staff members was to read aloud to him telegrams or other reports of any substantial length. Conversations with him tended to be monologues. Senator (then Representative) Mansfield, for instance, visited China in November 1944, and his report to President Roosevelt notes: "I saw Major General Pat Hurley and we had a very long talk. He talked for two hours and forty-seven minutes and I talked for thirteen minutes. . . ." (*Foreign Relations 1945*, p. 8). If a Congressman could do only this well, it can be imagined what chance a mere Second Secretary had.

1. Chinese history of the past forty or fifty years, but especially since the formation of the Chinese Communist Party;
2. Sun Yat-sen's *San Min Chu I,* and particularly the doctrine of "Political Tutelage" which was the theoretical basis of the Kuomintang's claim to a monopoly of power;
3. The nature and anatomy of Chiang Kai-shek's tenuous power, and the precarious but skillful way in which he maintained it by the manipulation of political and military groups, factions, armies, and individual leaders.

The one convincing lesson of the history of China since 1911, which was the only meaningful history known by both Chiang Kai-shek and Mao Tse-tung, could be summed up in the platitude: "Political power grows out of the barrel of a gun." The paramount issue in Chiang's mind was control of the Communist army. This was shown in Chiang's conversation with Ambassador Gauss on September 15 when he asked that "as a first essential I impress upon Lin that the Chinese Communists must submit unconditionally to the principle of unified military command under the Generalissimo. . . ."[26] It was the second of the KMT-approved five points that Hurley carried to Yenan on November 7.[27] The Communists, in the strength they had attained by late 1944, were never going to agree to this, even in principle, unless they had a significant share in the government that was going to control these unified forces. This would have meant an end, in substance as well as in name, to the Kuomintang monopoly of power. Chiang was wholly unwilling to agree to this; in truth, he could not afford to—for it would open a Pandora's box.[28] So Hurley's jubilation on his return from Yenan was coldly doused by T. V. Soong's: "The Communists have sold you a bill of goods. The National Government will never grant what the Communists have requested."[29] For all of Hurley's importuning, drafting of letters, and traveling of representatives between Yenan and Chungking, the negotiations never actually progressed beyond this early and immediate impasse.

Hurley never seemed to understand the basic incompatibility of the two parties he was trying to bring together. It was, in truth, a situation far different from the type in which he had previously been a successful mediator—such as arranging compensation by the Mexican government for the nationalization of American oil interests in that country. Here each side looked to eventual supremacy, and was interested in a political settlement only insofar as it would be useful in contributing to that end. The

---

[26] *Foreign Relations 1944,* p. 573.

[27] *Ibid.,* p. 666.

[28] History, including the passage from "tutelage" to constitutional government and the situation today in Taiwan, would seem to be indicative of the strength of the disinclination of Chiang and the Kuomintang to share political power, or to enforce the legal safeguards and political rights proposed by Hurley.

[29] *Foreign Relations 1945,* p. 195.

Kuomintang position, in essence, was: "Turn yourselves over to us, then we will reform on our terms." To this, the Communists replied: "Reform on our terms, then we will consider joining you." Control of the armies, and of the territories which the Communists had come to control, was crucial. It was the point on which neither party could yield.

IN THE HANDS OF STALIN

The third of Hurley's major misconceptions was that the Soviet Union wholeheartedly agreed with and was committed to support Hurley's exposition of American policy in China. He based this conviction on his conversation with Molotov in August 1944 when Hurley was on his way to China; it was reinforced by a second talk with Stalin and Molotov in April 1945.[30]

> . . . [P]lease distinguish between them [the Chinese Communists] and the Union of Soviet Socialist Republics, because they are different, and all of this time Marshal Stalin and Commissar Molotov had been telling me, and throughout the entire period of the vicissitudes through which we passed so far as I know they have kept their word to me, that, as I stated yesterday, Russia . . . does not recognize the Chinese armed Communist party as Communists at all. Russia is not supporting the Chinese Communist Party. Russia does not desire civil war in China. Russia does not desire the division of China and the setting up of two governments. Russia desires closer and more harmonious relations with China.
>
> Since these conversations with Mr. Molotov and Generalissimo Stalin, Russia has concluded with China the Sino-Soviet Pact and has exchanged letters solemnizing every one of these agreements.
>
> I have read that the Soviet has transgressed certain matters that involve the territorial integrity and the independent sovereignty of China, but frankly I have no evidence that would convince me that that is true. I believe that the United States and Russia are still together on policy in China.[31]

One intriguing feature of this particular statement of Hurley's view (similar in substance to many others) is that it shows that he clung to it as late as December 6, 1945—after he had resigned and ended his negotiations, while the USSR was holding and looting Manchuria, and at a time when large-scale civil war was already going on in China. Perhaps it was the unexpected difficulty of bringing the two parties together that helped to strengthen his certainty that Soviet influence was the key, and that a benevolent and helpful Russian attitude would bring Chinese Communist

---

[30] For the 1944 visit, *Foreign Relations 1944*, pp. 253–256. For the 1945 visit, *Foreign Relations 1945*, pp. 338–340. See also cautionary comments by Ambassador Harriman (*ibid.*, pp. 341–342) and George M. Kennan (*ibid.*, pp. 342–344).

[31] U.S. Senate, Committee on Foreign Relations, *Investigation of Far Eastern Policy* (mimeographed transcript, December 5, 6, 7, and 10, 1945), testimony of General Patrick J. Hurley on December 6, pp. 130–131.

submission to Kuomintang terms. This led him into contradictions, reversal of Washington's view of priorities, abandonment of his own views regarding the strength of the Communists, and finally the climactic—but fruitless—demands for a public statement of American policy that would support his position.

First of all, Hurley apparently never could see the logical inconsistency between his conviction that the Chinese Communists were "not Communists at all" and not supported, recognized, or encouraged in any way by the USSR, and his equally strong conviction that they would certainly and obediently accept the prompting, example, or dictation of the Soviet leaders.

> We are convinced that the influence of the Soviet will control the action of the Chinese Communist Party. The Chinese Communists do not believe that Stalin has agreed or will agree to support the National Government of China and the leadership of Chiang Kai-shek. Nothing short of the Soviet's public commitment will change the Chinese Communist opinion on this subject.[32]

This led logically enough to Hurley's argument that the Chinese Communists could not be expected to see the light until Soviet non-support was spelled out in a Sino-Soviet Treaty.

> . . . [T]he Chinese Communists still believe that they have the support of the Soviet. Nothing will change their opinion on this subject until a treaty has been signed between the Soviet and China in which the Soviet agrees to support the National Government. . . .
>
> The leadership of the Communist Party is intelligent. When the handwriting is on the wall, they will be able to read it. No amount of argument will change their position. Their attitude will be changed only by the inexorable logic of events.[33]

President Roosevelt and the State Department, on the other hand, had consistently held the view that Chiang's desire to improve relations with the Soviet Union would be more likely of satisfactory result if he first reached a settlement with the Chinese Communists. This was, indeed, the subject of the *only* message that Hurley seems to have received from Roosevelt relating to his negotiations.

> I wish you would tell the Generalissimo from me in confidence that a working arrangement between the Generalissimo and the North China forces will greatly expedite the objective of throwing the Japanese out of China from my point of view and also that of the Rus-

---

[32] Telegram 1139, Hurley to Secstate, July 10, 1945 (*Foreign Relations 1945*, p. 431).

[33] *Ibid.*, p. 432.

sians. I cannot tell you more at this time but he will have to take my word for it. You can emphasize the word "Russians" to him.[34]

Whether in the interest of consistency, or whether a reflection of his growing rejection of American official reporting on events in China and increasing closeness to Nationalist sources such as Chiang and T. V. Soong, Hurley gradually reversed his own early views on the strength and importance of the Communists. Certainly this shift does not appear to have been supported by any reports out of the American Observer Group in Yenan; most American observers of the scene in China continued to hold to their view, expressed for some time, that the Communists were steadily gaining strength and territory—time, in other words, was working in *their* favor. From talk of adding the equivalent of "one fully equipped American Army . . . worthy of much more consideration than it has heretofore received from America,"[35] Hurley's theme changed to depreciation of Communist strength:

> The strength of the armed forces of the Chinese Communists has been exaggerated. The area of territory controlled by the Communists has been exaggerated. The number of people who adhere to the Chinese Communist Party has been exaggerated. State Department officials, Army officers, newspaper and radio publicity have to a large measure accepted the Communist leaders' statements in regard to the military and political strength of the Communist Party in China.[36]

The strength of the Chinese Communists was not going to be changed by Hurley's wish or report. The chief problem with this fixation on first getting a treaty with the USSR as a means of bringing the Chinese Communists to terms was that it put the initiative, so far as timing was concerned, in the hands of Stalin. But Stalin was in no hurry. He was not willing to negotiate with the Chungking government until it knew of the Yalta agreement concerning China. But because the Yalta agreement also

---

[34] Telegram 123, Roosevelt to Hurley, November 18, 1944 (*Foreign Relations 1944*, p. 703). One can assume that preparations were already underway for the conference at Yalta. There are numerous other and more explicit statements of Washington's view that a KMT-CCP agreement should be antecedent to a Sino-Soviet pact. For example:

> Furthermore, the President in a message to the Generalissimo, transmitted through the Embassy as the Department's 955 of July 14, stated that a conference between Chinese and Russian representatives would be greatly facilitated if, prior thereto, the Chinese Government had reached a working arrangement with the Chinese Communists. . . . (Grew to Hurley, February 6, 1945, *Foreign Relations 1945*, p. 852; For the President's message to the Generalissimo, see *Foreign Relations 1944*, p. 245.)

[35] See footnote 23, above.

[36] Telegram 1139, Hurley to Secstate, July 10, 1945 (*Foreign Relations 1945*, pp. 432–433).

committed the Soviet Union to enter the war against Japan, Stalin was insistent—for fear of security leaks in Chungking and the resultant possibility of a preemptive Japanese attack on Siberia—that Chiang not be told until after Germany had been finally defeated and the USSR could shift sufficient forces to the Manchurian front. Thus he refused to receive Chiang's envoy, T. V. Soong, until July 1, 1945; the agreement was not signed until August 14; and not published until August 27. Hurley had learned of the Yalta agreement in March, and thus knew of the factor of delay that would be involved. Despite his view that the KMT-CCP agreement was primarily to aid the war against Japan, the course of action he (and Chiang Kai-shek) insisted on pursuing actually resulted in the negotiations being effectively halted until after Japan had been defeated and civil war had become a reality.[37]

The strategy that Hurley came to adopt focused more and more, as time went on, toward putting pressure on the Chinese Communists, whose strength was so "greatly exaggerated." My concern here is not to argue that this was unrealistic (though it was), but rather to point out that Hurley had backed himself into a corner where he had little other choice. The first steps were to reject the possible use of any "pressure" on Chiang, and to announce publicly to all and sundry that his mission was to "sustain" Chiang. The next steps were the manner in which he commenced the negotiations, and his continual reiteration that every move he took was "with the consent, advice and direction of the Generalissimo and members of his Cabinet."[38] These actions—of questionable wisdom and necessity—effectively tied Hurley's hands so far as dealing with Chiang was concerned. In November 1944 he had expressed the view "that if there is a breakdown in the parleys it will be the fault of the Government and not the Communists."[39] In May 1945 he was still willing to agree in a private report to President Truman that the Communists were holding back "in my opinion with some degree of reasonableness."[40] But having committed himself to Chiang, he could only follow along.

AMERICAN "UNANIMITY"

If the pressure of USSR support for only the National Government was to be effective on the Chinese Communists, it was logically essential that this pressure had to be matched by equal firmness and unanimity from the

---

[37] It should be recognized, however, that no one knew of the atomic bomb and the way in which its success would dramatically eliminate the expected last-ditch resistance of Japan.

[38] Hurley's report of December 24, 1944, to Secstate (*Foreign Relations 1944*, p. 747). This phrase in some form appeared in most of Hurley's reports. "Cabinet" may be more of an Americanism than a true description of Chiang's government.

[39] *Foreign Relations 1944*, p. 693.

[40] Telegram, Hurley to President Truman, May 20, 1945 (*Foreign Relations 1945*, pp. 107–114).

American side. So there was a steady intensification by Hurley of the theme: American policy was to support and sustain only the Generalissimo and the National Government; there could be no recognition or support of the CCP or other groups except as they recognized the authority of the National Government; there could be no military cooperation with such groups, and no granting—or even discussion of granting—of arms, aid, or other support without the prior approval of the Generalissimo.

Since such unanimity did not in fact exist among the Americans in China, vigorous and drastic steps were taken to achieve it. General Wedemeyer, though quickly coming to some views not greatly different from those of General Stilwell regarding the problems of activating and working with the Nationalist military organization, soon decided that it would be politic to leave "political" matters to General Hurley.[41] Staff officers who had served under General Stilwell were encouraged to transfer out of the Theater; others were shifted to troop training and other non-policy jobs.[42] All discussion of Chinese political affairs by U.S. Army personnel was sternly prohibited.[43] The Foreign Service Officers attached to the Army (whose services had only shortly before been requested by Wedemeyer on an urgent basis) were removed: General Hurley would do all the political advising. The Army Observer Group in Yenan was reduced to the status of collecting routine enemy intelligence and weather reporting.[44] American veterans of behind-the-lines work in Europe with partisans and maquis were becoming available in considerable numbers as enemy-occupied countries there were liberated; but it was impossible even

---

[41] It would seem, however, that General Wedemeyer disagreed with Hurley to the extent that he lacked Hurley's faith that "jawboning" (and a Russian treaty) would be successful. In a letter of July 9, 1945, to General Marshall, he stated:

If Uncle Sugar, Russia, and Britain united strongly in their endeavor to bring about coalition of these two political parties by coercing both sides to make realistic concessions, serious post-war disturbance may be averted and timely effective military employment of all Chinese may be obtained against the Japanese. I use the term coerce advisedly because it is my conviction that continued appeals to both sides couched in polite diplomatic terms will not accomplish unification. There must be teeth in Big Three approach. (Romanus and Sunderland, *Time Runs Out in CBI*, p. 383).

One may assume, I suppose, that General Wedemeyer was thinking of a coalition government rather than a "coalition of these two parties." For some Wedemeyer views regarding the National Government's military effectiveness, see, for example, *ibid.*, pp. 52–53.

[42] For example, Colonel Barrett; see *Dixie Mission*, p. 78.

[43] *Foreign Relations 1945*, p. 233. Every American officer was required to sign a statement that he had read and understood the policy.

[44] One of Colonel Barrett's successors as Commanding Officer of the Observer Group learned that the North Shensi hills abounded in pheasants (the Communists presumably keeping their ammunition for other purposes). Shooting pheasants became a much safer occupation than talking to such dangerous men as Mao Tse-tung.

to discuss plans for their use in the vital and extensive guerrilla areas of North and East China under Communist control.[45]

It was the Embassy in Chungking that went through perhaps the greatest upheaval. It was mainly staffed, for one thing, with officers who were China specialists. They had not only spent many years in the country, they had also had their training under career chiefs—like Ambassadors Nelson Johnson and Gauss—who had strong convictions about the need for full, free, and objective Foreign Service reporting. In recent years the Kuomintang, on the defensive concerning its own shortcomings, had come to regard with suspicion any official Americans who had been in China long enough to speak and read the language. Hurley now shared this view. It became an advantage to have not served in China, or at least to have not served there recently. This was called "bringing in a fresh, unprejudiced viewpoint." At Hurley's demand, his ranking subordinate and most of the reporting staff were recalled.[46] The new top men were a Foreign Service old-hand from Latin America and a gentlemanly (and capable) banker from Richmond, Virginia, who had volunteered for government service during the war. The Embassy's reporting became more cautious and limited. Officers reporting bad news learned that their confidential reports might be shown by Hurley to Chinese officials such as T. V. Soong, thus endangering their Chinese sources. Some were called on the mat to receive a lecture, in mule-skinner language, from the Ambassador—in Soong's presence.[47] How this looked from Washington is illustrated by a memorandum from the Office of Far Eastern Affairs to Under Secretary Grew and Assistant Secretary Holmes, the chief administrative officer of the Department:

> ... During General Hurley's visit here [in March and early April 1945], it was very evident from his remarks that he is extremely suspicious of and entertains a dislike for Foreign Service officers in

[45] Colonel Barrett describes the unfortunate results of one effort by OSS to discuss the possible use of these groups in Communist territory (*Dixie Mission*, pp. 76–77).

[46] From Hurley's point of view, most of these officers were guilty of insubordination, sabotage, and disloyalty for having joined in a telegram to the Department while George Atcheson was Chargé and while Hurley was in Washington for consultation. This suggested a new and more forceful approach to breaking the KMT-CCP deadlock; as such it was inferentially critical of the tactics and policy which Hurley had been applying (*Foreign Relations 1945*, pp. 242–246). Further discussion of this message will appear in a later section.

[47] One type of report which seemed particularly likely to inflame Hurley concerned the clashes spreading during the summer of 1945 between Nationalist and Communist armed forces, including claims by the Communists in some instances to have captured American-supplied arms. The sensitive point here may have been the new feature of General Wedemeyer's orders that "United States resources" were not intended for civil war; see, for instance, *Foreign Relations 1945*, pp. 406–410. Other incidents of suppression of reports, or of intimidation of officers writing them, are known to officers serving in Chungking during this period.

China. This antipathy has been confirmed by officers returning from Chungking, who have indicated the serious effect it has had upon their own morale and the morale of the other Foreign Service officers stationed at Chungking and at other posts in China. In consequence, it is becoming increasingly difficult to persuade Foreign Service officers who have served under General Hurley to return to China. Of an equally serious nature are the severe restrictions imposed by General Hurley upon political reporting by officers in China. We have definite reason to believe that General Hurley has ordered that only political reports favorable to the Chinese National Government may be made to the Department. This means that the Department will receive restricted and incomplete information concerning developments in China and it is apparent that we can no longer count on receiving factual and objective reports in regard to *all* aspects of the situation which the Department must have if it is to conduct its foreign relations in an intelligent and successful manner. It is hardly necessary to add that these restrictions have done much to undermine morale and have engendered a feeling among the Foreign Service officers with experience of Chinese affairs that our relations with China are being seriously mishandled.[48]

The press was not overlooked. The correspondents in China had been a group of rather unusual experience and competence, including such well-known reporters as Theodore H. White, Annalee Jacoby, Brooks Atkinson, Richard Watts, Harold Isaacs, A. T. Steele, John Hersey, Darrell Berrigan, and Jack Belden. Hurley soon realized that most of them, too, had doubts about the chances for success of "the mission with which I am charged."[49] Failing to have them removed (though a number did leave voluntarily to write the books and articles which it was impossible to get passed by the tight Kuomintang censorship), Hurley brought in a personally selected press attache (with no foreign service or China experience), and pulled wires to promote visits and assignments of friendly correspondents—who were apt to be pleasantly surprised by being asked to stay with the Ambassador.[50] Meanwhile the chief Chinese censor (whose position was actually under the Kuomintang rather than the National Government) gave an official explanation of his policy:

The censorship of the Chinese government does not permit anything to go out which will disturb the cordial relationship between

[48] *Foreign Relations 1945*, pp. 349–350 (emphasis in the original). The drafter was Edwin F. Stanton, who concluded a long and distinguished career by serving as Ambassador to Thailand from 1946 to 1953.

[49] See, for instance, a memorandum by Hurley (purpose not explained) complaining about Theodore White (*Foreign Relations 1944*, pp. 673–674).

[50] Henry J. Taylor was one of the visitors. For an unsuccessful effort by Hurley to arrange a visit by Henry Luce, who "has consistently supported both the Chinese National Government and the American policy," see *Foreign Relations 1945*, pp. 142–143 and 147–148. A subsidiary purpose of Hurley's generously extended hospitality was to minimize the visitor's contact with the regular press group at the Press Hostel.

the two governments (America and China). Ambassador Hurley represents the president and the American government; any attack by an American upon him on Chinese soil is therefore not permitted to go out.[51]

Since 1939 the Kuomintang had imposed a strict blockade of the Communist areas. One Kuomintang purpose being to suppress information about the Communists and the situation in their areas of operations (most of North China), this had included a rigid ban on all travel. This travel ban had finally been cracked in the spring and summer of 1944 when permission was given first for a press party and then for the U.S. Army Observer Group to visit Yenan. To supply the Observer Group and to provide mail and other services, a Headquarters plane began to make more or less regular overnight trips to Yenan. When space was available (which was frequently the case), the Headquarters had been fairly generous in allowing correspondents, senior officers, and representatives of other American agencies in China to take advantage of this means of making short visits or even, on occasion, to stay over between planes. Hurley, in the spring of 1945, reimposed the blockade: it now became an American as well as a Chinese affair. The Army agreed that it would transport no one not a member of the U.S. Army without his express approval in each case. Hurley's personal screening process extended to those he considered "ideological journalists."[52] Hurley's blockade, however, had a double purpose. He shared with the Kuomintang the desire to keep "favorable" news about the CCP from coming out. But he was also becoming increasingly suspicious that the Communists, by contact with Americans, might come to realize that not all of them saw American policy in Hurley's own monolithic terms. This was a cordon sanitaire with a vengeance.

So the pressures built up. American unanimity—of a kind—had been achieved. But still the long months of impasse dragged on. Perhaps uncomfortably aware of the isolation of his position, Hurley began to hope for a strong supporting statement of his policy from Washington.[53] None was forthcoming: Washington, as we shall see at a later point, was not with him. Meanwhile, Hurley searched the files for policy statements from which he could draw comfort and support. The best he could find was

---

[51] White and Jacoby, *Thunder Out of China,* p. 249.

[52] For details of an unsuccessful attempt by the Office of War Information to send an experienced representative into the Communist guerrilla areas for psychological warfare work, see Graham Peck, *Two Kinds of Time,* 1st unabridged ed. (Boston: Houghton, Mifflin Co., 1950) pp. 638–642.

[53] There are numerous references to this desire for a supporting statement of American policy in Hurley's testimony before the Senate Foreign Relations Committee in December 1945 (see reference cited in footnote 31, especially pp. 7, 8, 14, 40A, 40N). It is not clear from the record, however, just when, or through what channels, Hurley requested such a statement.

one of the terms laid down by Secretary of State Hull in his negotiations with Japanese representatives at Washington on November 26, 1941:

> The Government of the United States and the Government of Japan will not support—militarily, politically, economically—any government or regime in China other than the National Government of the Republic of China with capital temporarily at Chungking.[54]

Whatever its relevance for the situation in China in 1945, Hurley seized on this straw.[55] Henceforth he brought it out, on every possible occasion, as "the last public announcement of America's policy in China."[56]

AND, AGAIN, FAILURE

The final denouement came, after the long wait for a treaty with the USSR, when the Communists, astonishingly, refused to read "the handwriting on the wall."[57] In fact, the whole wall came tumbling down. Hurley's own pride, obviously, was deeply involved; and introspection does not seem to have been one of his conspicuous traits. He had been convinced that the parties were similar in aim, and actually close to agreement.[58] Furthermore, because Hurley had concluded that the Communists were weak rather than strong, it did not seem reasonable that they were determined to challenge the KMT (as all but Hurley had said they would) and fight rather than submit. Finally, he had the personal assurances of Molotov, and Stalin himself. There must be some other explana-

---

[54] See, for instance, Lohbeck, *Hurley,* p. 423. Hurley never noted the facts that: (a) this was not exactly a complete statement of policy; (b) the detail regarding the "National Government of the Republic of China with capital temporarily at Chungking" was to distinguish it from the Japanese-sponsored, Wang Ching-wei "National Government of the Republic of China," which had its capital at Nanking.

[55] For example, in his telegram (rather avuncular in tone) to President Truman on May 20, 1945 (*Foreign Relations 1945,* p. 110).

[56] There had, of course, been a great number of American statements on policy toward China in the period from November 1941 to mid-1945. Hurley might even, had he so chosen, have found support in a later statement given by Under Secretary Sumner Welles to Earl Browder on October 12, 1942:

> . . . [T]his Government desires Chinese unity and deprecates civil strife in China; this Government treats the Government of China as an equal; it does not dictate to the Government of China; it does not make United States friendship contingent; it regards unity within China, unity within the United States, unity within each of the countries of the United Nations group, and unity among the United Nations as utterly desirable toward effectively carrying on war against the Axis powers and toward creation and maintenance of conditions of just peace when the United Nations shall have gained the victory which is to be theirs. (*Foreign Relations 1942,* pp. 248–249.)

[57] See footnote 33, above.

[58] Almost every conversation with Hurley would include a confident insistence that he had the two parties "this close" (holding up his thumb and forefinger about an inch apart) to agreement. For Mao Tse-tung's familiarity with this conclusion, and what he thought of it, see *Foreign Relations 1945,* p. 273.

tion of such perverse and peculiar behavior of the Communists. No one was left to blame except the Foreign Service and State Department, and particularly those who, long ago before they had been "Hurleyed" out of China, had shared Hurley's hope of bringing about unity in China but had vainly tried to point out some of the very obstacles on which his barque had foundered.[59]

Hurley's attempt to bring about a settlement between the Kuomintang and Communists was largely a self-imposed task; it seems doubtful that it was specifically within the scope of whatever instructions or directives he ever received. This is not said in disparagement. He rightly recognized it as the principal problem in China. But no solution was possible by the methods and positions to which he inflexibly committed himself. Energy, persistence, and determination all proved of no avail in the face of the revolution, unseen by Hurley, which was already well started in China. So a long career in public life ended in bitterness, frustration, and failure.

The Hurley period was seen by the China Lobby, and apparently is still seen by Dr. Kubek and the government in Taiwan, as a high point in Chinese-American relations. To the student, it must certainly seem a low point for realism in the American conduct of its foreign affairs. It is useless to talk of "Who lost China?" It was never ours to lose (and if I were a Chinese, I would resent the suggestion of Americans like Dr. Kubek that it was). But what Hurley's ill-advised stubbornness lost us, and China, was time and opportunities. The time lost was a ten-month deadlock during the last, most critical months of the war. The opportunities lost were to seek more realistic means of averting, or blunting, civil war and of preserving our relations with China, if not as the close friend and ally we once hoped for, at least on a basis better than bitter enmity.

---

[59] Counselor of Embassy George Atcheson was certainly correct when he assured Hurley (in late January 1945): "There is no member of the staff that I know of who has not whole-heartedly hoped for the success of your negotiations. . . ." (*Foreign Relations 1945*, p. 191).

VI
Washington Insists on Flexibility

A continuing thread in American policy toward China was the tradition of non-intervention in Chinese internal affairs. It had one notable origin in the Open Door notes of John Hay in 1899 and 1900, and had long been a matter of considerable (self-congratulatory) pride to Americans. But the circumstances of 1945 were quite different from those of 1900.

Hurley, when he began to be defensive about his policy, argued that John Hay's phrase—"preserve Chinese territorial and administrative entity"—could mean only that the United States must support and sustain Chiang Kai-shek, the head of the recognized Chinese government, and accordingly that there could be no military cooperation or aid to forces within China except as Chiang himself approved.[1]

The State Department was not so sure. The Open Door policy had been designed to meet an external threat when it seemed that China was in danger of partition by imperialist powers seeking concessions and spheres of influence within Chinese territory. The American intent was friendly to China. But what the Open Door notes actually said, in their insistence on the most-favored-nation doctrine, was that others should not intervene in a way that was actually or potentially detrimental to the interests of American citizens in China. It could be argued that the Open Door policy had come to assume, with the passage of years, something of the nature of an American balance-of-power policy with regard to China. This was not, however, the sense in which Hurley was seeking to invoke it. He was using it as an argument for the limitation of American action toward internal events within China. The problem that was becoming increasingly important for American policy was a developing revolution in China. As our ally in the war against Japan, the government was receiving (and quite properly) American military aid in ever-increasing amounts. But, sooner or later, the issue was bound to arise whether we could go on insisting that such aid, limited to only one of the parties, was actually in its effect the non-interference and non-intervention that we preferred to think it. It took some time for this dilemma to become apparent.

It was, for instance, precisely the policy statement of 1900 that was cited by the Office of Far Eastern Affairs [FE] in October 1942 when it

---

[1] For example, Lohbeck, *Hurley,* pp. 247–248. Hurley actually argued that this American policy "was the immediate cause of our war against Japan" (*ibid.,* p. 423).

was attempting to guide Under Secretary Sumner Welles in preparing an answer to an inquiry from Earl Browder on American policy in China. From it, FE derived the conclusion: "It has been this Government's practice not to interfere in China's internal affairs."[2]

When I was temporarily in the State Department on consultation in January 1943, I prepared a memorandum for FE which made what may have been one of the first attempts to call attention to the issue:

January 23, 1943.

Kuomintang-Communist Situation

An outstanding impression gained during the past eighteen months spent in Chungking and in travel through Southwest and Northwest China is that the most careful study should be given to the internal political situation in China, particularly the growing rift between the Kuomintang and the Communists.

The "United Front" is now definitely a thing of the past and it is impossible to find any optimism regarding the possibility of its resurrection as long as present tendencies continue and the present leadership of the Kuomintang, both civil and military, remains in power. Far from improving, the situation is deteriorating. In Kuomintang controlled China the countering of Communism is a growing preoccupation of propaganda, of both military and civilian political indoctrination, and of secret police and gendarmerie activity. There is not only a rigorous suppression of anything coming under the ever widening definition of "Communism" but there appears to be a movement away from even the outward forms of democracy in government. It is now no longer wondered whether civil war can be avoided, but rather whether it can be delayed at least until after a victory over Japan.

The dangers and implications of this disunity are obvious and far reaching. Militarily, the present situation is a great hindrance to any effective war effort by China. . . .

Aside from the immediate war aspects, the political implications of this situation are also serious. Assuming that open hostilites are for the time being averted, the eventual defeat and withdrawal of the Japanese will leave the Kuomintang still confronted with the communists solidly entrenched in most of North China (East Kansu, North Shensi, South Chahar, Hopei, Shantung, North Kiangsu and North Anhwei). In addition the Communists will be in position to move into the vacuum created by the Japanese withdrawal from Suiyuan, Jehol and Manchuria, in all of which areas there is already some Communist activity. In the rest of China they will have the sympathy of elements among the liberals, intellectuals, and students. These elements are of uncertain size but of considerable influence in China, and the Kuomintang's fear of their power, and the power of whatever underground organization the Communists have suc-

---

[2] *Foreign Relations 1942*, pp. 250–251; see also Chapter V, note 55. Mr. Welles, it may be noted, was a bit more up-to-date in his reply to Mr. Browder. He did not invoke the Open Door doctrine with its overtones of equal trading rights for foreigners within China, but instead emphasized that China was to be treated as an equal among nations.

ceeded in maintaining in the Kuomintang area, is indicated by the size and activity of its various secret police organs.

But possibly the greatest potential strength of the Communists, and one reason why military action against them will not be entirely effective at the present time, is their control of the rural areas of North China in the rear of the Japanese. . . .

Non-Comunist Chinese of my acquaintance (as, for instance, the nephew of the well known late editor of the *Ta Kung Pao*) consider the likelihood of civil war the greatest problem facing China. They point out that the Communists are far stronger now than they were when they stood off the Kuomintang armies for ten years in Central China and that they will be much stronger yet if it proves that they have succeeded in winning the support of the population in the guerrilla zone. They point to numerous recent instances of successful Communist infiltration into and indoctrination of opposing Chinese armies (such as those of Yen Hsi-shan) and wonder whether this will not cause a prolongation of the struggle and perhaps make a victory for the Kuomintang, or for either side, impossible. There is undoubtedly a strong revulsion in the mind of the average, non-party Chinese to the idea of renewed civil war and the Kuomintang may indeed have difficulty with the loyalty and effectiveness of its conscript troops.

Belief in the certainty of eventual civil war leads these same Chinese to question whether the United States has given sufficient realistic consideration to the future in China of democracy. The question is raised whether it is to China's advantage, or to America's own interests, for the United States to give the Kuomintang Government large quantities of military supplies which, judging from past experience, are not likely to be used effectively against Japan but will be available for civil war to enforce "unity" in the country by military force. These Chinese also speculate on the position of American troops which may be in China (in support of the Kuomintang Army) if there should be civil war; and wonder what will be the attitude of Russia, especially if it has become by that time a partner in the victory over Japan. . . .[3]

It is almost laughable, after intervening events, to recall the waves of consternation and disapproval that were caused by this memorandum (which also had the added temerity to include what was probably the first written suggestion that the American government would be well-advised to try to find out what was happening in the other part of China by sending reporting officers to Yenan). The then presiding patriarchs of FE (Maxwell Hamilton and particularly the long-established, authoritarian Stanley K. Hornbeck) had not actually been in China for a great many years; they were still imbued emotionally with reports of China's brave and lonely resistance, and the hopeful but short-lived

---

[3] *Foreign Relations 1943*, pp. 193–199.

United Front of 1937–38. My views were dismissed as rash, exaggerated, and "immature."[4]

COMMITTED TO CHINA, NOT THE KUOMINTANG

By May 1944, events and trends in China were better known in Washington. On May 19—about six weeks before the President decided on the drastic step of asking that General Stilwell be put in command of all Chinese forces, and three months before General Hurley was sent to China to make it a reality—the Division of Chinese Affairs [CA] prepared a summary of American policy, particularly as it related to Sino-Soviet relations. This was approved by FE (now under new management) and submitted to the Secretary of State. One section is of interest:

> The United States is committed to fight by the side of China in the war against Japan and to extend aid to China in resisting aggression. Nevertheless, it is not committed to support the National Government in any and all circumstances, and in general does not sympathize with mutual fears and suspicions among the several United Nations or with attempts by any one of them to work for individual selfish advantage against the common interests of all. In respect to domestic problems in China it might be observed that the United States is not concerned with doctrinal questions between contending Chinese groups. It is desirous generally of seeing effected in China a program which will redound to the general benefit of the Chinese people without regard to the political complexion of the Chinese group which effects that program. It is the steadfast desire of the United States Government to see the Chinese people receive a greater share of the equities and goods of China and participate more fully in their government.[5]

During the next few months, the State Department was actively interested in the visit of Vice President Wallace to China and in supporting the proposal, already described, of Ambassador Gauss for a war council. Then Hurley arrived in Chungking and, failing in his mission to arrange the Stilwell command, immediately commenced his independent endeavor to negotiate an agreement between Chiang and the Communists. Even though he soon became the ambassador, the State Department entered a

---

[4] Some, but not all, of the waves can still be seen, congealed in the chill pages of *Foreign Relations 1943* (pp. 199, 201, 203–208). Mr. Hornbeck's comments (memorandum on p. 201) are considerably milder than some of his marginal notes, sensibly ignored by the editors, on my original text. We should, Mr. Hornbeck says, "maintain an attitude of intelligent skepticism with regard to reports emphasizing the strength of the 'Communist' forces in China." There was certainly nothing in my memorandum that suggested that quotation marks around Communist were appropriate.

[5] *Foreign Relations 1944*, p. 792. That the paper represented the current thinking of the State Department is indicated by the fact that copies were forwarded to Harriman in Moscow and Gauss in Chungking for their guidance (Feis, *China Tangle*, p. 142).

period of being merely a bystander to these events in China. Bystander, indeed, is hardly the correct word if one is to assume that a bystander can at least see what is going on. Hurley believed that he was obligated to report only to the President; and, as already noted, he did that in a sporadic and somewhat haphazard fashion.[6] The State Department was substantially uninformed concerning the details of the negotiations and the ambiguous basis on which Hurley had entered into and was conducting them.[7]

In December 1944, Hurley had hoped to make a short visit to the United States. A special plane was arranged (though his predecessor had always found it feasible to travel by regular Air Transport Command facilities). By the time the plane arrived, Hurley decided for a number of reasons (including non-arrival of his credentials, lack of agreement between "Communist troop leaders" and the National Government, and an unexplained fear that "many rumors would be created by my departure") not to make the trip. He sent a personal message to Stettinius, who had just recently moved up from Under Secretary to Secretary of State and with whom he was on a "Dear Ed" basis, explaining his decision and including the statement: "I am anxious to go to Washington for reports to President, to you and War Department. . . ."[8]

The State Department thought it saw an opening, and moved quickly to take advantage of it. A prompt reply was made in Stettinius's name:

> I appreciate your reasons for postponing your trip to Washington and, while I regret the delay in receiving a first-hand report from you, I concur in your decision. In the meantime I should appreciate very much receiving by telegraph a strictly confidential summary of the reports on the situation which you had planned to make in person.[9]

HURLEY STATES A GENERAL UNDERSTANDING

The message from the Secretary apparently hit the right note. Hurley now "recognized" the Department of State by sending it his first report of what he was trying to accomplish in China. This message subsequently became important because he included in it a statement of his "understanding" of American policy in China:

---

[6] Hurley was also fond of saying with a chuckle that he knew the President well enough to know that he "enjoyed" receiving information that the State Department did not have so he could "make them look silly."

[7] The paucity and largely secondhand sources of the information reaching the Department through official channels is indicated by the Embassy's telegrams of November 13 (*Foreign Relations 1944*, pp. 690–691) and November 24 (*ibid.*, p. 715). The published record seems to indicate that the White House did not actually know a great deal more, but at least it had the advantage of occasionally hearing direct from Hurley.

[8] *Foreign Relations 1944*, p. 210. For "Dear Ed," see *ibid.*, pp. 200–202.

[9] *Ibid.*, p. 744.

In all my negotiations it has been my understanding that the policy of the United States in China is:

(1) To prevent the collapse of the national government.

(2) To sustain Chiang Kai-shek as President of the Republic and Generalissimo of the Armies.

(3) To harmonize relations between the Generalissimo and the American Commander.

(4) To promote production of war supplies in China and prevent economic collapse and

(5) To unify all the military forces of China for the purpose of defeating Japan.

This is a broad outline of my mission.[10]

The Division of Chinese Affairs furnished the Secretary with its comment, stating (in part):

Ambassador Hurley's attached telegram of December 24 contains information new to the Department in addition to considerable background material.

The five points in which the Ambassador outlines his mission are basically sound. With regard to points one and two, it is desirable however to maintain sufficient flexibility in our attitude toward the political scene in China to avoid embarrassment in the unlikely event that Chiang with his Government is ousted and to take immediate steps to support the elements most likely to carry on resistance. . . .

. . . [I]n our thinking and planning with regard to relations with China, further disintegration of Chungking's authority is a contingency which must be taken into account.[11]

The Department chose to acknowledge this first report from General Hurley with a bland and noncommittal reply:

I have read with great interest and appreciation the report and analysis of the current situation in China contained in your telegram of December 24, as well as in your letter of December 6. The information you have given me, and your comment thereon, affords me a valuable insight into the problem with which you are faced and for which you are seeking solution with characteristic energy and acumen. China is now and will be in the postwar period

---

[10] *Foreign Relations 1944*, p. 745. It is this formulation that Lohbeck (*Hurley,* p. 310) cites as Hurley's "new directive" on becoming ambassador. However, to the first point he adds: "and keep the Chinese Army in the war." And he adds a sixth point: "Support the aspirations of the Chinese people to establish a free, united, democratic government." Lohbeck also states (p. 497, note 3) that Hurley "asked the Secretary of State to advise him of any changes that should be made in this directive." The text as published in *Foreign Relations* contains no such question or request; nor does it indicate that the text is not complete.

[11] *Foreign Relations 1944*, pp. 750–751.

of major and vital importance to us. I trust you will keep me fully informed. . . . With best wishes for the New Year.[12]

This episode has been set out in detail because it is this exchange of telegrams—Hurley's report of December 24 and the reply of Secretary Stettinius on January 2—that has provided the basis for the assertion, down through the years to Kubek, that Hurley's conception of American policy in China was not "questioned or corrected" by the Secretary of State or the President. By Hurley, and by those who have agreed with his version of this period, this instance of non-reaction in Washington has been taken as clear approval and concurrence.[13] Herbert Feis characterizes the Secretary's comment, with justification, as "anemic." He suggests that it was an indication that the State Department and White House "were unsure and wavering" about the best way "at this juncture" to handle the Chinese internal quarrel. He seems, however, to leave the clear inference that Hurley can therefore hardly be blamed for the policy he continued to follow.[14] The scholarly account by Feis has naturally influenced many other writers interested in this period, who did not have access to the documents that have only relatively recently become publicly available.[15] Eventually, as we shall see (and as Feis also noted at a later point),[16] Hurley was informed that Washington had a different view of China policy—particularly as it concerned any all-out commitment to support Chiang Kai-shek and the Nationalist cause. But this episode has had such a pervasive effect in the literature that it should be placed in context.

In the first place, the Department was trying to establish some sort of a working relationship with the new ambassador in China, without which it could hardly hope to have an effectively functioning embassy. Every ambassador nominally works for the State Department; but he is appointed by the President and is a personal representative of the President. These blurred lines of responsibility can (and frequently do) pose a problem for the Department's efforts to keep a rein on a freewheeling ambassador. This is especially the case if the ambassador is a political

---

[12] *Ibid.,* p. 215. The letter of December 6, referred to, congratulated Stettinius on becoming Secretary of State and dealt in only a very cursory way with events in China: no mention was made of the KMT-CCP negotiations (*ibid.,* pp. 200–202).

[13] See, for instance, Lohbeck, *Hurley,* p. 310 and p. 497, note 3.

[14] Feis, *China Tangle,* pp. 179, 213, and 219.

[15] For instance, Earl Latham, *The Communist Controversy in Washington: From the New Deal to McCarthy* (Cambridge: Harvard University Press, 1966), p. 257:

> Hurley had no clear instructions as to how he was to deal with the Chinese Communists, nor any directive that it was American policy to keep the Chiang regime in control of the government of China. Although Hurley's definition of his mission was a substantial modification of American policy, he was never contradicted in his assumptions.

[16] Feis, *China Tangle,* pp. 292–293.

(non-professional) appointee, and even more so if the incumbent President is inclined to conduct the country's foreign relations without much reference to the State Department. All these problems were exemplified to the *nth* degree in the case of Hurley. He was a person of formidable force and self-importance, with an extremely broad conception of his mission, claiming the most sweeping kind of carte blanche authority directly from the President, and operating completely independently of the Department of State in a critical situation of great delicacy and vital concern to the interests of the United States.[17]

During Roosevelt's tenure, there were two ways to take care of such a situation. One was for the President himself to take note and act. Now, however, the President's attention was elsewhere. The climactic phases of war in Europe and around the world, and such matters as the approaching talks at Malta and Yalta, were more than enough to fill his attention.

---

[17] One illustration may be sufficient. Before his departure for Yenan in November 1944, Hurley had a conversation with Ambassador Gauss. Learning of Hurley's plans, the ambassador told him of the instruction which he (Gauss) had received from the Department on September 9 regarding any approach to the Communists (*Foreign Relations 1944,* pp. 567–569). On that basis, Gauss suggested that Hurley not allow himself to become too directly involved in trying to mediate between the two parties. Hurley brushed off this proffered advice with the statement that his understanding with the President was that he could do anything he considered desirable to increase the Chinese war effort. There is only a pale shadow of this talk in Gauss's telegram of November 13 (*Foreign Relations 1944,* pp. 690–691); but Gauss had returned to Washington on November 24 and it can be assumed that by late December the Department had some inkling, despite the lack of reports from Hurley himself, of the way in which the new ambassador was operating.

There was also a later echo of this incident. In February 1945 Hurley reported the Chinese desire to open negotiations with the USSR and seemed to be suggesting that he might be of assistance (*Foreign Relations 1945,* pp. 851–852). The Department's "tentative comment" (*ibid.,* pp. 852–853) was that "while we are at all times anxious to be helpful to the Chinese Government, we should not permit the Chinese Government to gain the impression that we are prepared to assume responsibility as 'adviser' to it in its relations with the USSR." It also referred to the previously expressed American view that "a conference between Chinese and Russian representatives would be greatly facilitated if, prior thereto, the Chinese Government had reached a working agreement with the Chinese Communists." In this connection, it cited the September 9 message to Gauss "regarding the importance of reaching such a 'working arrangement.' " Although the Department did not refer to that part of the September 9 message that limited the mediating role that the American Ambassador was authorized to play in any KMT-CCP negotiations, the mere reference to the message seems to have hit Hurley on a sensitive nerve. He immediately jumped to the conclusion that criticism of his prominent part in the current negotiations was intended:

In your message you appear to have reduced my role in these negotiations to the position of merely making a suggestion without implementing the suggestion. That is the method followed by Ambassador Gauss when he transmitted the President's and the Secretary of State's message on September 9th last. That message, as you now know, obtained no results whatever because it lacked vigorous implementation. . . . I believe our position is weakened and accomplishment delayed by lack of vigorous implementation of suggestions. (*Foreign Relations 1945,* pp. 229–230).

China, since the Stilwell recall, had been pushed to the back of the stove. The second possibility was for the State Department to take the initiative in consultation with the President. This needed an effective channel to the President: someone broadly competent in world affairs, sensitive to the Department's interests and concerns, with ready access to the White House, and enjoying the President's friendship and confidence. Sumner Welles had, of course, been such a contact until his resignation as Under Secretary in late 1943. Stettinius was not a wholly successful replacement. These thoughts must have been in the minds of the men at the working level in the State Department when Hurley showed his first inclination to be cooperative by submitting his report of December 24. So, even though CA did raise a cautionary note, the drafters of the Department's reply apparently decided that a placatory (even if "anemic") reply was the appropriate tactic to reinforce Hurley's tentative willingness to enter into relations with the State Department. In view of those drafters, the key sentence in their message was undoubtedly: "I trust you will keep me fully informed."

There was, however, still another consideration that influenced the non-reproving tone of the Department's message of January 2. This was the simple fact that the policy issue in China had not yet been brought to the surface. Hurley stated his "understanding" of American policy in broad, general terms. It was not until a month or two later that the lines of the policy cleavage between Washington and Hurley became clearly drawn when Hurley, reacting to the impasse in his negotiations, began to spell out in words and actions his own extreme definition and interpretation of such terms as "prevent the collapse of the national government" and "sustain Chiang Kai-shek." So much for Washington's failure to "contradict" Hurley's assumptions in this early episode.

FLEXIBILITY REAFFIRMED

It was not long after this (apparently on January 16, 1945) that Secretary of War Stimson asked the State Department to furnish guidance on China policy for his staff and for General Wedemeyer. The Division of Chinese Affairs responded with a memorandum of January 29 to Acting Secretary Grew. Omitting some reference to Hong Kong which is not relevant here, its substance was:

> The short-term objective of the United States Government is to assist in mobilizing all of China's human and material resources for prosecution of the war against Japan. We are using our influence to bring about a greater degree of political and military unity, and to achieve greater efficiency and volume in the production of war material. We are supplying China with materials for direct military use and for industrial purposes connected with the war effort.
>
> Our long-term objective in China is to assist in the development

of a united, democratically progressive, and cooperative China which will be capable of contributing to security and prosperity in the Far East.

The mission of our military authorities in China, we believe, should be focused for the present upon the short-term objective described above. Undoubtedly measures devised to "contain" Japanese forces, in cooperation with the Chinese, will result in a degree of rearmament of Chinese forces, but it is believed that measures undertaken at this time to rearm China in order that it might become a strong Asiatic power would be impracticable.

We would like to see the rearmament, to such extent as may be practicable, of all Chinese forces willing to fight the Japanese, but the present unsatisfactory relations between the Chinese Government and the Chinese Communists makes it impolitic to undertake measures for the rearmament of the Chinese Communists even though it is generally conceded that they could effectively use quantities of small arms ammunition and demolition materials. *However, if operations are undertaken along the China coast it is suggested that our military authorities should be prepared to arm any Chinese forces which they believe can be effectively employed against the Japanese, and that they should at an opportune time so advise the Chinese military authorities.*

It is our purpose, as indicated above, to utilize our influence to bring about, both as a short-term and as a long-term objective, the unification of China. *It does not necessarily follow that China should be unified under Chiang Kai-shek.* However, with regard to the short-term objective, Chiang appears to be the only leader who now offers a hope for unification. The alternative to the support of Chiang for the attainment of our immediate objective might be chaos. *With regard to our long-term objective, it is our purpose to maintain a degree of flexibility which would permit cooperation with any leadership in China that would offer the greatest likelihood of fostering a united, democratic, and friendly China.* Developments in this regard would have a bearing on any plans to assist in the peacetime rearmament of China.[18]

This policy statement was approved by the Department of State and forwarded to the Secretaries of War and the Navy about February 1.[19] Secretary Stimson found it "OK" and sent it on to General Wedemeyer with the comment that it was for his "guidance."[20] The policy view set forth was amplified but not substantially altered in another statement in May (which will be referred to again). There can be no doubt, therefore, that it was an authoritative statement of American policy in China.

It was also supported, it may be noted, by a Briefing Book Paper on American long-range policy objectives in China, prepared on January 12, 1945, for the Malta and Yalta meetings, which stated in part:

---

[18] *Foreign Relations 1945,* pp. 37–39; emphasis added.
[19] *Ibid.,* p. 37, n. 52.
[20] Romanus and Sunderland, *Time Runs Out in CBI,* pp. 336–337.

1. Political: a strong stable and unified China with a government representative of the wishes of the Chinese people:

a) We should seek by every proper means to promote establishment of a broadly representative government which will bring about internal unity, including reconcilement of Kuomintang-Communist differences. . . . While favoring no political faction, we continue to support the existing government of China as the central authority and we look for the establishment within its framework of the unified and effective type of government that is needed.

b) Should these expectations fail of achievement and the authority of the existing government disintegrate, we would reexamine our position in the light of the manifested wishes of the Chinese people and regard sympathetically any government or movement which gave promise of achieving unity and of contributing to peace and security in eastern Asia.[21]

Hurley's subsequent response to this policy statement of January 29 was an angry denial that he was ever informed or supplied with a copy.[22] Several facts may, however, be noted. A copy was "transmitted to the Ambassador in China by the Acting Secretary in instruction no. 40, February 9 [1945]."[23] A copy, as noted above, was also sent by the War Department to General Wedemeyer in Chungking, with whom Hurley was in close and constant association. Hurley indicated that he was familiar with the contents of the statement when he testified before the Senate Foreign Relations Committee in December 1945.[24] Furthermore, it would appear that Hurley actually had a copy in his personal possession, since it was he who introduced its text into the MacArthur Hearings in 1951.[25] In his testimony here, he found parts of the policy statement acceptable; but in regard to other sections he insisted: "I call attention to the fact that this is in conflict with the policy. . . ." This would seem to raise the question, not normally considered as needing debate, whether the final authority for making foreign policy rests with the government in Washington or an ambassador in the field.

Again, a parenthetical note. The reader who goes back to the tran-

[21] *Foreign Relations of the United States: The Conferences at Malta and Yalta, 1945*, p. 356.

[22] See, for example, Lohbeck, *Hurley*, p. 340.

[23] *Foreign Relations 1945*, p. 37, n. 51.

[24] U.S. Senate, Committee on Foreign Relations, *Investigation of Far Eastern Policy* (mimeographed transcript, December 5, 6, 7, and 10, 1945), testimony of General Patrick J. Hurley on December 5, pp. 83–84.

[25] U.S. Senate, 82nd Cong., 1st sess., Hearings Before the Committee on Armed Services and the Committee on Foreign Relations, *Military Situation in the Far East*. (Washington: Government Printing Office, 1951), pt. 4, pp. 2929–2930. This document had not previously been published and was still classified. This is confirmed by the fact that the State and Defense Department censors, who went over the transcript of these hearings before their publication, made a partial deletion from the document. The full text, however, can now be read in *Foreign Relations 1945*.

scripts of these investigating committee hearings in 1945 and 1951 [footnotes 24 and 25] may be surprised to find that Hurley's motive in trying to have the policy statement of January 29 placed on record is not so much to debate its policy implications as it is to use it as the basis for one of his favorite and most unquenchable allegations: that I personally delivered a copy of this American policy statement to Mao Tse-tung when I made my second trip to Yenan in March 1945. His proof? That he had discovered during the spring of 1945 that Communist forces, presumably on the basis of this information supplied by me, were expanding southward into areas along the East China coast. But this is precisely what Chen Yi and other Communist leaders had told me *in August of 1944* that they intended to do. My reports of those intentions, submitted at the time, were of course on file in Hurley's own Embassy.[26] The plain fact is that there is not the slightest iota of basis for, or truth in, this accusation. I never saw, read, held a copy in my hands, or even knew of the existence and contents of this policy statement of January 29 until I read it in 1951, to my considerable surprise, in the published transcript of the MacArthur Hearings. I did not, accordingly, deliver a copy or divulge its contents to Mao Tse-tung or to any other member of the Chinese Communist Party. Nor, I may add, would I have done so had I such knowledge. This happens to be one of the more astonishing products of Hurley's suspicious imagination and quick vindictiveness. But it is not untypical of this remarkable man.

No Dictation to the Generalissimo

In February 1945 it became apparent that the Kuomintang-Communist negotiations were deadlocked. Ambassador Hurley and General Wedemeyer decided to go to Washington for consultations. And the Embassy staff in Chungking and the Office of Far Eastern Affairs in the Department, both acting independently, believed that it was time to take a fresh look at the situation. Both, it happened, came up with generally similar policy suggestions.

So far as consideration by the State Department was concerned, the first of a number of reports and papers was one by the Chief of CA on March 1. It included these recommendations:

> . . . [W]hile continuing to exert our influence to bring about Chinese political and military unity, we should be prepared, in the event of American military operations which could be aided by the cooperation of Chinese Communist forces, to supply those forces with arms and ammunition.

---

[26] See my report No. 19 from Yenan, August 31, 1944 (*Foreign Relations 1944,* pp. 527–532; also *Amerasia Papers,* Document 142, pp. 817–821). A memorandum by Green H. Hackworth, Legal Advisor to the State Department, discussing this and other charges by General Hurley, is to be found in *Foreign Relations 1945,* pp. 740–744.

There should be no question of choosing between Chiang and the Communists; of withdrawal of support from Chiang. But likewise there should be no question of an exercise of our prerogative, dictated by military necessity, to utilize all forces in China capable of cooperating with us in the fight against Japan. Chiang, having failed to effect military unity, should be told that he has forfeited any claim to exclusive support.

Chiang's initial reaction would probably be unfavorable—but without practical effect because it is extremely doubtful that he would be prepared actively to oppose aid to the Chinese Communists. There is also the probability that, faced with a positive statement of our stand and intentions, Chiang might actually be moved to effect, on a military level, the unity of forces for which we have been striving.[27]

On the following day (March 2) a much fuller statement of a proposed "American Policy with Respect to China" was completed by a group of senior officers in CA and FE. This did not differ greatly in its conclusions from the March 1 memorandum but it did reintroduce the Gauss proposal for a "war council," and it stressed the need for flexibility:

a) To the extent that Chiang Kai-shek is sincerely willing (1) to accept American counsel, (2) to cooperate wholeheartedly with the United States in bringing about the defeat of Japan, and (3) to carry out measures designed to achieve internal reform and the promotion of national unity, it would appear to be in the interests of the United States to support him and his Kuomintang-sponsored government. But it is clear that it would be in the American interest to maintain a flexible policy in this respect vis-à-vis Chiang for two reasons: first, the United States may wish to be in a position to withdraw support from Chiang in the event that his government and administration deteriorate to a point reaching impotence; and, second, the United States appears to possess, in its discretion to grant or to withhold support and assistance, a weapon which may be used to induce Chiang to cooperate, reform the administration of his government, and put China's maximum effort into the prosecution of the war.[28]

Coincidentally with this activity, the State Department received a telegram dated February 28 from George Atcheson, Counselor of Embassy at Chungking, who, as the ranking officer, was Chargé d'Affaires in the absence of the Ambassador. Although, as already noted, it offered recom-

---

[27] *Foreign Relations 1945*, pp. 247–249. This memorandum, by Mr. John Carter Vincent, ended with a parenthesized note: "Since preparing the foregoing, I have read Atcheson's telegram no. 324 of February 28 and feel that it should receive the most serious consideration."

[28] *Ibid.*, pp. 249–253. Although it contains no reference, it is probable that this paper was drafted after receipt of the Chungking message of February 28 (see n. 30, below). As an intended policy paper, it would be normal to omit reference to telegrams or other correspondence.

mendations similar to those already proposed in the Department, it was this message which seems to have become the principal focus of the debate over China policy that took place in Washington during the ensuing several weeks of the Hurley visit. On March 2 it was sent by Acting Secretary Grew to President Roosevelt with a memorandum stating that developments in China "emphasize the need of flexibility in applying our policies. . . ."[29] It may be worthwhile, therefore, to set forth the complete text.

The situation in China appears to be developing in some ways that are not conducive to effective prosecution of the war, nor to China's future peace and unity.

1. The recent American attempt through diplomatic and persuasive means to assist compromise between the factions in China was a necessary first step in the handling of the problem. Unity was correctly taken to be the essence not only of the most effective conduct of the war by China but also of the peaceful and speedy emergence of a strong, united and democratic China.

But the cessation of Japanese offensives, the opening of the road into China, the rapid development of our Army plans for rebuilding Chiang's armies, the increase of other assistance such as the WPB [War Production Board], the expectation that the Central Government will share in the making of important decisions at San Francisco, and belief that we are intent upon the definite support and strengthening of the Central Government alone and as the only possible channel for aid to other groups—these circumstances have combined to increase greatly Chiang's feeling of strength and have resulted in unrealistic optimism on his part and lack of willingness to make any compromise. (See our 301, February 16, 4 p.m.)

This attitude is reflected in, among other things, early hopes of a settlement with Russia without settlement of the Communist problems, when nothing was finally offered but an advisory inter-party committee without any power or place in the Government, and in recent military-political appointments which place strong anti-Communists in the strategic war areas and name to high administrative posts reactionaries such as Admiral Chan Chak (Tai Li subordinate) to be mayor of Canton and General Ho Kuo-kuang (former commander in chief of Gendarmerie) as chairman of Formosa.

2. The Communists for their part have come to the conclusion that we are definitely committed to the support of Chiang alone, and that we will not force Chiang's hand in order to be able to aid or cooperate with them. In what they consider self-protection, they are therefore following the line of action (forecast in statements of Communist leaders last summer if they continued to be excluded from consideration) of actively increasing their forces and aggressively expanding their areas southward, regardless of nominal Kuomintang control, to reach southeast China. The Department is referred to our 284, February 24, 9 a.m., reporting

---

[29] *Foreign Relations 1945,* p. 254.

large movements and conflicts with Central Government forces already taking place. In grasping time by the forelock, the Communists intend to take advantage of the isolation of East China by the Japanese capture of the Canton-Hankow Railway, to make themselves as nearly invincible as possible before Chiang's new armies now in process of formation in Yunnan are ready, and to present us the dilemma of accepting or refusing their aid if our forces land anywhere on the China coast. Communists close to the leaders are now talking of the necessity of their seeking Soviet assistance. The party itself is broadcasting demands for Communist and other non-Kuomintang representation at San Francisco, and is actively considering creation of a unified council of their various independent guerrilla governments.

3. The conclusion seems clear that, although our intentions have been good and our actions in refusing to deal with or assist any group but the Central Government have been diplomatically correct, if this situation continues and our analysis of it is correct, chaos in China will be inevitable and the probable outbreak of disastrous civil conflict will be accelerated. Even for the present it is obvious that this situation, in which we are precluded from cooperation with the large, aggressive and strategically situated armies and organized population of the Communist areas, as well as the forces such as the Li Chi-shen and Tsai Ting-kai group in the southeast, is unsatisfactory and hampering from a purely military standpoint. As indicated above, the situation is also dangerous to American interests from a long-range point of view.

Unless checked, this situation is apt to develop with increasing acceleration as the tempo of the war in China and the whole Far East is raised and the inevitable resolution of China's internal conflict becomes more urgent. The time is short and it will be dangerous to allow affairs to drift.

4. If the high military authorities of our Government agree that some cooperation with the Communists and other groups who have proved themselves willing and are in position to fight the Japanese is or will be necessary or desirable, we believe that the immediate and paramount consideration of military necessity should be made the basis for a further step in American policy. The presence of General Wedemeyer in Washington as well as General Hurley should be a favorable opportunity for discussion of this matter.

Predicated on the assumption that the military necessity exists, the first step we propose for consideration is that the President inform the Generalissimo in definite terms that military necessity requires that we supply and cooperate with the Communists and other suitable groups who can assist the war against Japan (this would not under present conditions include forces such as the Szechwan warlords who are not in actual position to attack the enemy) and that we are taking direct steps to accomplish this end. We can assure the Generalissimo that we are not contemplating reducing our aid to the Central Government (any aid we give the Communists or other groups must because of transport difficulties be at first on a small scale and will probably be less than the natural increase in the flow of supplies into China). We must include in the statement that we will keep the Central Government informed of the extent and types of such aid. We can also tell the Generalissimo that we will be able to use the lever of our supplies and cooperation to limit independent and aggressive action on their part, restricting them to their present areas. And we can point out the advantage of having the Communists helped by us rather than seeking Russian aid or intervention, direct or indirect.

At the time of making this statement to the Generalissimo, he might also be told, if it is considered advisable, that although our effort to persuade the various groups of the desirability of unification has failed and we can no longer delay measures for the most effective prosecution of the war, we consider it obviously desirable that our military assistance to all groups be based on unity and the coordination of military command; that we are prepared to continue to lend our good offices to this end, where feasible and when asked for; and that while we believe that the proposal should come from the Generalissimo, we would be disposed to support: (1) The formation of something in the nature of a supreme war council or war cabinet in which Communists and other groups would have effective representation and some share in responsibility for the formulation and execution of joint war plans, and (2) the nominal incorporation of Communist and other selected forces into the Central Government armies under the operational command of American officers designated by the Generalissimo on the advice of General Wedemeyer, on agreement by all parties that these troops would operate only within their present areas or specified extended areas. It should be made clear, however, that our decision to cooperate with any forces able to assist the war will not be delayed by or contingent on the completion of such internal Chinese arrangements.

Such a *modus operandi,* we believe, would bridge the present deadlock in China and serve as a preliminary move toward full solution of the problem of ultimate complete unity. As one result of the recent negotiations the principal and over-riding issues have become clear. The Generalissimo and his Government will not at this time on their own initiative take any forward step which will mean loss of face, prestige or personal power. The Communists will not, without guarantees in which they have confidence, take any forward step which will involve dispersion and eventual elimination of their forces upon which their present strength and future political existence depend. The step we propose taking will exert on both parties the force necessary to break this deadlock, and the *modus operandi* embodied in those two proposals should initiate concrete military and, as an inevitable result, political cooperation and accordingly provide a foundation for increasing future development toward unity.

These proposals would not exclude the political consultation committee plan which, if adopted, could function alongside the war council and the Government. In fact, it should be expected that the committee would be greatly strengthened.

The statements to Chiang should, of course, be made privately. But the possibility of the logical and much more drastic step, in the event of his refusal to accept it, of a public statement of policy such as that by Churchill in regard to Yugoslavia would be clearly understood.

Even though not made public, however, the fact of our assistance to the Communists and other forces would soon become generally known throughout China. This, we believe, would have profound and desirable political effects in China. There is tremendous internal pressure in China for unity based on a reasonable compromise with the Communists and a chance for the presently liberal groups to express themselves. However, these liberal groups, even within the Kuomintang such as the Sun Fo group, and the minor parties were ignored in the recent negotiations by the KMT but not by the Communists (with whom they present what amounts to a united front) and they are disillusioned and discouraged by what they feel is American commitment to the present reactionary leadership of the Kuomintang. By the steps we propose we would prove that we are not so committed, we would greatly raise the morale and prestige of these liberal groups, and we would exert the strongest possible influence through these internal forces to impel Chiang to put his own house in order and make the concessions necessary to unity.

There is no question that such a policy would be greatly welcomed by the vast majority of the Chinese people (although not by the very small reactionary minority in control of the Kuomintang) and that it would raise American prestige.

The statement has been made to a responsible American by Sun Fo himself that if Chiang were told, not asked, regarding United States aid to Communists and guerrillas, this would do more to make Chiang Kai-shek come to terms with them than any other course of action. The majority of Chinese believe that the settlement of China's internal problem is not so much a matter of mutual concessions as reform of the Kuomintang itself. They also declare, with justification, that American "non-intervention" in China cannot help but be in fact intervention in favor of the present conservative leadership.

Also by such policy, which we consider realistically accepts the facts in China, we could expect to secure the cooperation of all of China's forces in the war, to hold the Communists to our side rather than throw them into the arms of Russia (which is otherwise inevitable if Russia enters the war against Japan), to convince the KMT of the undesirability of its apparent present plans for eventual civil war, and to bring about some unification which, even though not immediately complete, would provide the basis for peaceful future development toward full democracy.

5. This telegram has been drafted with the assistance and agreement of all the political officers of the staff of this Embassy and has been shown to General Wedemeyer's Chief of Staff, General Gross.[30]

---

[30] *Foreign Relations 1945*, pp. 242–246; also paraphrased in *China White Paper*, pp. 87–92. (One deletion in *Foreign Relations* has been made good by substitution from the *White Paper* version.) The last paragraph, unusual (perhaps unprecedented) in a Foreign Service message of this kind, was a spontaneous decision by

This telegram, it may be noted, was consistent with the Washington formulations of a flexible policy. But the Department of State had somewhat vaguely talked about short-range support of Chiang (except in the case of coastal landings encountering non-KMT forces), and seemed to treat flexibility as a long-range consideration. The Embassy argued, on the other hand, that the situation within China was moving so sharply toward a crisis that it needed the application of flexibility now, when it had some chance of being effective and while we had still had a valid military basis for invoking it, rather than delaying until some indefinite future date, when it would be too late. The telegram assumed that Chiang would find it possible, for his own preservation, to accommodate himself to this policy and to emerge as the head of a broadly-based united front or coalition government. But it was implicit that the American interest in a friendly, united China should have priority over the personal support of Chiang Kai-shek.

Included in the message was the statement (first paragraph in section 4): "The presence of General Wedemeyer in Washington as well as General Hurley should be a favorable opportunity for discussion of this matter." These discussions, entered into by Hurley with considerable heat, now commenced. On March 5 (in person), on March 6 (by telephone), and on March 7 (again in person), Hurley had long conversations with senior officers of FE and CA.[31] Neither side appears to have made any progress in convincing the other. Hurley then took the discussion to the White House level. In these talks with President Roosevelt (there seem to have been at least two, possibly more), no representative of the State Department has been mentioned as being present. Nor has any record been brought forward by Hurley, or discovered by the many historians and government figures who have dealt with this period. One must assume, therefore, that no record was kept, and that the full details of the deliberations will never be known. Only one fact is\clear: Hurley stayed on as ambassador. In its official account in 1949, the State Department was able to offer only the laconic statement:

---

all those involved. Although assigned to the Army, I was nominally a member of the Embassy staff and joined gladly in the drafting of the telegram. Under ordinary circumstances, the offering of such recommendations would be a matter of course and considered a normal Embassy responsibility. But under Hurley, circumstances were not normal; we already had reason to expect that his reaction would be neither calm nor rational. It was in an effort, then, to demonstrate that the responsibility was not that of Mr. Atcheson alone, as well as in the hope that explicit unanimity might lend our views more weight, that we all insisted (over Atcheson's original demurral) on signing the original copy of the telegram and including this statement. Since I was the one who took a copy of the message to Chief of Staff Gross, I can report that his comment also was one of strong approval. All of the signers of the telegram, including Atcheson, were shortly removed from China on Hurley's demand (see also Chapter V, note 46).

[31] *Foreign Relations 1945*, pp. 260–264.

General Hurley strongly opposed the course of action recommended above [in the February 28 telegram from Chungking] and it remained the policy of the United States to supply military material and financial support only to the recognized Chinese National Government.[32]

I think, however, that it is possible to probe through this murky obscurity with a reasonable confidence of finding the road. Despite what seemed to most observers to be a deadlock between the Kuomintang and Communists, Hurley was still optimistic of success (he was, one might note, temperamentally inclined to be optimistic, particularly where his reputation and persuasive powers as a negotiator were at stake). But several developments at about this time could be interpreted—by persons not immediately in touch with the situation in China—as seeming to lend credence to this optimism.

One was Chiang Kai-shek's agreement, urged by Hurley and supported by a message from Roosevelt, to the Chinese Communist request for representation in the Chinese delegation to the forthcoming conference at San Francisco to set up the United Nations.[33] This seemed a concession that might augur at least some relaxation of tensions.

A second apparently favorable development was the agreement concerning China which had just recently been reached at Yalta.[34] Certainly it must have seemed to Hurley that this fitted precisely with the strategy which he himself in Chungking had come to believe (in concert with Chiang?) to be the only means of bringing the Communists to terms. As recently as January 14 he had bypassed the State Department and sent a long message direct to the President which included the following categorical assurance:

> . . . In your heralded forthcoming meeting, secure the approval of Churchill and Stalin of your plan for: (1) Immediate unification of all military forces in China and (2) A post-war, free, unified, democratic China. When you have secured that agreement we will be able to place in your hands complete plans for the unification of the

[32] *China White Paper*, p. 92.

[33] *Foreign Relations 1945*, pp. 268–269, 278–279, 283–284, 298, 307. Lohbeck, for instance, states that this Communist request "might be an opportunity to move the contending Chinese factions a step closer toward unification, and Ambassador Hurley so presented the idea to President Roosevelt" (*Hurley*, p. 379).

[34] I am aware that this interpretation is very different from the various "reminiscent" accounts given by Hurley himself in later years, particularly in his extensive testimony before the MacArthur Hearings in 1952 (*Military Situation in the Far East*, pp. 2883–2893) at a time when blanket denunciation of Yalta was highly fashionable; see also Lohbeck *Hurley*, pp. 358–377. Herbert Feis does a thorough job of pointing to the discrepancies between these later statements by Hurley and the contemporaneous evidence: Hurley's own statements at the time, his own telegrams reporting to President Truman immediately after his talks with Churchill and Stalin, and statements of other participants such as Ambassador Averell Harriman (*China Tangle*, pp. 278–280, 283–288).

military forces of China; for the recognition of the Chinese Communist Party as a legal political party; for representation of all parties in the administration of the Chinese Government; for the promotion of democratic processes and the establishment of fundamental individual rights and the reconstruction of a free, united, democratic China.[35]

From the fragmentary evidence, discussion of Yalta seems to have dominated these talks between Hurley and the now failing President. Hurley was allowed to see and make a "pencilled copy" of the agreement itself so that he would be able to brief the Generalissimo at the appropriate time. There was also some discussion of colonies in the China area, and Hurley's suspicions of the policies in China of the imperialist powers.[36] It was decided that Hurley would return to China by way of London and Moscow "to obtain cooperation from the British and Soviet Governments for the American policy to support the National Government of China; to unite the military forces of China to bring the war to a speedy end and to support all reasonable efforts of Chinese leaders for the purpose of creating a free, united, democratic China."[37]

In this somewhat euphoric setting (Roosevelt himself was hopeful about the results of Yalta), there seems to have been scant consideration of the recommendation by the Embassy staff and State Department that more positive action be taken within China to end the deadlock there. There was, however, one rather odd note that helped to bolster the rationale that Hurley had been developing.

Hurley, Lieutenant General Wedemeyer, and Commodore Miles discussed the Chinese military problems with the Joint Chiefs of Staff on March 27. They were all of the opinion that the rebellion in China could be put down by comparatively small assistance to Chiang's central government.[38]

---

[35] *Foreign Relations 1945*, pp. 176–177.

[36] Roosevelt hoped that the British could be persuaded to relinquish Hong Kong, and was against giving the French any help to regain Indochina. Hurley had come to a somewhat obscure but firm conviction that the British were among the "imperialist bloc of nations" who opposed his policy and wished to "keep China divided against herself." He may also have noted a remark by Mao Tse-tung in a heated exchange with Colonel Barrett in Yenan on December 8, 1944: "We have fought the Japanese for seven years without any outside help, and we will keep on fighting them no matter what happens. If the United States will not help us, there is still England and the Soviet Union" (*Foreign Relations 1944*, p. 730).

[37] Telegram, Hurley to Secstate, April 14, 1945 (*Foreign Relations 1945*, pp. 329–332). Churchill was quite willing to express support of American policy in China but "Hong Kong will be eliminated from the British Empire only over my dead body."

[38] Fleet Admiral William D. Leahy, *I Was There* (New York: McGraw-Hill, 1950), p. 337. Commodore Milton E. Miles commanded an American Naval Group that operated in China as part of SACO (Sino-American Cooperative Organization) of which General Tai Li, the chief of Chiang Kai-shek's principal secret police organization, was the director and Commodore Miles the deputy director (Vice

There seems to have been no summing up of the decisions reached in these disjointed talks between different groups and at several levels. The only participant in all was Hurley; and he tells us merely: "The President sustained my position and said that it was in keeping with the traditional American policy in China."[39] Coming down a little closer to specifics, Hurley succeeded in having the Embassy proposal set aside by convincing the President that he would be able to deliver a Kuomintang-Communist agreement "by the end of April."[40] Hurley based this confidence on the expectation that the Communists would promptly be swayed by the assurances of support for American policy which he counted on receiving from Churchill and Stalin during the trip on which he was about to start.[41] The State Department, on its part, conceded that *if* the deadlock in China was broken in the near future—as Hurley so confidently expected—"then the question of adopting any alternative plans, including that of Mr. Atcheson, does not arise."[42] For the time being, then, the decision was that there would be no dictation to Chiang Kai-shek. I shall return to the background of this decision at a later point in this chapter.

But Also No Commitment

The limited nature of the decision on China policy that Hurley took back with him to Chungking was immediately made apparent. Hurley had won his point that there should be no American military cooperation with the Communists unless Chiang Kai-shek approved—though he conceded that this might not apply in a landing on the China coast, in which case the U.S. Army "would have the right to arm all forces in such a condition that would assist the American landing force."[43] But the basic American policy—that the United States was *not* irrevocably committed to the support of Chiang Kai-shek and should maintain a degree of flexibility—still stood. Indeed, it was promptly reaffirmed, in categorical terms.

On the actual day (April 3) that Hurley was leaving Washington, the State Department completed a statement of United States postwar mili-

---

Admiral Milton E. Miles, *A Different Kind of War* [New York: Doubleday, 1967] pp. 108–111).

[39] Lohbeck, *Hurley,* p. 383.

[40] FE memorandum of March 7 (*Foreign Relations 1945,* pp. 262–264).

[41] Hurley seems to have assumed that this secondhand statement of Stalin's support would impress the Communists, though his earlier quotation of Molotov had not. Furthermore, he seems to have expected this Communist compliance to be almost instantaneous: Hurley left Washington on April 3, interviewed Stalin on April 15, and did not arrive in Chungking until near the end of the month. There is nothing in the published record to show whether he communicated directly with the Communists on his arrival. But very soon after that arrival he announced this British and Soviet support at a press conference on April 28 (*Foreign Relations 1945,* pp. 374–378). As we have already seen, Yenan still showed no willingness to accept the Kuomintang terms, and Hurley was forced to fall back on the still indefinite date when the expected Sino-Soviet treaty would be concluded.

[42] See footnote 40, above.

[43] See footnote 24, above.

tary policy with respect to China. The issue that prompted this was the extent to which the United States should commit itself in long-range projects "such as the giving of United States assistance toward the establishment of an effective Chinese air force." The State-War-Navy Coordinating Committee (which at that time had a function generally similar to the present National Security Council) considered this paper and approved it—without change. This approval was formalized in SWNCC 83/1 of May 29, which stated (in part):

> . . . [T]he political policy of the United States with respect to China is as set forth in the enclosure [the State Department paper of April 3].
> *a.* No commitment looking toward the implementation of a military policy of assisting the Chinese Government to create and maintain a modern post-war army and airforce should be made until the interested Departments of the United States Government have been consulted and have expressed opinion that certain necessary political and economic conditions have been fulfilled by the Chinese Government. . . .
> The Joint Chiefs of Staff have advised the Committee that they perceive no objection to these conclusions from the military point of view.[44]

The State Department's paper of April 3, which set forth this now agreed-on policy, drew upon the language of its earlier paper of January 29 and included that paper as an annex.[45] It also incorporated language from the briefing paper prepared for the Yalta meeting.[46] In some respects, however, it went beyond these earlier policy statements in qualifying American support for the Generalissimo's government.

> 3. . . . A well-trained and well-equipped Chinese national *(non-political)* army, supported by a modern air force, would unquestionably contribute materially to the maintenance of a strong China. In the opinion of the Department of State, however, the achievement of internal unity and the establishment of a stable government supported by the people are prerequisite thereto.
> 4. Existing political conditions in China are such as to require the greatest caution and flexibility in the application of measures designed to implement the objectives set forth in paragraph 2.
> *a.* The American government recognizes and supports the National Government of the Republic of China under the leadership of Chiang Kai-shek. However, the unrepresentative character of the present government which is strictly controlled by a single party, namely, the Kuomintang, the inefficiency of its governmental, administrative and judicial machinery, the inefficiency and corruption prevalent in the present Chinese army and air force, the lack of

---

[44] *Foreign Relations 1945,* pp. 116–117.
[45] See footnote 18, above.
[46] See footnote 21, above.

protection accorded to persons and property and the absence of freedom of speech and freedom of the press, constitute factors which have created widespread dissatisfaction with the present National Government. . . .

It appears to the Department of State to be of the utmost importance that our support of the present Kuomintang-controlled National Government should be realistically alert to these political factors which may conceivably result in the overthrow of the present government *or the outbreak of civil war.* . . .

8. With respect to the post-war period and with particular reference to the problem stated in the directive under consideration, the Department of State feels that it would be unwise to commit ourselves in any way with the present National Government of China to assist in the development and maintenance of a modern post-war Chinese air force unless and until:

a. International political unity and stability have been achieved in China.

b. The Chinese Government has obtained the support of the Chinese people. . . .[47]

President Roosevelt died on April 12. President Truman, unbriefed and still inexperienced even in the job of Vice President, had much to learn. The end of the war in Europe, the Potsdam Conference, and then the events leading up to the Japanese surrender were soon upon him. Stettinius, never effective in the position, was replaced by Byrnes as Secretary of State in August. No one expected the sudden ending of the war in the Far East: the China situation had a low priority. Hurley, disappointed that his talks with Churchill and Stalin had not moved the Chinese Communists, carried on in his inflexible course with his eyes set on the mirage of a Sino-Soviet treaty. The State Department, thoroughly aware by now that its ambassador in China was following a policy that was different from its own, made several efforts to bring him into line. These did not, apparently, receive the strong support at the top of the government which would have been necessary—with Hurley now firmly in the saddle in Chungking—to make them effective.

On April 27 the Acting Secretary of State (Grew) sent to President Truman a memorandum, prepared by FE on April 18, which was presumably intended to provide the Secretary and the new President with a brief but comprehensive summary statement of American policy toward China. This was essentially a condensation of the several previous policy papers already noted (the Yalta briefing paper and those of January 29

---

[47] *Foreign Relations 1945,* pp. 74–79; emphasis added. The fact that the Kuomintang regarded the military forces as a Party army *(Tang-chün)* [F. F. Liu, *A Military History of Modern China* (Princeton: Princeton University Press, 1956), pp. 15–16, 19–20, 274–275] was something that never seems to have been clear to Hurley. The Kuomintang's political commissar system in the army was discontinued (under American urging) in 1947—but was later reinstituted (Barrett, *Dixie Mission,* p. 87).

and April 3); the introductory paragraphs will be sufficient to indicate its tone.

> Toward both the immediate objective of defeating Japan and the long-term objective of peace and security, we seek to promote establishment of a broadly representative Chinese government which will bring about internal unity, including reconcilement of Kuomintang-Communist differences, and will effectively discharge its internal and international responsibilities.
>
> While favoring no political faction, we continue to support the existing Government of China, headed by Chiang Kai-shek, as the still generally recognized central authority which thus far offers the best hope for unification and for avoidance of chaos in China's war effort. However, with regard to our long-term objective and against the possible disintegration of the authority of the existing Government, it is our purpose to maintain a degree of flexibility to permit cooperation with any other leadership in China which may give greater promise of achieving unity and contributing to peace and security in east Asia.[48]

At about this time, according to Feis, the State Department again considered doing something about the impasse in China.

> On May 2nd William Phillips, who was briefly serving in the Department, called a meeting to discuss a new instruction for Hurley, which might provide a more positive approach to the problem of inducing or influencing political unity in China under a "coalition" government (Vincent memo, May 2nd); and it was apparently decided that a summary of the memo of April 18th was adequate for this purpose.[49]

Whatever may be the reason, *Foreign Relations 1945* includes no material relative to this meeting, nor does it include the Vincent memorandum of May 2 that Feis refers to.[50] The editors of *Foreign Relations 1945* indicate that the FE memo of April 18 was "transmitted to the Ambassador in China by the Acting Secretary of State in instruction No. 133, May 15, not printed."[51] Such an instruction would have gone forward by mail (courier pouch). The reference by Feis to a "summary of the memo of

---

[48] *Foreign Relations 1945*, pp. 93–95. The Acting Secretary's transmitting memorandum stated that it was prepared "at the request of the Secretary of State for use in connection with the San Francisco Conference."

[49] Feis, *China Tangle*, p. 292, n. 3. William Phillips was a Foreign Service and State Department veteran of towering prestige and seniority. His career, which commenced in 1903, had included service in Peking and as the head of FE, six years as Assistant Secretary of State, two tours as Under Secretary, ambassadorships in five countries, assignment as OSS representative and political adviser to General Eisenhower in London in 1942, and most recently as American diplomatic representative in New Delhi. After retiring in late 1944, he had been recalled to active duty as a Special Assistant to the Secretary of State.

[50] John Carter Vincent was head of CA during this period.

[51] *Foreign Relations 1945*, p. 93, n. 28.

April 18th" is apparently to a telegram which the Acting Secretary sent to Hurley on May 7. Unfortunately, this message is also not included in *Foreign Relations 1945*. However, from the account by Feis, it obviously included more than a mere summary of the FE memorandum.

> Hurley was told that it was deemed most important that we maintain complete flexibility with regard to the means of reaching our ends. He was told also to be sure to make it entirely clear to Chiang Kai-shek and his government that our support was not a blank check; that they must share their power and mend their ways, to the end that internal unity and stability might be achieved as soon as possible, that the prosecution of the war might be facilitated, and that a sound basis could be laid for firm and friendly relations with Russia.[52]

A part of this attempt to obtain a high-level curb on Hurley may be also reflected in the FE memorandum of April 28 to Grew and Holmes. It is hard to see how the State Department's disagreement with "General Hurley's 'policy' " could be stated in terms more clear and blunt.

> We have for some time noted with concern that General Hurley's approach to the very complicated political problems in China is characterized by an intransigent and inflexible attitude. It had been our hope that upon General Hurley's return to Washington it would be possible to talk freely and frankly with him on policy matters and to impress upon him the very great importance attached by officers of the Department to a completely flexible and realistic approach to these problems. However, the few conversations had with General Hurley were unsatisfactory and fruitless. Experienced Foreign Service officers and responsible officers of other Government agencies who have recently returned from Chungking share our concern in regard to the enunciation by General Hurley of a policy which has been described, by intelligent observers of the political situation in China, as "blank check" support of the Generalissimo and his one-party (Kuomintang) government. In our opinion General Hurley's "policy" is increasing Generalissimo Chiang Kai-shek's intransigence in dealing with the problem of internal unification, is unwisely restricting our military aid to China exclusively to the Generalissimo's forces, thereby preventing us from making use of other Chinese forces which might be effectively used against the Japanese. His policy, we believe, is vitiating the influence and leverage we possess to induce the Generalissimo to bring about the military, economic and governmental reforms essential to the establishment of internal unity and stability. *In brief, Ambassador Hurley is conducting this Government's relations with China along lines which we do not approve and which we fear will lead China toward internal chaos and serious external complications.*[53]

---

[52] Feis, *China Tangle*, pp. 292–293.
[53] *Foreign Relations 1945*, p. 349; emphasis added. This is a part of the same memorandum already cited in Chapter V, n. 48.

This unusual situation, in which the government in Washington had one policy and its ambassador in China quite a different one, persisted until Hurley's dramatic resignation in November 1945. This event, and the fact in the background that open civil war was spreading by that time in China, marked the final failure of the tactics and policy that Hurley had so rigidly pursued into a blind end.[54] It also forced President Truman and Secretary Byrnes, for the first time, to give serious attention and study to the problem of American policy in China.

What emerged from that belated but intensive study was the comprehensive instruction given to General Marshall as he commenced his mission to China. Relevant portions of that instruction were:

> The U.S. recognizes and will continue to recognize the National Government of China and cooperate with it in international affairs and specifically in eliminating Japanese influence in China. The U.S. is convinced that a prompt arrangement for a cessation of hostilities is essential to the effective achievement of this end. Incidental effects of U.S. assistance upon any dissident Chinese elements will be avoided insofar as possible. Beyond these incidental effects, U.S. support will not extend to U.S. military intervention to influence the course of any Chinese internal strife.
>
> The U.S. is cognizant that the present National Government of China is a "one-party government" and believes that peace, unity and democratic reform in China will be furthered if the basis of this Government is broadened to include other political elements in the country. Hence, the U.S. strongly advocated that the national conference of representatives of major political elements in the country agree upon arrangements which would give those elements a fair and effective representation in the Chinese National Government. It is recognized that this would require modification of the one-party "political tutelage" established as an interim arrangement in the progress of the nation toward democracy by the father of the Chinese Republic, Doctor Sun Yat-sen.
>
> As China moves toward peace and unity along the lines described above, the U.S. would be prepared to assist the National Government in every reasonable way to rehabilitate the country, improve the agrarian and industrial economy, and establish a military organization capable of discharging China's national and international responsibilities for the maintenance of peace and order. . . .[55]

---

[54] Hurley, of course, never conceded this failure; he preferred scapegoats. But he certainly read the newspapers and telegrams with their discouraging news of the breakdown of the KMT-CCP talks and the daily spread of open civil war in China. It is hard to find any other explanation of his long stay away from China—from September 22 to his resignation on November 26—at a time when events there were steadily falling apart. If he had thought there was a hope of saving the situation, one would have expected him to return.

[55] *Foreign Relations 1945*, pp. 770–773. The preceding twenty-five pages (pp. 745–770) give full details of the discussion, papers, and various drafts from differ-

Dr. Kubek tells us that the policy that guided General Marshall in China was a wholly new policy.

> The slanted words of the career diplomats [Davies and Service] released the steam, therefore, to reverse the wheels at this juncture and change the direction of United States policy in the Far East.[56]

> ... [I]n 1945 the anti-Nationalist faction in the Untied States was manufacturing its disastrous policy of direct American intervention in China's internal affairs. According to Dr. Stanley K. Hornbeck, this was the critical juncture: "It was, then, in the year 1945— and not before then—that the government of the United States, first having taken action inconsistent with tradition and commitment in regard to China, embarked upon what had become a course of intervention in regard to the civil conflict. . . ." [57]

> When the United States unwittingly assisted the wrong side in gaining control of China proper, Korea and Vietnam became inevitable involvements for the nation that has had to assume the mantle of leadership in the free world. History will set it down as simply as that. What needs to be added to the record, however, is this detail of chronology: The United States Government shifted its policy in China in 1945, making its tragic blunder at the very moment that the Amerasia affair was making headlines.[58]

> ... the tragic reversal . . .[59]

> ... that calamitous change of policy . . .[60]

The fact, however, is very different. The Marshall directive was essentially nothing more than a continuation of the American government's policy of conditional aid to Chiang Kai-shek and the Nationalist Government that can be traced back through a long series of policy statements to at least the policy paper of May 4, 1944.[61] What had been achieved

---

ent sources that finally led to this agreed-on policy statement. In addition to Vincent (then head of FE), these discussions and drafting contributions included Generals Hull and Handy, Fleet Admiral Leahy, Under Secretary Dean Acheson, Secretary Byrnes, President Truman, and General Marshall himself at every stage. Nonetheless, Dr. Kubek asserts (*Papers*, p. 27) that "all of Marshall's directives had been drafted by John Carter Vincent."

[56] *Papers*, p. 30.

[57] *Ibid.*, pp. 26–27. Dr. Hornbeck left the Department in September 1944 to become Ambassador to the Netherlands.

[58] *Ibid.*, p. 113. Probably not all historians "will set it down as simply as that."

[59] *Ibid.*, p. 30.

[60] *Ibid.*, p. 113.

[61] See footnote 5, above: "The United States . . . is not committed to support the National Government in any and all circumstances." As noted in Chapter III, the actual initiation of the policy of conditional support had come in the several months immediately preceding the State Department policy paper. This was in the President's strong response to Chiang's virtual ultimatum in January 1944 for a billion-dollar loan; and in the War Department's threat to cut off lend-lease when Chiang refused (in March and April) to activate the Y-Force on the Salween River front.

was not a new policy, but the effective consolidation and implementation of long-existing policy. This came about under the force of an emergency, and by the notable elimination of Hurley's independent and contradictory theme of unconditional support of Chiang Kai-shek. General Marshall, one might note parenthetically, had long advocated, and sought to have implemented, a policy of conditional support.[62]

It is quite clear, I suggest, that Dr. Kubek cannot support his version of China policy by the actual policy documents—which are not to be found in *The Amerasia Papers*. Admittedly, American policy toward China during 1944 and 1945 was not always clear, well-defined, and free of contradictions. That, after all, was one reason for the title—*The China Tangle*—that Herbert Feis selected for his study. But it is also true that the policy was not unconditional support of Chiang Kai-shek, as Dr. Kubek would have his readers understand.[63] If the United States ever came close to agreeing to unconditional support, it was in two instances which Dr. Kubek, ironically, may not wish to consider as such.

The first of these was when Roosevelt requested that Stilwell be placed in command of all Chinese forces. Just what this would have involved in terms of American commitment was never spelled out; but that it would increase American responsibilities in the Theater and involve some commitment to Chiang seems unquestionable. When Chiang Kai-shek refused to accept Stilwell, President Roosevelt's reply included the statement: "... I am now inclined to feel that the United States Government should not assume the responsibility involved in placing an American officer in command of your ground forces throughout China."[64] General Wedemeyer, as already noted in Chapter III, was not authorized to accept command of Chinese troops. And the American feeling of "responsibility" toward China steadily declined.

The second instance was actually in the secret, unpublished instructions to General Marshall himself. On December 11, 1945, General Marshall had his next-to-last meeting with President Truman before his departure for China. Also present were Secretary Byrnes and Admiral Leahy. It was General Marshall himself, in his characteristically meticulous and thorough manner, who prepared a memorandum of the conversation. In it we find:

> The President stated that he wished to have a clear and complete understanding among us as to just what was the basis on which I was to operate in China in representing him. . . .

---

[62] Marshall's consistent advocacy toward China of what Romanus and Sunderland call a *quid pro quo* policy went back to at least November 1941 (*Stilwell's Mission to China*, p. 41, and numerous other indexed citations in this and succeeding volumes under "Marshall" and *"quid pro quo* policy").

[63] See Introduction to Part Two, notes 1–5.

[64] Roosevelt to Chiang, October 5, 1944 (Romanus and Sunderland, *Stilwell's Command Problems*, p. 459).

Finally, General Marshall stated, that if the Generalissimo, in his (General Marshall's) opinion, failed to make reasonable concessions, and this resulted in the breakdown of the efforts to secure a political unification, and the U.S. abandoned continued support of the Generalissimo, there would follow the tragic consequences of a divided China and of a probable Russian reassumption of power in Manchuria, the combined effect of this resulting in the defeat or loss of the major purpose of our war in the Pacific. Under these circumstances, General Marshall inquired whether or not it was intended for him, in that unfortunate eventuality, to go ahead and assist the Generalissimo in the movement of troops into North China. This would mean that this Government would have to swallow its pride and much of its policy in doing so.

The President and Mr. Byrnes concurred in this view of the matter; that is, that we would have to back the Generalissimo to the extent of assisting him to move troops into North China in order that the evacuation of the Japanese might be completed. . . .[65]

Two questions may well be raised concerning the picture of American policy in China during 1944 and 1945 as I have set it forth. First: if Hurley was not accurately representing American policy, why was he left as ambassador in Chungking? Second: if the actual policy in China during this period was one of conditional support for Chiang, why has this fact not been clearer to students of the period?

An answer to the first question must, unfortunately, be largely speculative. While Rosevelt was President (up to April 1945), a number of possibilities come to mind. Orderly administration was apparently not a matter of great concern to Roosevelt. He was inclined to conduct foreign relations in a highly personal manner, and often with scant reference to the State Department. He had used Hurley on a number of other missions during the war, and had come to have some confidence in him.[66] Some of the reports of Roosevelt's failing physical and mental powers during this period can probably be discounted.[67] But one may wonder, at the same time, how thoroughly the President was briefed, and how clearly he understood the dispute over American policy in China as Hurley was representing it. No State Department voice, for instance, seems to have been

---

[65] *Foreign Relations 1945*, pp. 767–769. The history of this period would be a great deal clearer if Hurley had followed this example of General Marshall, and the earlier example of Ambassador Gauss (see Chapter IV), in recording important conversations.

[66] See, for instance, Leahy, *I Was There*, p. 227.

[67] Note, for instance, Wedemeyer's account of a talk with Roosevelt in March 1945: "I had not seen the President for several months and was shocked at his physical appearance. His color was ashen, his face drawn, and his jaw drooping. I had difficulty in conveying information to him because he seemed in a daze. Several times I repeated the same idea because his mind did not seem to retain or register . . ." (Albert C. Wedemeyer, *Wedemeyer Reports!* [New York: Henry Holt, 1958], p. 340). For similar statements by Hurley and William B. Bullitt, see Lohbeck, *Hurley,* pp. 353, 366–367, 368.

heard in the White House talks during March 1945 when these issues were being raised.[68] One finds seeming clues that Roosevelt did not really realize that the focus of the China debate had come to be whether American support of Chiang was to be conditional or, as Hurley was insisting, unconditional. For instance, Roosevelt wrote his old friend Evans Carlson on November 15, 1944: "I am hoping and praying for a real working out of the situation with the so-called Communists."[69] In December, Mao Tse-tung chided Hurley with the fact that he [Mao] had received a letter from President Roosevelt (not printed in *Foreign Relations 1944*) saying that he "was willing to cooperate with all anti-Japanese forces in China."[70] As late as mid-March 1945 (while Hurley was in Washington), Roosevelt had a long private talk with another old friend, Edgar Snow. Some parts of Snow's detailed report are of interest.

> Roosevelt liked to tell anecdotes and I liked to hear them, so that our conversation was very far from systematic; but if there was one recurrent subject on which it was less desultory it was China. He was baffled and yet acutely fascinated by the complexity of what was happening there, which nobody explained satisfactorily to him: myself included. He understood that our wartime aid was actually a form of political intervention in China and he genuinely desired, I concluded, that it be used in ways which would both keep China in the war and bring about social, economic and political progress. But how to do it?
>
> By 1945 Roosevelt was more than ever puzzled by Chiang Kai-shek as a man and a politician. When I last saw him he had just heard about a breakdown in negotiations Pat Hurley was then conducting between Yenan and Chungking. It was "very disappointing news," coming after earlier reports that a formula had been worked out. The President said Chiang Kai-shek had "raised some perfectly absurd objections" to the Communists' requests for certain guarantees along lines of a bill of rights which appeared "perfectly reasonable" to F.D.R. . . .
>
> By now he recognized the growing strength of the Chinese Communists as the effective government of the guerrilla areas. He was considering giving them direct help against Japan, as a matter of military expediency. . . .
>
> The President asked a few questions about what, concretely, the Eighth Route (Communist) Army could do with our aid in North China. He then said that we were going to land supplies and liaison officers on the North China coast, as we drew closer to Japan. All this was of course off the record. Heretofore, we had given no mil-

---

[68] As already mentioned, the State Department lost its effective link with the White House when Sumner Welles resigned in 1943. Stettinius does not seem to have had much interest in China.

[69] Letter, Roosevelt to Lt. Col. Evans F. Carlson, USMC, November 15, 1944: cited by Barbara W. Tuchman, *Stilwell and the American Experience in China* (New York: Macmillan Co., 1971), p. 486 n.

[70] *Foreign Relations 1944*, pp. 740–741.

itary help to the Communist forces. I assumed that in any such commando operation we would try to find Kuomintang people to work with also. I wondered how the Reds, who controlled most of the North China population beyond the roads, railways and cities garrisoned by the Japanese would react to that.

"I suppose the position is that as long as we recognize Chiang as the sole government we must go on sending all supplies exclusively through him? We can't support two governments in China, can we?" I asked.

"Well, I've been working with two governments there." The President threw his head back decisively. "I intend to go on doing so until we can get them together."

This last conversation reflected a certain new coolness in attitude toward Chiang Kai-shek and a growing impatience with his obstinate resistance to basic reforms necessary for his own self-preservation. . . .

Just what did Roosevelt, who then had these secret terms of Yalta concerning Manchuria and China fresh in mind, foresee as the possible future of our own relations with the Chinese Communists? What did he mean when he said that day, "I'm working with two governments [in China] and intend to go on doing so . . ."? [71]

Roosevelt, it should be remembered, was speaking at the very time that Hurley was in Washington arguing against the Embassy's proposal to commence military cooperation with the Communists. He asked Snow about the capabilities of the Communist forces, indicated that he expected the United States to land "supplies and liaison officers" on the North China coast (where the Communists were the only Chinese force), and then made it clear that this cooperation with the Communists would be direct and without regard to objections by Chiang Kai-shek ("I've been working with two governments there. I intend to go on doing so . . ."). This was not full acceptance of the Embassy proposal; but it was precisely in accord with the State Department's guidance paper of January 29. And it was far from unconditional support of Chiang Kai-shek.

Hurley, himself, clearly recognized that there were limits to our support of Chiang Kai-shek. He was, in fact, very sensitive to the charge that he favored unlimited or blank-check support. For instance, during his report of a controversy with members of his staff in Chungking in June 1945, he made the statement: "Both Ringwalt and Smyth know that the rumors they report to the effect that the U.S. policy is to give 'unlimited support to the Kuomintang' is [sic] untrue."[72]

My own belief, which I have already noted and of which there is admittedly no proof, is that it was Yalta that was the principal factor in

[71] Edgar Snow, *Journey to the Beginning* (New York: Random House, 1958), pp. 347–349. Reprinted by permission of the author. In addition to showing the difference of Roosevelt's attitude from Hurley's, these passages are of interest in showing Roosevelt's relations of confidence in at least one member of the press.
[72] *Foreign Relations 1945*, pp. 409–410.

Hurley's being kept on and being sent back to China without clarification of these policy issues. For one thing, Yalta loomed so large that it pushed these troublesome and difficult disputes into the background. And from it, Hurley acquired a new expanded mission: to get British and Soviet support for his negotiations that could be used to bring pressure on the Communists in advance of an eventual Sino-Soviet treaty to be based on the Yalta agreement; to assist Chiang in his preparations for the treaty with the Russians; and to brief him on the provisions and background of the Yalta agreement itself when the appropriate time came.

In this catalog of considerations, Roosevelt must have had some awareness of the dilemma involved in the fact that it was he alone, over the scorn of Churchill and the shrug of Stalin, who had insisted on elevating Chiang and China to Big Four status. Perplexed and disappointed in Chiang as Roosevelt had increasingly become since the unhappy meeting at Cairo and its bickering aftermath, less important though China had become for the war and immediate future, and optimistic though the President seems to have been of a satisfactory working relationship with the USSR, the embers of this old illusion probably had still enough life to make it uncomfortable for him to adopt a bluntly harsh attitude toward the Generalissimo. This reluctance may have been increased if Roosevelt felt any uneasiness about the concessions at China's expense, still secret from Chiang, that had been agreed on at Yalta.

There is one more factor that undoubtedly contributed to making this a thorny problem that Roosevelt preferred not to grapple with. The Cold War had not yet commenced; in fact, the Yalta agreements seemed—to Roosevelt and Hurley—to hold the promise of Soviet cooperation in many areas of concern. Nonetheless, Roosevelt was astute enough as a politician to be keenly aware that China policy was a sensitive subject, that Chiang Kai-shek had a large and fervent band of American supporters, and that "Communist" was a dirty word to important segments of American public opinion.

What actually happened was that Roosevelt postponed the issue by ignoring it. Yalta seemed likely to Roosevelt to provide the answer to Chinese unity. In the meantime, Hurley was confident that his negotiations would be successful within the next month. There was no need, if this was true, to grasp the nettle of taking some other positive, and certainly unpleasant, action to end the deadlock in China. The Embassy and State Department proposal for direct military cooperation with the Communists was therefore set aside. Hurley was sent back to China to continue doing what he had been doing.

What would American policy be if the situation in China continued to deteriorate? If Yalta (or the advance British and Soviet support of our policy) did not bring the Communists to accept the terms offered by Chiang? If a sudden end of the war found China hopelessly divided? If civil war on a broad scale commenced? One can assume that, in March 1945, these eventualities seemed distant and remote: Roosevelt probably felt that they could be dealt with if and when the need arose. At any rate, nothing seems to have been done in these White House talks to try to answer them. The extent, nature and duration of our support of Chiang were thus left undefined.

One is tempted to make two observations. Even though Hurley himself conceded that American support of Chiang was not "unlimited," it seems obvious that his conception of the extent of that support was considerably broader than Roosevelt's. For one thing, Hurley wanted to use the claim of American support for Chiang as a heavy counter in his manipulative game to get agreement in China. But the failure of Roosevelt to define this support—as in the earlier case of Washington's failure to clarify Hurley's "understanding" of American policy in his December 24 statement—seemed to lend veracity to Hurley's claim that he alone was representing American policy.

The second point is the obvious one that the attempt to differentiate between short-term and long-term policy is usually illusory. Confronted with Hurley's return to China, and the putting aside of the proposal to commence military cooperation with the Communists, the State Department continued to stress the long-range policy of flexibility. But what is done today cannot help but affect the future: short-term actions thus come to determine long-range policy.

After Truman became President, there was bound to be a period of uncertainty. Still, there was a general expectation in Washington, as the new administration began to settle down and catch its breath, that the tenure of Republicans such as Hurley might be limited because of a stronger feeling that good jobs should go to good Democrats.[73] Again, however, it was the Yalta agreement concerning China that operated to make Hurley seemingly indispensable. It was an American diplomatic commitment, probably unprecedented in nature, of the utmost gravity and delicacy. Hurley had been made one of the very limited group who even knew of the existence of the commitment. Furthermore, he had been informed of all its details, and was to have an important role in securing its implementation. Not surprisingly, Hurley lost little time in acquainting

---

[73] I mentioned this, for instance, in a personal letter from Washington to Theodore H. White in Chungking on April 16, 1945 (*Tydings Transcript*, pt. 1, p. 1357). This got into the Tydings Committee hearings because the Committee's minority counsel, in a preview of Dr. Kubek's use of my personal papers, obtained and introduced copies of my personal correspondence which had been taken from my desk at the time of my arrest (and later returned to me). Since I was writing under wartime censorship, Hurley's name was not mentioned; and instead of saying "good Democrats," I said "good party members." Unfortunately, in the atmosphere of 1950, this suspect phrase took some explaining—although it did not require much effort to see that I had started to write "Republican officeholders" and then scratched it out (*ibid.*, pp. 1337–1339).

the President with these circumstances. This was done in a private message (bypassing the State Department) on May 10.

> Knowing the great strain under which you must be working I have hesitated to burden you with problems by which we are confronted here. In my last conference with President Roosevelt he entrusted me with two specific missions in addition to my duties as Ambassador to China.
>
> The first mission was to bring Churchill and Stalin to an agreement on the policy that the United States had been pursuing in China. . . .
>
> The second mission entrusted to me by President Roosevelt in my last conference with him pertains to a decision affecting China reached at the Yalta Conference. Before my last visit to Washington and before I had been informed by the President of the Yalta decision pertaining to China including particularly the all-important prelude, the Generalissimo had discussed with me China's position on the same problems decided upon at Yalta and had given me his attitude relating to them. . . .
>
> Both Roosevelt and Stalin advised me that it was agreed between them that I would not open the subject of the Yalta decision with Chiang Kai-shek until the signal was given me by Stalin. Stalin said he would give me carte blanche and let me use by own judgment as to when and how to present the subject. However, both Harriman and I were of the opinion that it would be best to delay the presentation because of the possibility of leakage which in turn might bring undesirable results. I explained this to Stalin and it was finally decided that I am not to present the subject to Chiang Kai-shek until we have advised Stalin that, in our opinion, the time is opportune and until we have received the signal from him.
>
> I want to emphasize to you that prior to my recent visit to Washington I had discussed with Chiang Kai-shek all phases of the Chinese-Russian problem before we knew what was contained in the Yalta Agreement, and since coming back to Chungking we have again thoroughly covered the same subjects without alluding to the primary subject. We are therefore in a position to proceed with dispatch on the Yalta Agreement when we are authorized to submit the particulars thereof to the Generalissimo. . . .[74]

There was, of course, more involved in the whole Yalta package than merely the agreement concerning China. At the highest levels of the government in Washington during May there was active consideration (initiated by Grew) of whether the Yalta decision should be reconsidered. Feis provides a cogent summary:

---

[74] *Foreign Relations 1945*, pp. 865–868. President Truman replied promptly on May 12, again by non-State Department channels: "Please continue your efforts to accomplish the purposes outlined to you by President Roosevelt. . . . We will endeavor to get to Chiang Kai-shek, through you at the earliest date, all the available information on this subject that can be disclosed without damage to the overall prospect" (*ibid.,* pp. 868–869).

The whole consultation ended in a mild conclusion: we would not try to revise the terms of the Yalta Accord; but before asking Chiang Kai-shek to concur we would try to get Stalin to re-endorse protective principles. We would again test whether the Soviet government honestly intended to allow the Chinese government to exercise unimpaired sovereignty over all of China and Manchuria, and whether it would fall in with our effort of unification. . . . Hopkins set off to talk . . . with Stalin. Truman, who was taking up the task of finding whether he could work with the Soviet Union, a task which had worn away the last weeks of Roosevelt's life, had asked Hopkins to risk the journey. It was thought that he, if anyone, could on the one hand reassure Stalin that Roosevelt's policies would be continued, and on the other induce Stalin to carry out faithfully with Truman the agreements reached with Roosevelt. The mission was regarded as a crucial attempt to restore the trustful working accord which Roosevelt and Hopkins thought had been formed at Yalta, particularly in regard to whether Stalin would act fairly toward Poland and adhere to the American understanding of what had been arranged for the Far East.[75]

This was undoubtedly the reason why, despite the impressive auspices of William Phillips, the State Department's attempt in early May to solve its "Hurley problem" was so ineffectual that it had to be limited to the (once again, "anemic") action of sending him a copy of the policy memorandum of April 18 and an exhortation "to make it entirely clear to Chiang Kai-shek and his government that our support was not a blank check."[76] The problem was—and it must have given Hurley considerable amusement—that no one on the operating levels in the State Department even knew of the existence of the Yalta agreement on China. The State Department, except perhaps for Stettinius, had not been consulted in the reaching of the agreement, and no representative of the State Department conversant with Far Eastern affairs was present at Yalta. The head of FE did not learn about the agreement until July 1945 (five months later), while he was en route with the American delegation to the Potsdam Conference.[77]

---

[75] Feis, *China Tangle*, pp. 308–309.

[76] See footnotes 49 and 52, above.

[77] Characteristically, these facts did not deter Hurley when convenient whipping boys were wanted:

> There is a tendency now to charge the Yalta Secret Agreement to President Roosevelt. President Roosevelt is dead, but I can say that he is not guilty. He was a very sick man at Yalta, and the surrender of China to the Communists in the Secret Agreement of Yalta was engineered by the officials of the American State Department under the brilliant leadership of a young American, Alger Hiss. (Letter from Hurley to the *Atlantic Monthly*, September 28, 1950; cited in Lohbeck, *Hurley*, p. 368.)

I know of no evidence that the role of Hiss at Yalta was more than that of a staff member of the American delegation's secretariat.

I come then to the second question: why has the fact not been clearer that American policy in China during 1944 and 1945 was actually one of conditional support of Chiang Kai-shek? The answer, I suggest, lies outside of the policy papers and discussions—for these show a consistent development of policy leading to the Marshall directive.[78] Instead, the answer is in American domestic political conflicts, because it was the heat generated by these political attacks that apparently persuaded the Democratic Administration to seek refuge in reticence. One might also note, parenthetically and in the expressive words of Herbert Feis: "There are few harder stunts of statesmanship than at one and the same time to sustain a foreign government and to alter it against its fears and inclinations."[79]

China policy, it hardly needs saying, had been a subject of acrimonious, partisan debate in the United States since at least the early stage of World War II, when the decision had been made to concentrate American energies first on the defeat of Germany. The Stilwell recall in October 1944 had provoked a flurry of controversy and charges of dictation to Chiang. Roosevelt had tried to smooth it over as nothing more than "a conflict of personalities."[80] A storm was stirred up by the Hurley resignation in November 1945. The State Department's protective reaction was, again, to deny that there had been policy differences.[81] Perhaps this could be justified as an attempt to defuse Hurley's angry accusations; but one

---

[78] Historians who have examined the record closely have noted this element of continuity but have not, generally speaking, given it emphasis. Perhaps the clearest statement is in Tsou, *America's Failure*, pp. 298–299. Tsou also notes (*ibid.*, p. 142) that "the Truman-Marshall policy . . . was nothing but an extension of the wartime policy . . ."; but he seems to be referring here more narrowly to unification by peaceful means. Feis sees the disagreement between "the dissenters in the State Department" and Hurley more in personal terms. He states: "The Far Eastern specialists went on advocating 'a flexible and realistic approach' "; but he seems to minimize the fact that their approach had been established as official policy (see, for instance, *China Tangle*, pp. 273–274).

[79] *China Tangle*, p. 272.

[80] Tuchman, *Stilwell and the American Experience*, p. 506:

> Obliged to comment at a press conference, Roosevelt was never more bland. It was all a conflict of personalities. Chiang Kai-shek and General Stilwell had "certain fallings-out—oh, quite a long while ago—and it finally ended the other day." No politics were involved, not even Chinese politics; no (in reply to question after question), not strategy, not policy, not Lend-Lease, nor the Hump tonnage, nor Hurley-Nelson, nor Gauss's resignation, nor the "so-called Communists" had anything to do with it. It was "just personalities."

[81] The clearest example of this is the statement of Secretary of State Byrnes on December 7, 1945, before the Senate Foreign Relations Committee in its investigation of Hurley's charges. The closest he would come to an admission of differences between the State Department and Hurley was: "The phase of that policy upon which Ambassador Hurley has placed the greatest emphasis is our support of the National Government of Generalissimo Chiang Kai-shek" (*Investigation of Far Eastern Policy*, pp. 189–200, and specifically p. 191).

effect was certainly to make Marshall's mission appear as more of a new policy venture than it actually was.

By the spring of 1949, the collapse of the Kuomintang Government on mainland China was irreversible and nearly complete. But the partisan attacks on the Administration's China policy showed no signs of abatement: on the contrary, they were steadily more frequent and more violent. President Truman and Secretary of State Acheson decided to publish the record of the events and policy of the United States in China during the preceding five years. It was this publication, appearing in August 1949, that has become known as the *China White Paper*. It has been, and rightly so, a valuable and authoritative source book for the history of this period. But it could not completely escape the circumstances in which it was written.

Lyman Van Slyke, in his Introduction to the recent republication of the *China White Paper,* points out:

> By implication, the decision to publish the White Paper reflected the feeling that since we could no longer effectively influence events in China, we should not be entangled in them. . . . [T]he Administration plainly hoped this record would show that we had done as much as we could, that our course had been basically correct, and that the impending fall of China to the Communists was in no way attributable to American policy. The White Paper was issued to counter largely Republican criticism. . . .[82]

> By now, too, a new note had been added—the question of Communist influence on China policy in the State Department. . . . There had been sporadic charges made earlier against certain career China specialists, beginning with Hurley's letter of resignation in 1945, but by 1949 the atmosphere had grown feverish. . . . The White Paper was thus published in the midst of acrimonious controversy over United States China policy, the containment of Communism abroad, and the fear of subversion at home.[83]

Whatever the reasons, the *China White Paper* omitted the fact that there existed a long line of policy papers, prepared in most instances by the State Department but also backed by the approval and authority of the War Department, Joint Chiefs of Staff, and the State-War-Navy Coordinating Committee, stating that the policy of the United States in China during 1944 and 1945 was one of flexible, conditional support of the Kuomintang government.[84] The existence of these papers has, not

---

[82] Lyman P. Van Slyke, "Introduction," *China White Paper* (Stanford: Stanford University Press, 1967), 5th unnumbered page.

[83] *Ibid.*, 4th unnumbered page.

[84] For the convenience of the reader, the following are the policy papers, memoranda, and messages to which I have made reference (together with the number of the footnote in the text above—Chapter VI—where each was first cited):

surprisingly, become known to scholars who have researched the history of the period. All of them are referred to, in greater or less detail, by either Feis, Romanus and Sunderland, or Tsou. But the official disclosure of the actual texts had to await the publication—eighteen and twenty years respectively after the appearance of the *China White Paper*—of the *Foreign Relations* China volumes for 1944 and 1945.

This reticence on the part of the State Department has had several rather obvious effects. In his Letter of Transmittal that serves as foreword to the *China White Paper,* Secretary of State Acheson noted:

> When peace came the United States was confronted with three possible alternatives in China: (1) it could have pulled out, lock, stock and barrel; (2) it could have intervened militarily on a major scale to assist the Nationalists to destroy the Communists; (3) it could, while assisting the Nationalists to assert their authority over as much of China as possible, endeavor to avoid a civil war by working for a compromise between the two sides.[85]

There was, in fact, a fourth, unmentioned alternative: to seek to avoid civil war by working for a compromise, but to keep the United States in a flexible position, basically uncommitted to the extension of Nationalist, or any other power in China, and ready to adjust itself to the further evolution of that country.[86] This had, indeed, during the critical years of 1944 and 1945, been the State Department's own now-forgotten alternative.

Another result, perhaps inevitable in the circumstances of the time but not without effect for the long-run future, was that the Chinese Communists made the *China White Paper* the focus of their first mass anti-American campaign. Van Slyke sums it up:

May 19, 1944	(State Department paper)	note 5
Jan. 12, 1945	(Yalta Briefing paper)	note 21
Jan. 29, 1945	(State Department paper)	note 18
April 3, 1945	(State Department paper)	note 47
April 18, 1945	(State Department memo)	note 48
April 28, 1945	(FE memorandum)	note 53
May 7, 1945	(telegram, State to Hurley)	notes 49, 52
May 29, 1945	(SWNCC 83/1)	note 44

It should be noted that this list, though including what I consider the principal documents, does not include all papers and messages which discuss some aspects of a flexible policy, such as readiness to supply non-Kuomintang military forces in the event of a coastal landing. See, for instance, CA memo of "about January 12" prepared for the JCS and transmitted "to the Ambassador in China by the Secretary of State . . . to 'be helpful to the Embassy as indicating general lines of policy and thinking in the Department with regard to China. . . .'" (*Foreign Relations 1945*, pp. 169–172 and n. 27).

[85] *China White Paper,* p. x.
[86] See, for instance, Lawrence K. Rosinger, "The White Paper in Brief," *Far Eastern Survey,* September 7, 1949 (Vol. 18, no. 18), pp. 205–208.

There had been much Communist-inspired criticism of the United States in the past, but there remained in China considerable reservoirs of good feeling, particularly among the intellectuals and bourgeoisie in the cities. These reservoirs the Party now set out to drain, as a part of the larger movement to eliminate Western influence from China.

The last five articles in Volume IV of Mao's *Selected Works* denounce the United States in general and the White Paper in particular. Mao's editors describe the goals of the campaign when they say that these pieces "exposed the imperialist nature of United States policy toward China" and "criticized the illusions about U.S. imperialism harbored by some of the bourgeois intellectuals." . . .

The Chinese Communists did not find it necessary, or desirable, to translate the White Paper. Instead, they concentrated almost entirely on extracts from Acheson's Letter of Transmittal: the amount of aid given to the Nationalists; the assertion that the United States had done all it could to support Chiang; the claim that the "Communist leaders have foresworn their Chinese heritage" and are subservient to Russia; and above all, the statement that the United States should encourage developments to "throw off the foreign yoke." [87]

To come down to a less world-shaking plane, the omissions from the *China White Paper* history of American policy left some of its officers in what might be described as a slightly exposed position in the subsequent years of strife. For instance, the February 28 (1945) telegram from the Embassy staff in Chungking was quite properly included: as one of its co-authors, I would like to think of it as a policy recommendation worthy of such notice. But it was severed from all context. The reader had no way of knowing that a similar view was independently arrived at by responsible officers of the Department, and that the Department itself had strongly urged the adoption of the policy recommended in that telegram.

In retrospect, it may have been hopeless for a beleaguered Administration to try to publish a convincingly objective account during the bitter controversy over the "loss of China." At the time, however, I shared the belief that it would reduce the controversy and thus serve a useful purpose.[88] All of us failed to foresee the venom and public hysteria of the ensuing McCarthy period.[89] The effort was a conscientious one. But from

---

[87] *China White Paper,* "Introduction," 6th and 7th unnumbered pages.

[88] I readily agreed, for instance, to the inclusion of excerpts from my reports in one of the annexes to the *White Paper* (Annex 47, "Memoranda by Foreign Service Officers in China, 1943–1945," pp. 564–576). Hurley's accusations, and publication of selected fragments of my reports (by such sources, for instance, as pro-Kuomintang members of Congress), had already created distorted impressions of my views; it seemed to me that actual publication of the reports themselves could only be a good thing.

[89] One irony of the situation was that no amount of reasoned argument or objectivity would have succeeded in mollifying the Administration's critics. Thus we find Lohbeck, who appears throughout his book to be speaking for Hurley, dismissing the *China White Paper* with the statement: "The *United States Relations With China* followed exactly the policy that had been promoted by General Stil-

a record so voluminous, it was unavoidable that there had to be a drastic selection based on relevance. By 1949, the policy papers of 1944–1945 were down the drain. Furthermore, they represented a flexible policy that both Roosevelt and Truman left blurred, and which had been effectively nullified by the words and actions of Hurley. Most of the criticism of the *China White Paper* has come from persons friendly to the Kuomintang. It is also ironic that the incompleteness of the picture it presented worked a hardship on its own officers who had to wait for more than twenty years for the full record to be published in *Foreign Relations*.

---

well, John Patton *[sic]* Davies, John Stewart Service, and George Atcheson in China . . ." (*Hurley,* p. 456). White is thus made black, facts are no longer facts, and reasoned discourse becomes impossible.

VII
The Rejected View From the Field

The preceding four chapters have attempted to find out what American policy in China actually was during 1944 and 1945. Since Dr. Kubek says that I "actively opposed and subverted" American policy, the logical next step should be to look at what it was that I reported and recommended. I propose now to do this, even though under the ground rules that Dr. Kubek has adopted, it may be effort largely wasted.

Dr. Kubek, as we have seen, essentially reduces American policy in China to the unlimited support of Chiang Kai-shek. It follows—in Dr. Kubek's mind, as in General Hurley's—that the reporting of factual information unfavorable to the Chiang regime, and the drawing of conclusions from those facts, are the same thing as subversion of the policy. Furthermore, to foresee the failure of the Kuomintang government is automatically taken by Dr. Kubek to be the "espousal" of that failure. The logic behind this mental jump is a bit obscure. Apparently it is based on Dr. Kubek's conviction that it was the mere submission of these critical reports that became the direct cause of the "fall of China." But Dr. Kubek does not stop there: "Just as these documents of World War II provide a clue to the catastrophe that befell China a few years later, so will the Amerasia Papers be seen to pertain irresistibly to the present perplexities of American policy in the Far East."[1] Never, it might be said, has such a strong claim been made for the potency of Foreign Service reporting.

Dr. Kubek's line of reasoning has certain advantages. Since his real concern is what he alleges to be the *effect* of the reports, the actual content of each report has no relevance except as it may contain something which Dr. Kubek considers to be derogatory to the Kuomintang or favorable to the Communists. Thus it is entirely unnecessary for him to confront the question of the truth or falsity of the information reported. This confrontation, it may be noted, is conspicuously absent.[2] Similarly, what

---

[1] *Papers,* p. 113.

[2] One indication of this is a check of Dr. Kubek's footnote sources. The now massive Western scholarship on the history and nature of the Chinese Communist movement is completely ignored except for the single exception of Karl A. Wittfogel's "A Short History of Chinese Communism," in *General Handbook of China* (1956), vol. 2, prepared by the Human Relations Area Files for the U.S. Army. Although Dr. Kubek's focus is on the war years, no mention is made of such authoritative contemporary sources as the so-called Peabody Report, *The Chinese Communist Movement: A Report of the United States War Department, July 1945.*

some scholars might regard as significant agreement regarding the situation in China by isolated reporting officers scattered all over that large country need not, again, be related to the question of whether this unanimity might indicate something about the probable validity of their reports. On the contrary, to Dr. Kubek it is only suggestive of conspiracy.

I doubt that there is need to waste time in debating Dr. Kubek's quaint concept of the function of Foreign Service reporting and the responsibility of Foreign Service officers. Secretary of State Byrnes testified at some length on these specific points in his refutation of the charges made by General Hurley at the time of his resignation.

> Of course, it is the duty of every officer of the United States to abide by and to administer the declared policy of his Government. But conditions change, and often change quickly in the affairs of governments. Whenever an officer honestly believes that changed conditions require it, he should not hesitate to express his views to his superior officers.
>
> I should be profoundly unhappy to learn that an officer of the Department of State, within or without the Foreign Service, might feel bound to refrain from submitting through proper channels an honest report or recommendation for fear of offending me or anyone else in the Department. If that day should arrive, I will have lost the very essence of the assistance and guidance I require for the successful discharge of the heavy responsibilities of my office.[3]

One problem in trying to discuss my reporting is its sheer volume. It accumulated over a long period in response to a constantly changing and often rapidly developing situation in China. It seems practical, therefore, to deal with it here in only a summary way, and—when it seems desirable for clarity—to disregard strict chronological sequence. This may be permissible if, as I believe, there was an overall consistency in the point of view. Although I will try to indicate—and quote from—some reports that I, personally, consider to be the more important, I hope that the reader interested in fuller detail will go to the reports themselves.[4]

This was originally published as an appendix to the Internal Security Subcommittee's 1951 hearings, *Institute of Pacific Relations,* but has been reprinted in 1968 by Stanford University Press under the editorship of Lyman P. Van Slyke.

[3] U.S. Senate, Committee on Foreign Relations, *Investigation of Far Eastern Policy,* p. 199. The context of this statement by Secretary Byrnes had particular reference to Hurley's allegations concerning reports made by George Atcheson and myself.

[4] Appendix A lists (and shows available published sources for) all of my reports from Yenan, as well as a number of other papers drafted or co-authored by me which may be indicative of the development of my views. *The Amerasia Papers,* it will be noted, is a good source for the Yenan reports (largely, as I have shown, by Dr. Kubek's use of my personal papers); but it lacks most of the other papers. The *Foreign Relations* volumes have some material from most of the reports of substantive importance; but, for reasons presumably of space, they often include only the summary and conclusions, omitting the factual presentation and argument. Complete documentation, however, is not always possible. Many memoranda have

It should be understood, at the outset, that I am thoroughly aware that not all that I predicted happened; and much that did happen was not as I expected. Furthermore, timeliness was important: my information was not always correct, and the reports often written in haste. Usually directed toward a particular current problem or some aspect of an over-all situation, they were seldom comprehensive. I was, after all, a field reporter: the research-analysis and policy men in Washington could fit the bits and pieces into the whole. It should be obvious, too, that these reports were not written with the thought that they might some day be published. They were directed to the men on the China desk in the State Department and others in Washington, who already had some background on the China situation and a familiarity with the common terms of discussion concerning it. They were not, therefore, ever intended as definitive works of political exposition.

Despite these obvious shortcomings, I have not felt impelled, during the years since they were written, to revise or apologize for these reports and views. Certainly, if I were to write them today, they would be different in form and detail—though not, I believe, greatly different in their general recommendations. But I would also be a man of 61 rather than 35, wiser (perhaps) with the benefit of hindsight, removed from intimate proximity to world-shaking events, and possibly inclined toward a more sedate manner of presentation. History, after all, will judge their value or folly without regard to afterthoughts and excuses. So far as I am concerned, they represent a conscientious effort, on the spot and at the time, to report what I saw, heard, and believed to be the truth of the situation—and to recommend what I thought best for the long-term interests of the United States.[5]

THE VIEW FROM CHUNGKING

It was apparent, by the beginning of 1943, that the internal situation within China was going to have a vital importance for American interests there. The rivalry between the Kuomintang and the Chinese Communists could hamper the prosecution of the expected long war against Japan on

---

never been published, and I have no copy. Some details of my thinking were simply a product and part of the constant and vigorous discussion, debate, and argumentation that went on during these years.

[5] The reader may be struck by an excessive use of the "first person perpendicular." Though personally uncongenial, often awkward, and sometimes misleading, the choice of "I" rather than "we" is a deliberate one. The intent is not to give any seeming confirmation to Dr. Kubek's extravagant inflation of my role: far from it. The reader having only a slight familiarity with the history of the period, with essential source books such as the *Foreign Relations* volumes, or even with Dr. Kubek's own selection of documents, will realize that I was generally not alone in my views and recommendations. I am discussing, though, events of twenty-six or more years ago: events which had an aftermath that gravely affected the subsequent lives and careers of the American participants. I think it fair—except when contemporary signed documents are involved—to speak, therefore, for myself alone.

the mainland of China; it could be even more destructive of the peace, unity, and stability that we hoped China would achieve in the postwar period. Since the Chinese Communists, apparently growing in strength behind the Japanese lines in North China, were largely an unknown quantity, the United States would be wise to get firsthand knowledge of them. The most complete statement of my views at this time was in a memorandum (already referred to near the beginning of Chapter VI) prepared on January 23, 1943, while I was temporarily on consultation in the Department of State.[6]

Returning to China in April, I was sent back to the Northwest—where I had also spent the summer and fall of 1942.[7] After two months in Lanchow, I was recalled to Chungking for duty with General Stilwell's staff. This put me in an unusual position for a civilian and Foreign Service officer. My specified duties were relatively few and assigned missions quite infrequent. On a continuing basis I served as a liaison between the Army headquarters and the Embassy, and also as liaison (for intelligence from North China) between the headquarters and the Communist representatives regularly stationed in Chungking. The freedom of the job, and some assigned missions, provided opportunities for even more travel than in the past: Chengtu, Sian, Assam, Kunming, and a long trip (to guide an engineer officer on a survey of motor roads—including those in operation as well as those made "impassable" to impede any possible Japanese advance) that took me by jeep, junk, horseback, and foot through the provinces of Yunnan, Kweichow and Kwangsi.

By the spring of 1944, the war was not going well in China. Japanese drives in East China were threatening. Stilwell was advancing slowly in a bitter campaign in North Burma, but Chiang was holding back on a commitment to have the American-trained Y-Force coordinate in a drive westward across the Salween River. In the acrimonious aftermath of Cairo and the revision of Allied plans agreed on there, we were embroiled in Chungking on a whole range of issues: the exchange rate, financial support, construction of the B-29 bases at Chengtu, and—as always—the quantity and allocation of tonnage over the "Hump."[8]

I settled down now in Chungking. As a consultant, I became peripherally involved in many of these negotiations proceeding between American and Chinese officials, and in trying to bring about better coordination

---

[6] Chapter VI, note 3. For available texts see Appendix A, Part 3, (a).

[7] On this second trip to the Northwest, I was privately and "unofficially" told by the Embassy that if I should find it possible to enter the Communist base in North Shensi by slipping through or around the KMT blockade (as, for instance, by traveling down the Yellow River to approach from the less well guarded north), I should do so. I found the blockade too tight, and a foreigner in those strategic areas too conspicuous, for hope of success: a request for clearance to visit Ninghsia was sharply refused by the Chinese authorities.

[8] For this period see Romanus and Sunderland, *Stilwell's Command Problems,* Ch. VIII.

between the Army and other agencies: OSS, OWI, and so on. Occasionally I was called on for confidential interpreting or drafting.[9] But my principal continuing function evolved as providing political background and consultation to the Chief of Staff and the Assistant Chief of Staff (Intelligence). By agreement with all concerned, I started preparing informal memoranda over my own signature. Reports on some topics or persons were specifically requested. But I was also encouraged to submit memoranda on any subject that seemed timely, significant, or useful to the Headquarters. The original of these went, of course, to the Headquarters itself. A second copy was supplied to the Embassy, which then decided whether or not to incorporate it into its own reporting to the Department of State. A third copy went to John Davies, the senior among the Foreign Service officers attached to Stilwell's staff, who was spending most of his time during this period in India.[10]

On March 20, with the Burma campaign in the balance and Chiang stubbornly refusing to allow the Y-Force to move, I reflected the crisis mood of the Headquarters in some general observations on the problems of the alliance and the desirability of a *quid pro quo* policy.

[Chiang expects America to defeat Japan for him. And in the process to strengthen his external position by diplomatic support, and his internal position by financial aid and by improving and supplying his armies. The fundamental consideration today of Chiang and the Kuomintang is not the war against Japan but the continuing struggle for internal power, the desire to liquidate the Communists, and the almost certain inevitability of civil war.

Chiang believes that by bluff and by taking advantage of our weakness and lack of unity in dealing with him, he can evade American efforts to jolt him out of this course. He believes that we are so committed to him that he can "have his cake and eat it too."]

. . . Chiang *will* cooperate if the United States, upon which he is dependent, makes up its mind exactly what it wants from him and then gets hard-boiled about it. Until the President determines our policy, decides our requirements, and makes these clearly and unmistakably known to Chiang, Chiang will continue in his present ways. . . .

This may mean taking an active part in Chinese affairs. But unless we do it, China will not be of much use as an ally. And, in doing it, we may save China.[11]

---

[9] See, for instance, Chapter III, note 4.

[10] Davies and I worked together in a loose way. We consulted on areas and topics to be covered, and generally avoided duplication of effort. One result of this is that my own reporting was not complete; the best statement of my own view on some subject may often be something that Davies had already written. It should also be borne in mind that our reporting was not coordinated with that of the Embassy; we did not have access to the Embassy files and usually were uninformed regarding the coverage of, and views expressed in, the Embassy's reporting.

[11] Appendix A, Part 3, (b). *Foreign Relations 1944* omits the bracketed paragraphs and some additional remarks critical of Chiang Kai-shek. Presumably this

In this instance, as we know from Chapter III, Roosevelt did get "hard-boiled"—though my memorandum did not reach Washington until ten days after his message of April 3 to the Generalissimo.[12]

In May, it was learned in Chungking that Vice President Wallace would be visiting Chungking in late June on a special mission from President Roosevelt for talks with the Generalissimo.[13] We were not informed in detail of the purpose of the visit. Several topics seemed likely: the deteriorating situation in China and our difficulties in gaining Chiang's cooperation; recent tension between China and the Soviet Union; the continued KMT blockade of the Communists; and Chiang's refusal of Roosevelt's request (made in February) to send American observers to Yenan. With the campaign in Burma still critical, it seemed unlikely that General Stilwell would be able to come to Chungking.[14] We were not sure whether Wallace, in the General's absence, would consult with Headquarters or desire any briefing from it. Should the need or opportunity arise, I began to prepare a general summary (omitting, of course, the strictly military aspects—on which I was not qualified).

As I got into the task, it began to outrun the proportions of a normal briefing paper. The deterioration of the situation in China—militarily, politically, and economically—seemed to be moving toward a crisis. Changsha, for instance, fell to the Japanese on June 18; it was becoming

---

was under the editorial rule: ". . . certain omissions of documents are permissible . . . to avoid giving needless offense to other nationalities or individuals" (*ibid.*, p. iv). Dr. Kubek prints the whole text.

[12] Chapter III, n. 12. As for advocacy of a *quid pro quo* policy, Tang Tsou cites an authoritative parallel. On April 21, 1949 (the day before Nanking fell to the Communists without serious resistance), Chen Li-fu, leader of the Kuomintang's conservative CC clique, had a conversation in Canton with the minister-counselor of the American Embassy:

> . . . [Chen] is sanguine that the Kuomintang, with united ranks, will be able to rally sufficient support to prolong the struggle until the U.S. can be persuaded once again to intervene. Should that time come, he hopes that we will lay our cards frankly on the table and demand a definite *quid pro quo* for anything we give. This is the only way, he said, we could assure the accomplishment of the ends we desire. (*America's Failure*, pp. 118–119; and *China White Paper*, p. 306.)

Dr. Kubek, incidentally, considers "CC clique" to mean "the Chinese Communist Clique in Kuomintang politics" (*Papers*, p. 527) when, of course, it actually referred to the political polar opposite from the Communists—namely, to the clique of the two Chen brothers, Chen Li-fu and Chen Kuo-fu, who represented the extreme right wing of the Kuomintang.

[13] *Foreign Relations 1944*, pp. 227–230.

[14] Our expectations were correct: Wallace and Stilwell did not meet. "The Generalissimo in Chungking and Chennault in Kunming absorbed Wallace's time and energies, so that Stilwell's staff found little opportunity to present the theater commander's point of view, nor did Wallace feel that he could spare the time to visit General Stilwell in Burma" (Romanus and Sunderland, *Stilwell's Command Problems*, p. 375).

apparent that our airbases in south and east China could not be defended. (This was, as already noted in Chapter III, the situation that led to the JCS recommendation in early July that Stilwell be put in command of the Chinese armies.) The urgency of the time seemed to call for an attempt to analyze the roots of the China problem, and to suggest what the United States might do about it. Essentially, this was trying to think through and spell out the problems briefly alluded to in my memorandum of March 20, three months earlier. My draft, in various stages, was passed around. Views and suggestions were contributed by a number of people in the Embassy, Treasury, OWI, and Army. The final product, then, was not all my own, though I agreed with all that it contained. It was finished on June 20, the day that Wallace arrived in Chungking. He received a copy—but the tightness of his schedule probably meant that he never read it. The Embassy, of course, also received a copy, which it transmitted to the State Department.

The paper reached Washington at a time (in early July) when a great many people were apparently concerned about the alarming situation in China. It was forwarded by FE to the Secretary of State with favorable comment; and I was later given to understand that copies reached the White House. Copies also seem to have been made, duplicated, and circulated rather widely in several government agencies involved with China affairs.[15] Several months later I even recognized a familiar ring in some magazine articles.[16] Eventually, the State Department on September 13 instructed the Embassy in Chungking to inform me that the memorandum had been commended.[17] It should be clear from this commendation (al-

---

[15] For reasons unknown, most of these copies made in Washington were neither accurate nor complete. This has been responsible for uncertainty as to the date of the memorandum, and confusion over paragraphs that appear in one copy but not in another. Some copies carried a SECRET classification and omitted my name (credit in one case was anonymously given to "a close observer of the Chinese scene"). However, I have seen another copy that omitted all classifications and *included* my name. At any rate, my authorship and at least the substance of my views seem to have become well known among the China-watching fraternity at the time (although I myself did not arrive in Washington for another four months). With the proven efficiency of Chinese intelligence in Washington, and the somewhat exuberant way in which this memorandum was circulated, it may safely be assumed that the Kuomintang representatives in Washington also obtained knowledge—and probably copies—of it.

[16] For instance in an article that appeared in *Collier's* in January 1945 (*Tydings Transcript,* pp. 2328–2329). This was written by Gayn some four or five months before I ever met him. I saw, however, no reason for concern. From at least early 1943, the White House, State Department and OWI had seen the need for a more informed and realistic American public opinion about China. Furnishing of background information to American writers was an accepted practice. In this memorandum, I myself had urged that this be done on a regular and expanded basis (see Appendix B: Section III, D, 2, d).

[17] Department's UNRESTRICTED instruction no. 807, September 13, 1944, to the Embassy in Chungking (copy in my possession). "Mr. Service's very timely and able analysis and his constructive suggestions, together with the careful appraisal

most a month after Hurley had received his briefing on American policy preparatory to leaving for China), that this memorandum was not regarded in Washington as subverting or opposing American policy.

Something less than half of the memorandum was devoted to an analysis of the shortcomings and deficiencies of the Kuomintang in 1944; the remainder of the paper dealt with positive political factors in China, and proposed an American policy combining conditional aid and political pressure to bring about a broadening of the base of the government. It was, however, the critical analysis that seemed to attract most notice and has been frequently quoted.[18] Despite (or, perhaps, because of) this notoriety, the memorandum was not included or referred to in *Foreign Relations 1944*. Scattered excerpts (amounting to about one-fourth of the whole) had earlier been printed in several sections of the *China White Paper* annex, "Memoranda by Foreign Service Officers in China."[19] Two versions have been published elsewhere than by the State Department; but neither was the original text. Apparently based on copies that were made in Washington agencies, both are incomplete and contain numerous errors (e.g., "newsreel" instead of "reversal," "security" for "society").[20] The memorandum is lengthy; but since there is no complete and

---

thereof and thoughtful statement of views presented in the Embassy's covering despatch, have been of especial value to the Department in connection with the current critical situation in China and its relation to the military effort and the general interests and policies of the United States." I have never seen the Embassy appraisal and comment referred to.

[18] For example, Feis, *China Tangle,* p. 164 and n. 9; Tang Tsou, *America's Failure,* pp. 195–196 and n. 66; Harold M. Vinacke, *The United States and the Far East, 1944–1951* (Stanford: Stanford University Press, 1952), pp. 25–26; Carsun Chang, *The Third Force in China* (New York: Bookman Associates, 1952), pp. 98–100 [Mr. Chang, founder and chairman of the Chinese Democratic-Socialist Party, comments: "I do not think that the most fervent supporters of Chiang Kai-shek can take exception to this able analysis of the pathological political condition of China during this period."]; Rupert Emerson, *From Empire to Nation* (Cambridge: Harvard University Press, 1962), p. 264; Pichon P. Y. Loh, *The Kuomintang Debacle of 1949: Conquest or Collapse?* (Boston: D. C. Heath, 1965), pp. 27–32. [Although Mr. Loh begins his lengthy excerpt with "B" he fails to inform his reader that he is presenting only an excerpt of a much longer report, nor does he indicate deletions which he has made within the body of the excerpt printed.]

[19] Annex 47, pp. 564–576.

[20] See Appendix A, Part 3, (d), for the various sources. One version, stated to have been found in Amerasia, is printed by Dr. Kubek; he notes one instance (p. 587, n. 7) where this text is incomplete, but there are several others. A second, slightly different, version was introduced by me into my hearings before the State Department Loyalty Security Board and thus appears in the *Tydings Transcript* (pp. 2035–2046). At the time, the State Department had not been able to locate its own file copy of the memorandum (presumably because I did not have the reference to the Embassy's transmitting despatch). The only copy I had then been able to obtain was one that had apparently been made and circulated in OSS. The *Tydings Transcript* text was subsequently reprinted by the Internal Security Subcommittee in its 1951 hearings, *Institute of Pacific Relations* (pp. 816–827). The two garbled, incomplete versions have thus been printed in three places: two of them by the Internal Security Subcommittee.

accurate text available for reference, it is included here as Appendix B. Summarization is not easy, but the following may be indicative.

> The situation in China is rapidly becoming critical. The Japanese have succeeded in their gamble that the Kuomintang would accept slow strangulation in preference to the political hazards of warfare based on mass mobilization. There is a progressive internal breakdown. The Kuomintang is proving incapable of averting this debacle: its policies—internal, economic, military, and foreign—are actually precipitating the crisis. The fundamental cause of this suicidal trend is that the Kuomintang, steadily losing popular support (which, as a result of the practical experience of the war, is becoming more politically conscious), is concentrating more and more on putting the preservation of its shrinking power above all other considerations.
>
> These policies, unless checked by the internal opposition they evoke and by friendly foreign influence, seem certain to bring about a collapse which will be harmful to the war and our long-term interests in the Far East. We cannot afford to sacrifice these interests and withdraw from China. But if we aid the KMT on its own terms, we will be gaining only a brief respite from the ultimate day of reckoning. It is useless, therefore, to continue giving American aid in the past haphazard manner.
>
> The crux of all important Chinese problems—military, economic, and political—is democratic reform. We must base our support on a positive policy of attempting to aid this democratic reform. But it must depend on and be brought about by the significant, latent forces within China. The implementation of our policy therefore depends on close coordination of our activities in China, the tactful exertion of suggestive pressure on the KMT, and the careful encouragement of these democratic forces.

This proposal for active political intervention may have seemed more of a departure in 1944 from customary, old-fashioned, hands-off diplomacy than it seems today. But it was certainly a less direct form of intervention than seeking American command of the Chinese armies—which was recommended by the JCS and approved by Roosevelt before my paper reached Washington. Except for being stated in active rather than passive terms, my recommendation was not very different in substance from the rather hopeful statements of long-range policy which the State Department itself was drafting in 1944 and 1945; perhaps my chief divergence was that I urged that the long-range be brought down to the short-range.

THE VIEW FROM YENAN

One thing accomplished by Wallace's visit was that Chiang gave his permission, long denied, for the U.S. Army to send an observer group to the Communist areas in north China.[21] The War Department had already

---

[21] *Foreign Relations 1944*, pp. 460–463.

accepted, in early March, the State Department's suggestion that I be included in the group to provide political reporting.[22] I flew to Yenan on July 22 as a member of the first contingent.[23] In the second contingent on August 7 was Raymond P. Ludden, a fellow Foreign Service officer also attached to General Stilwell's staff, who had been working with the Headquarters of the Twentieth Bomber Command—which was flying B-29 long-range bombers over North China to Japan and Manchuria from the new fields built near Chengtu.

The first question, and a basic one, was to get a realistic assessment of Communist strength. One indicator would be the extent of their territorial control. During the previous three years in Chungking, the several Americans and British who had escaped from Japanese-occupied cities and traveled through the Communist areas had been interviewed intensively. Once we were in Yenan, we had ample opportunity to learn the Communist claims. The Observer Group had for several weeks what amounted to a daily seminar with a particular army commander or representative from one of the Communist base areas. There was, however, no really convincing substitute for actual inspection. Several groups were sent out into the guerrilla areas. Since travel was by foot, this was a time-consuming operation. One group spent seven weeks in the Shansi-Suiyuan Border Region. Ludden started off with another group that spent four months and traveled some 1200 miles in visiting the Shansi-Chahar-Hopei Border Region.[24] One factor that proved of great incidental aid was the steady increase in American air operations, since this resulted in American air crews being rescued pretty much all over the map. As information accumulated, I submitted a number of reports on the extent of Communist control. The last of these, and the one based on the most complete information, was prepared on March 17, 1945.

Even since the arrival of the U.S. Army Observer Section in Yenan and the establishment of direct contact with the Headquarters of the Communist armies, there has been some hesitancy to accept the Communist claims to have effective control of the countryside of those parts of North and Central China which are under nominal Japanese occupation. Until we had seen for ourselves, such hesitancy was justified: the extent of Communist claims surprised even those who had made efforts to collect all previously available information on their activities.

Due to lack of personnel, absence of facilities such as air assistance, and the slowness of overland travel by foot, the Observer

---

[22] *Ibid.,* pp. 345–346, 355–357, 373–374.

[23] For a general account of the U.S. Army Observer Group in Yenan, see Barrett, *Dixie Mission.*

[24] For reports by Ludden on this trip, see *Papers,* pp. 1329 and 1342 (*Foreign Relations 1945,* pp. 200 and 212). Another report, "Development of Eighth Route Army Regular Forces in the Shansi-Chahar-Hopei Base Area," does not appear to have been published.

Section has made relatively slow progress in inspecting the various Communist bases behind the Japanese lines. Officers of the Section have, however, covered northwest and northeast Shansi, southeast Shansi and west Hopei (including visits to the Peiping and Paoting areas).

Officers of other organizations have visited the Hankow area and North Chekiang.

But by far the greatest aid to our verification of the extent of the Communist areas has been the large number of American airmen (now some 70) who have dropped to safety in those areas.

The attached map shows the approximate routes traveled by American observers on assigned missions and by these rescued airmen. (Although a number of flyers have been rescued in the East River Communist area near Canton, their routes are not shown because the area is relatively small and well-known.)

It will be noted that routes traveled include all of the major Communist bases except the Shantung Peninsula (which apparently has not been the scene of air activity). From their points of rescue some of the air crews have traveled as far as 1,000 miles through Communist-held territory.

Crews have traveled under Communist protection from the seacoast near Shanhaikuan (just south of the border of Manchuria) around Peiping to Yenan. Others have landed on the coast of North Kiangsu and traversed that province and Anhwei. Another party dropped just across the river from Nanking and was brought to Shansi.

The Communists have rescued men near Shanghai, Hankow, Canton, Nanking and Taiyuan—all important Japanese-held bases in China. Flyers have dropped safely within a mile of Japanese airfields or blockhouses.

Over a hundred American crossings of Japanese-held railway have been made safely.

It is axiomatic that it is difficult to hide an Anglo-Saxon traveling through China. But except when crossing railways or in areas very close to the Japanese, practically all travel was done by day without any attempt at concealment. In fact, public celebrations, mass meetings and speeches along the way were customary. Newspapers published in the base areas noted the passage of American visitors. Some of the parties did not even take the bother of exchanging their American Army uniforms for Chinese clothing.

Passage across solidly held areas of Chinese control, in which there were no Japanese forces, sometimes took a week or more of steady travel.

The rescued aviators I have had a chance to talk to have agreed with the officers of the Observer Section in their favorable impression of the Communist forces with which they had contact. The so far unequaled opportunities for extensive observation enjoyed by these men makes the collection and compilation of their reports a most important source of information concerning the Chinese Communists.

The following conclusions are now justified:

(1) We must accept as substantially correct the Communist claims

to control the countryside of North and Central China behind the line of Japanese penetration.

(2) Our past consideration of the territory as "Japanese occupied" should be revised. The Japanese hold only a thin skeleton: the rest of the area is controlled by forces on our side.[25]

The areas under Communist control were scattered and diverse, from dry, sparsely populated hills to the rich, heavily populated plains of north and east China. Population statistics in China were not generally reliable; and even if they were, there would still be a problem of precise delineation of guerrilla areas where neither side held full control. The Communist estimates of their population increased steadily from 85 million in August 1944 to 100 million in March 1945.[26] We took it for granted that these figures represented an optimistic maximum. But they were indicative, and could not be dismissed out of hand. They were some ten times the total of the maximum claimed population of all the various Communist areas during the Kiangsi Soviet period in the 1930s.[27]

---

[25] For available published texts, see Appendix A, Part 2, report no. 17. The map referred to is not available. However, a comprehensive map of the Communist base and guerrilla areas (which we concluded was generally reliable) appears facing p. 122 of Harrison Forman, *Report From Red China* (New York: Henry Holt, 1945). Unfortunately, it has been much reduced in reproduction. A considerably clearer, translated version, based on the same source, will be found as the frontispiece to the Stanford University Press reprint of the *Peabody Report*.

A copy of the same map (hand-drawn and about three by five feet) was given me by General Yeh Chien-ying, the Communist Chief of Staff, as I was leaving Yenan for Washington in October 1944. When I received it, I asked General Yeh whether it should be treated as having any security classification. He replied with a laugh: "None at all: the Japanese know very well where we are." The map, after all, was on the scale of 1:2,000,000 (about 32 miles to the inch), did not indicate unit locations, and was hardly of the topographical and other detail necessary for military operations. Soon after I reached Washington, I was asked to appear for a "de-briefing" session in the Military Intelligence Division of the War Department. This map attracted considerable attention, since it was more complete and specific than anything that MID had yet received. I readily agreed to the MID request that I loan them the map so that it could be reproduced and translated. When I returned to the Pentagon a few days later to pick up the map, I was surprised to find that it had been copiously imprinted with classification stamps rendering it officially SECRET. My protests and explanations were unavailing: it was soberly insisted by the colonels assembled that this classification was required because it "showed the location of allied forces" (although the "allied forces" involved did not desire the classification or consider it necessary). I was, however, allowed to keep the map that General Yeh had given me, and presumably to wrestle with my own conscience as to whom I might allow to see it. The fact, of course, was that anyone who could buy or borrow Forman's book was shortly able to view the identical map to his heart's content without any risk of security infringement.

[26] There was considerable confirmed expansion of the Communist areas during this period. See, for instance, Appendix A, Part 2, report no. 8; Ludden's memorandum of February 7, 1945 (*Foreign Relations 1945*, pp. 212–215); and despatch no. 24 of May 30, 1945, from Edward E. Rice at Sian (*Foreign Relations 1945,* pp. 397–398).

[27] Edgar Snow, *Red Star Over China* (London: Victor Gollancz, 1937), p. 82. The total of 9 million was given by Mao Tse-tung in a conversation with Snow at

Before the Sino-Japanese War, the Communists had held only the relatively small Shen-Kan-Ning base area (in which Yenan was located), and had mustered a military force of possibly ninety thousand.[28] This expansion of territory and population had been achieved under war conditions, behind the Japanese lines of penetration into China; and it had been successful, without outside sources of supply or manpower, against Japanese, puppet, and sporadic Kuomintang military efforts to consolidate, control, and administer the areas. Obviously it required, in the first instance, an effective army—one much larger than the Communists had started with. The army, then, became another subject of immediate and continuing study. And, as with the question of territorial control, the picture became steadily clearer as what we were told and could observe in the Yenan base area received amplification and confirmation from the growing number of reports from Americans in the field who had had a chance to observe the Communist army in actual combat, on the move, and in widely scattered areas. Their findings were in uniform and sharp contrast to the reports, also based on direct American military observation, of the physical condition, morale, and general fighting qualities of most of the Kuomintang armies.[29] I did not, myself, report—except incidentally—on the Communist army. Many reports are available. The conclusions of the *Peabody Report* chapter on "The Chinese Communist Army" may be adequate.

> The consensus of opinion of U.S. observers is that the Chinese Communist Regular Army is a young, well-fed, well-clothed, battle-hardened, volunteer force in excellent physical condition, with a high level of general intelligence, and very high morale. Training of these troops may be rated as fair for their present capabilities even though it is woefully inadequate judged by American standards. Military intelligence, for their purposes, is good. The most serious lack of the Communist forces is in equipment.
>
> The outstanding weaknesses of the Communist forces include lack

---

Yenan in 1936. Mao's figure for the maximum population of the Kiangsi Soviet itself was 3 million. Snow noted that these figures were much lower than some estimates that had appeared. "Mao laughed when I quoted him the figure of '80,000,-000' people living under the Chinese Soviets, and said that when they had that big an area the revolution would be practically won." Cf. Chalmers A. Johnson, *Peasant Nationalism and Communist Power* (Stanford: Stanford University Press, 1962), p. 192, n. 1.

[28] Snow, *Red Star*, p. 271. The Kuomintang figure for Communist strength in 1937 was 26,000 (memorandum dated August 1943 supplied to the American Embassy at Chungking by General Ho Ying-chin in September 1944; see *Papers*, p. 911).

[29] I know of no report by any American observer that is critical of the physical condition, morale, leadership, or general fighting qualities of the Communist armies during the Sino-Japanese War. Most criticisms have been of obvious deficiencies (such as arms and equipment), by people who never saw them (such as Hurley and Wedemeyer), or on questions of whether their equipment and training made them able or willing to launch and carry through a large-scale offensive against the incomparably better equipped Japanese.

of sufficient small arms ammunition, lack of artillery, lack of engineers and other technical personnel, lack of signal equipment in general and especially of radio communication below regiment level, complicated and irregular organization, and heavy casualties among officers with consequent weakness in junior leadership. . . .

These shortcomings of the Communists are, however, offset in part by certain organizational advantages. The small units of the Communist forces, carrying the lightest possible equipment, have high mobility and are well adapted to guerrilla warfare. These units are equipped and trained to operate independently. They exist off the country, apparently having full support of the populace in the areas. This facilitates quick dispersal and mobility. The organization of the forces enables coordination of the operations of these individual units, within the limits of existing communication facilities, through a centralized command. This command takes in not only the regular forces of the area, but also the local detachments and other units within the People's Militia, and the whole population enlisted in the People's Self-Defense Corps. The Communists claim that the political work throughout the army guarantees high morale, excellent discipline, and the whole-hearted support and cooperation of the people.

The capabilities of the Chinese Communist Army may be viewed in the light of the following two factors. First, the Communists are capable of continuing indefinitely the present program of harassment against the Japanese while slowly increasing their strength and supplies. Second, they are not capable of independent, decisive operations to dislodge the Japanese from North or East China unless the Japanese situation has deteriorated seriously or is on the verge of collapse.[30]

The clearer the facts became of a remarkable Communist expansion of territory, population, and armed forces, the more important it was to find out how this expansion had been accomplished; what it meant in terms of political strength; and what it indicated for the future in terms of the willingness of the population to continue to follow and actively support Communist leadership.

One obvious factor was Japanese aggression.[31] In contrast to their unsuccessful civil war during the Kiangsi period, the Communists now were waging a nationalistic war of defense against a hated foreign invader. This

---

[30] Lyman P. Van Slyke, ed., *The Chinese Communist Movement: A Report of the United States War Department, July 1945* (Stanford: Stanford University Press, 1968), pp. 205–207. By the time this comprehensive report was prepared, reports were available from American observers in a number of Communist areas not covered by the Observer Group based on Yenan; see, for example, the very interesting OSS report by an Air Force observer with the New 4th Army which gives broad corroboration of much of the information reported by the Yenan group (*Papers,* pp. 1312–1322).

[31] The fact of Japanese aggression, and the opportunity it gave the Communists to gain support through the appeal of nationalism, was indeed so obvious that I tended to give it only incidental attention in my reports. As will be seen, I came to concentrate more on other elements in the Communist success in gaining popular support, which I believed would be likely to have a lasting political effect after the end of the war with Japan.

brought them much support, particularly from patriotic youth and intellectuals. But Mao had also been farsighted in choosing the areas behind the Japanese as his battleground. For one thing it ensured direct contact with the enemy. The Japanese and their eventual puppet allies needed, if nothing else, to ensure their own security and to obtain the grain and produce of the countryside. Communist initiatives to organize and control the countryside brought Japanese counteractivity. As the war stretched on year after year, there were few villages that had not been raided, sacked, or destroyed—most, in many areas, several times. The war was literally brought into the home of every peasant in the guerrilla areas. The ruthlessness of Japanese tactics actually had the effect, in the long run, of strengthening the Communist appeal. By contrast, to a peasant in the Kuomintang rear (as, for example, in uninvaded Szechwan) the war meant little except the constant fear of the death sentence of conscription, steadily higher tax demands, and the unending impositions of half-starved soldiery. In the second place, warfare behind the Japanese lines could only be mobile, guerrilla operations—the kind of war that Mao and the Communists knew best and excelled at. Finally, the Communists had an area of activity in which they were relatively free from Kuomintang interference.

It was clear, though, that the appeal of nationalism—important as it was—did not provide the whole explanation of the Communist success in gaining popular support. Two considerations seemed relevant. One was the fact that the long-suffering Chinese peasant had always been excluded from government and was apolitical: he had no tradition of rising in defense of the homeland. Secondly, there had been periods—early in the war, and later when the Kuomintang made unsuccessful efforts to reestablish control in some areas behind the Japanese lines—when the peasant had a choice between supporting the government or the Communists. His support invariably went to the Communists. I discussed these problems in a memorandum that tried to analyze the reasons for the spectacular growth of the New Fourth Army, which operated in central and east China areas where Kuomintang competition was more of a factor than in the 8th Route Army areas of north China.

> (a) It might be assumed, for instance, that a patriotic desire to fight the foreign invader was responsible for this popular support. This is partially true.
> But to the Chinese peasant (who is the only important class involved, both because of his overwhelming numerical superiority in China and because the Communists have had to operate entirely away from the cities) the idea of active *personal* resistance was entirely new. In the past the peasant had regarded all governments merely as something to be endured; there was little, as far as he was concerned, to choose from between them; and even if one was slightly better or worse than another, it was no concern of his and

there was nothing he could do about it.

So the peasant needed a great deal of education and indoctrination—and some tangible evidence that it would benefit his own interests—before he was willing to take up arms. The fact that the Communists were able to accomplish this—while the Kuomintang was not—indicates a closeness to and an ability to appeal to the common people in terms which they understand. . . .

(b) Furthermore, the people, if they were willing to fight, almost always—certainly in the early years of the war—had two choices: they could fight with either the Kuomintang *or* the Communists. It would have been more natural for them to have turned to the Kuomintang because it was *the* government. Instead they turned to the Communists, who have come more and more to be regarded and treated by the Government as rebels. It would seem therefore that the peasants received better understanding and treatment from the Communists. . . .

(c) It might be argued that the Communists have the advantage of a "cause," that they use such direct appeals as distributing the land of the landlords to the peasants, that they spread a rabble-rousing Communism, or that they have found an equivalent of the fervor which gave such impetus to the Taipings or the Boxers. But, in fact, this argument is never heard. Even the Kuomintang does not bother to advance it. If they did, it would be refuted by the evidence of every foreign observer who has traveled through the Communist guerrilla areas. The Communists are not even actively preaching *Communism*—though it cannot be denied that they are, sometimes by not too subtle means, trying to create support for the Communist *Party*.

(d) It can also be claimed this popular support is chiefly due to the Communist skill in propaganda. The Communists *are* masters of this art, and it does have a part—but only a relatively small one. The war has lasted more than seven years—longer than mere propaganda without positive results could hope to hold the stolid and practical Chinese peasant. Furthermore, the guerrilla warfare into which the Communists have drawn their supporters is the type which is hardest of all military forms on the peasant because the whole area is continually a battleground.

(e) Another argument, little heard because it is so obviously untenable, is that the Communists have *forced* the people to support them and to join their armies. But the Communist armies were small when the war began: they did not have the military power necessary to have forced the people. Their armies, relatively speaking, are still small. They are, for instance, much smaller than the Kuomintang uses to *garrison* areas of equivalent size far in the rear and away from any enemy. It is obvious therefore that the Communist army does not need large forces to maintain its own rear—as it would if it carried out Kuomintang policies of conscription and taxation and was plagued by the same resultant problems of banditry and internal unrest. It is also true that these relatively small regular forces could not successfully fight off the Japanese and hold these areas unless they had the active assistance and participation of the people in large irregular auxiliary forces, which can only, by their nature, be voluntary. The Communists claim over 2,000,000 local volunteers,

151

the Peoples Militia, who are an active force in resisting and harassing the enemy. This figure may be exaggerated—though the evidence we have so far been able to gather indicates that Communist statistics of this nature are not inflated. But an organization of this type cannot be created and made effective by the threat of military force. And the Kuomintang does not even claim to have such an organization.

3. The conclusion therefore seems justified that the peasants support, join, and fight with the Communist Armies because they have been convinced that the Communists are fighting for their interests, and because the Communists have created this conviction by producing some tangible benefits for the peasants.

These benefits must be improvement of the social, political or economic condition of the peasants. Whatever the exact nature of this improvement, it must be—in the broader sense of the term as the serving of the interests of the majority of the people—toward democracy.[32]

By saying that nationalism was not the whole answer to the Communist success, I did not mean that their nationalism was not genuine. Mao insisted: "We are, first of all, Chinese."[33] I do not think that any of us who knew Mao and the other Communist leaders, or who had traveled in the guerrilla areas, had any doubt of the sincerity of this feeling. But guerrilla war, in a favorite Communist analogy of the fish and water, required mass mobilization and popular support. And mass mobilization could obviously lead beyond the immediate goal of defeating Japan. I tried to sum this up in a memorandum in March 1945:

> They [the Communists] insist that effective prosecution of the war demands full mobilization of the people; that this requires political indoctrination and the granting of political rights and economic reforms benefiting the mass of the population. . . . Fundamental to this argument is the Communist conception of the war against Japan as a national war of liberation which must at the same time, in order for its success, be an important and progressive stage in the Chinese revolution. The primarily conservative Kuomintang fears this "revolutionary" potentiality of the war—which means democracy and economic reform as a basis for popular resistance.[34]

We heard a great deal, with varying emphases and details, about the Communist programs to gain this popular support. One version which perhaps has the advantages of being clear, succinct, and systematic, developed out of several long conversations I had with Chen Yi, then the Acting Commander of the New Fourth Army.

---

[32] Appendix A, Part 1, report no. 22. The quoted passages (*Papers*, pp. 837–838) are not included in the brief summary that appears in *Foreign Relations 1944*.

[33] Appendix A, Part 1, report no. 15. This report is the account of a lengthy and important interview with Mao. The quoted statement appears in *Papers*, p. 792, and *Foreign Relations 1944*, p. 608.

[34] Appendix A, Part 2, report no. 11.

(a) First it was necessary to win the people's confidence, in a military sense. Fortunately the original cadres were old and experienced guerrilla fighters. In their first engagements, the Japanese were not used to their tactics and were unprepared and over-confident because of their easy defeats of other Chinese troops. During the first year they had uniform success: after that they had newly trained and capable forces. The Communists always follow the policy of using their best troops in important engagements, holding their newer troops as reserve or to throw in after the enemy is retreating to give them experience.

(b) The first step after coming into an area is intensive propaganda to explain the war and secure popular support.

(c) This is followed by the creation of mass organizations of the people. These include farmers, youth, women, militia, and so on. All of these are for the purpose of carrying out some function in resisting the enemy. But they are also encouraged to interest themselves in their own problems. For instance, the farmers are told that in the well-established guerrilla bases rents and interest have been reduced.

(d) Through and from these mass organizations, democratically elected governments are set up. At first these are on the village level. As the area becomes stabilized the system is extended until the hsien governments, and finally the base governments, are elected by the people. Nominations and elections are carried out in general village meetings.

(e) As soon as some sort of government control is established, rents and interest are reduced. This is done moderately. The minimum standard is 37½ % for rent. But in the first stage rents are not usually reduced by more than one-quarter. This is to avoid driving the landlords away and into the Japanese camp. In many areas into which the N4A has gone, the power of the landlords has been very great and they have been able to hang on to their control and even in some areas to dominate the local governments. In such areas the Communists move slowly by strengthening the organization of the people until they gain control by democratic methods.

(f) Taxes are reduced because of the moderate requirements of the N4A and the elimination of corruption through popular election of officials.

(g) Taxation is made moderately progressive. At present the poorest approximately 20% of the farmers pay no tax. The highest rate on the rich landlords usually does not exceed 35%.

(h) Banditry is vigorously attacked and the welfare of the people is improved by the maintenance of peace and order. In addition to direct attack, the other policies of the Communists are effective in removing this old burden of banditry.

(i) As important as any of these is the practical demonstration of the unity of the army and the people. The Army takes as one of its major tasks the protection of the people (to the degree that this often determines its military operations). It takes positive measures to prevent enemy interference with the sowing and harvest. It actually assists when possible in farm work. When and where able its troops produce a part of their own needs. It avoids any sort of arbitrary demands on the people, pays for what it takes, and replaces

153

breakage or damage. It helps the people cope with disasters such as breaks in dikes. In times of poor crops it reduces its own rations to the level of subsistence of the people. It continually harps on the idea that the army and people are "one family."

(j) There is never any forced conscription. Except for the encouragement of the formation, on a volunteer basis, of such organizations as the Militia, it avoids in the early stages of its control of an area, any attempt at recruiting.

(k) Within the Army it takes special measures to care for families of soldiers; emphasis is given to care of wounded; such practices as beating of soldiers are prohibited; and there is a democratic relationship—outside of purely military matters—between officers and men.

(l) Various other phases of the program include women's rights, intensive advancement of popular education, promotion of all types of cooperative societies, and so on.[35]

Partly perhaps because he was a military commander (though among the Communist leaders there was never a completely sharp differentiation of political and military roles), and partly also because our talks were focused on the history and growth of the New Fourth Army, Chen Yi was speaking primarily from the army point of view. Thus he emphasized measures to create the peasant support that provided the army's manpower and made possible its existence and expansion. There were, however, additional factors in the equation. Peasants were the overwhelming majority, but there were also other economically essential elements in the guerrilla areas. In contrast to the Kiangsi Soviet days, the Communists were applying broad United Front economic and political policies that obviously were holding non-peasant support and making it possible for their base areas to be self-sustaining. Furthermore, they had attracted, and seemed able to use and win the support of, large numbers of students and intellectuals—groups of relatively high prestige, political awareness, and influence in China. These were factors that could have major long-term political significance. As our information accumulated, and as I had opportunities to talk at length to a cross-section of leaders from various base areas, I attempted an analysis of "The Development of Communist Political Control in the Guerrilla Bases." Since only a much abbreviated version appears in *Foreign Relations 1944,* it may be appropriate to include the main portion here.

> 1. The Chinese Communist Party has overwhelming political influence in the various guerrilla bases. In effect, this influence amounts to control. Although the governments of these bases are nominally independent of each other, their form of organization, and their policies and administrative programs, are all similar. Furthermore these policies are identical with those of the Communist Party. . . .
>
> As the Japanese Army advanced through North China at the be-

---

[35] See note 32, above.

ginning of the war, most of the provincial and local governments collapsed. The officials and leading Kuomintang members—usually the same men—fled south with the Central Government troops. Many of the wealthy landlords also fled south, or took refuge in the large cities where there were foreign Concessions or which, even under Japanese occupation, were relatively quiet. . . .

The Communist Armies rapidly over-ran these areas in their eastward advance during late 1937 and 1938 which extended from Shensi to the sea. . . .

After occupation, it was necessary that organized governments be set up to administer these areas and to enable them to serve as supporting bases for the Communist armies. The Political Department of the 8th Route Army (in other words the Communist Party) set about this task as rapidly as possible. Intensive propaganda and indoctrination of the peasants could create support for the Army's government. But it could not immediately produce leaders. What local government and Kuomintang leaders there once had been had mostly left. The influential local citizens (landlords and gentry) had either fled (the Communist name frightened them into continuing this even after the immediate Japanese danger was passed), or those who did remain were dubious of Communist promises and skeptical that resistance against the Japanese had any hope of success. So these people cautiously remained in the background.

The *only* important, politically conscious and experienced group that the Communists found, in the areas and willing to join them, were large numbers of liberals and intellectuals. Most of these were university professors and students from the great educational center of Peiping. Since the student demonstrations there in December, 1935, they had been demanding resistance against Japan. In the first great tide of war enthusiasm they had left Peiping and other cities ahead of the Japanese occupation and gone into the countryside to organize popular resistance. Most of these groups had stayed behind after the Government and its defeated armies fled south. But they were not organized, and were operating individually or in small groups with whatever followings their eloquence could attract.

A few of these people were Communists. A larger number were nominally Kuomintang members. Many belonged to no party. But the great majority of them were strongly liberal and in favor of the Communist plan of people's guerrilla warfare based on democracy. This was, in fact, what they were already actively trying to start. The need of coordination, and the organization of governments which could serve as bases, was obvious. Most of these groups therefore willingly—by inclination, and by the logic of circumstances—accepted Communist leadership and joined with them on a United Front basis.

The first governments were thus mainly composed of these two elements, the Communists and these unorganized liberals, with the addition of the few influential local citizens who remained in the regions and could be persuaded to cooperate. These cooperating local elements were also liberal in tendency—as would be indicated by the fact that they had not fled and were non-defeatist enough to believe, in this gloomy and uncertain time, in the possibility of resistance.

155

The "democratic" nature of these first governments was "confirmed" by the followings of the Communist armies and these liberal groups, and by numerous mass meetings organized by them—which often went through the gesture of voting (by acclamation) for the government which had been set up.

The liberals were very useful in this early stage for providing the bulk of the immediately needed administrative officials and hsien magistrates. As democratic machinery was not yet set up, they were appointed to these posts by the government, or in very newly occupied areas by the political officers of the Army (who among many other duties fulfill the function of our Army's civil government officers).

Most of the partisan bands which had gathered around the liberals were absorbed into the Communist Army: this was one important source of their rapid growth in this early stage of the war.

The Communists were not only the leaders in setting up these governments: they were also the only group ready with a complete and well-thought-out program. They were preparing for a long war and had determined that they would fight behind the enemy lines with guerrilla tactics. Mao Tse-tung's famous booklet *Protracted Warfare* was published at this time. (The broader question of the motives behind these Communist tactics, of choosing a theater where they could be separated and independent of the Kuomintang and develop warfare on a democratic basis, is outside the scope of this discussion.)

In brief, the Communist plan was the following. The apathetic peasant had to be aroused by convincing him that he had something immediate and concrete to fight for. It was also necessary to create a well-rounded, productive, self-sufficient base that could survive being cut off from the cities. This demanded the support of *all* classes, and the return and cooperation of the landlords, local capitalists, handicraft entrepreneurs, and merchants. These conditions dictated moderate policies. Even if there had not been the United Front pledges to the Central Government, extreme policies would frighten away what little local capital existed and leave the base economically disorganized and unable to support the Army. Politically it was also desirable to bring all classes into unified resistance and to prevent the possibility of division by the Japanese. The most effective measure as far as the farmer was concerned was the reduction of rents and interest. But this reduction was to be moderate and *limited;* and the government would protect the interests of the landlord by guaranteeing the payment of these reduced rates. Private enterprise was guaranteed non-interference and was offered assistance to increase production. Thus the fears of the landlord-merchant group would be calmed. Finally democracy would be instituted. This would interest all groups in joining the government, through the democratic process, in order to protect or advance their own interests in such matters as rent and interest reduction and taxation.

The Communist leaders stress the importance and precedence of these measures: *first and basic,* limited rent-interest reduction to win the active support of the peasants, who are the bulk of the population; *second,* democratic self-government to bring all classes, particularly the landlord-merchants, into active participation and hence support of the government. This conception of the importance of democracy as a means of obtaining the participation and support of the capitalist groups is interesting and significant in the study of present and probable future Communist policies. They have no illusions that China can hope to build a proletarian state in anything like the near future.

The Communist program was logical and, objectively viewed in the light of the circumstances, reasonably fair to all. Even though it was only carrying out unenforced laws as far as rent reduction was concerned, it might have been opposed by the landlord-conservative (or even the orthodox Kuomintang) groups. But these were not at the time—for the reasons described above—important participants in the governments. The liberal groups, without any strong organization or alternative program of their own, followed the Communist lead. The original Communist program was therefore adopted by these impromptu coalition governments as they were established —first in Shansi-Hopei-Chahar and later in other areas.

The program worked out as intended. As the governments became well established and showed ability to withstand Japanese attack, and as the peasants through education (by the Communists) in their new democratic powers began to exhibit interest in more drastic rent-interest reduction and progressive taxation, the landlord-capitalist group was driven to active participation to preserve its own interests.

Within one year most villages were under elected governments. By 1939–40 the democratic election of hsien governments was general. And by 1942 most of the bases were governed by popularly elected Peoples Political Councils.

In all of these grades of government there is substantial, though not large, representation of both the landlord-capitalist and peasant-laborer groups. This landlord-capitalist participation has been rewarded (by means of Communist support) with some reduction of the early high tax rates on large incomes, and more extensive government assistance to private productive enterprise.

This institution of political democracy has not, however, been accompanied by political development along definite party forms.

The landlord-capitalist element has formed pressure groups, without unified party organization or leadership. Their main object has been merely the preservation of their own interests.

The Kuomintang has not established itself in an organized manner because (1) it had no strong original foundation in the regions, and (2) the central Kuomintang authorities (Chungking) have generally taken the attitude that these are "traitor areas" and "illegal" governments. When the Kuomintang *has* tried to come back into some of these areas, it has done so with the backing of military force and government mandates abolishing the governments already set up and functioning. . . .

The increasingly politically conscious peasants have tended to gravitate toward the Communist Party. This can be regarded as natural. In the first place they regard the Communists as responsible for setting up the bases and for the practical improvement in their social-political-economic condition. In the second place, there is no other party with anything to offer the peasants or actively seeking their support. Even if the Kuomintang were active in these areas, it could give little practical attraction to the peasant.

It must, of course, be recognized that the Communists have controlled all political indoctrination and propaganda and have not discouraged this tendency of the peasants to regard them as their benefactors. Furthermore, the Communist Party has actively expanded its Party organization in its newly won areas and has established branches down to the villages. Of the approximately 1,000,000 present members of the Party, it is claimed that more than one-half are peasants. It is reasonable to assume that most of these are in North China.

The only other important group, the liberal-intellectuals, have also failed to set up a separate party organization. They have remained in close support and cooperation with the Communists. Some have actually joined the Communist Party. But it seems that this tendency is not at present encouraged—since the overwhelming domination of the Communist Party is something that the Communists, for political reasons described below, wish to avoid—and that many of those outside the Communist Party might as well, as far as thinking goes, be considered in it.

Even without party organization or their own following, this liberal-intellectual group has remained politically important as holders of elective offices. Reasons for this can be assumed to be: (1) the shortage of men in the areas with their qualifications of education and experience; and (2) during their first, appointed terms they generally made a good impression on the people by their patriotic enthusiasm, democratic leanings, and honesty. Thus many of them have continued to hold posts as magistrates and high administrative officials.

The actual situation, therefore, is that no strong opposition has developed to the Communists and they have remained the undisputably dominant political factor.

This dominance tended to become so pronounced that in 1940 the Communist Party decided, as a purely Party measure, to restrict itself to one-third of the membership of any elective government body, and to advocate that the other two-thirds be divided between Kuomintang and non-party members. The one-third limitation on the Communists was a maximum, not a minimum limit. It was hoped that this would improve the all-around representative character of the governments, thus helping to keep the support of the numerically small landlord-merchant groups and countering Kuomintang charges of monopoly and violation of the United Front.

This self-restriction of the Communist Party has not had much effect on its leading role. It generally elects its solid one-third (in a few areas it actually continues to hold slightly over this ratio in the Peoples Political Councils). The Kuomintang representation is made up of *individuals* who were former officials or Kuomintang members but now have no Party machine back of them and are usually of liberal tendencies. It is usually difficult to find enough of these persons, with suitable qualifications, who are willing to join the government: with the present situation between the two parties, a "regular" Kuomintang member knows that he jeopardizes his Party standing and will be accused by Chungking of being a "Communist" if he participates in an "illegal" Communist government. As a result the Kuomintang (it would be more correct to say "nominal Kuomintang") representation in most governments is below the sought-for one-third. The remainder of the government is then made up of a few representatives of the landlord-merchant groups (who may also find some representation through the Kuomintang members) and a larger number of the liberal-intellectuals.

The typical composition, then, is one-third Communists, plus a few liberal Kuomintang (or ex-Kuomintang) members, plus a large number of liberal-intellectuals, and finally a relatively small group of the landlord-merchant group.

With this strong representation and a predominantly liberal and sympathetic majority, it is not surprising that the Communists have been the chief initiators of the policies followed by the base governments. Furthermore, since the Communist Party holds the same dominant position in each government, and since it is the one connecting link between these separate governments, it has secured the adoption by all of them of its program.

Related to this development of predominant Communist influence in the guerrilla bases are a number of other factors which should be mentioned, even though detailed study of some will be left for following reports.

(a) The Communists have kept their program moderate and within the limits that the liberal-Kuomintang and liberal-intellectual groups affiliated with it would continue to support. This has promoted unity. It has also increased and held support. It might also be said that it has robbed any important potential opposition of any issues.

(b) The Communist program has introduced democracy and improved the economic condition of the great majority of the population. This is the first experience the people have had of these benefits, and their political experience has not had a chance yet to go beyond the stage of being grateful. Nobody opposes Santa Claus.

(c) The Communists at times have played a balancing role. In areas where the landlords were too successful in gaining control over local governments, either through the old awe in which they were held by the peasants or their power over their tenants, the Communists have stepped up their assistance to the people through indoctrination in democracy and active support of the people's organizations. On the other hand, in areas where the peasants "felt their oats" and used their new political powers to monopolize the local governments, the Party used its influence to obtain the election of landlord representatives. Wherever used, this policy makes grateful friends. And the Communists admit that when they use their influence to aid the election of a landlord, it is a "progressive" landlord—in other words another supporter of their policies.

(d) The Communists have accepted and incorporated into their own program some proposals put forth by other groups. An example was the policy to "refine the Army and reduce the Government" (generally translated as "rationalization"), which was originally introduced into the Shen-Kan-Ning Peoples Political Council by a landlord representative. The Communists make much of this willingness to accept suggestions from others as an indication of their democracy. And they explain this incorporation into their own program as the most expeditious and sure means, since they are the only party common to all governments, of having these improvements universally put into effect. There is a great deal of merit in these arguments. But it must be recognized that the Communist Party, in a very smart and hardheaded political way, gets the credit for these improvements because the original introducer is not widely known and soon forgotten, and it becomes known as another item of the Party program.

(e) The Communist control of propaganda has already been mentioned. This propaganda, except in special instances, does not attack the Kuomintang or other groups. But it does tend to put these other groups in a bad light. And it invariably works to promote the Communist Party.

(f) Finally, the Army is the army of the Communists. This is important because the political effect of the 8th Route and New 4th Armies is tremendous. This effectiveness comes in several ways. The Political Department, which is used in indoctrination of the people, especially of newly occupied areas, is highly organized and experienced, and under wholly Communist leadership (contrary to the rest of the Army). But even greater than this direct effect is the example of the behavior and attitude of the army toward the people, its volunteer character, its completely different attitude of unity with the people, its high morale, and the fact that it fights.

6. I have attempted to show that the political control of the Communist Party in the guerrilla bases has developed from its leadership in establishing and holding these bases, the absence of strong opposition, the adoption of moderate, democratic policies which have benefited the great majority of the population, and political astuteness combined with control of propaganda and the influence of the Army. The *policies* of the Communist Party have been democratic and there is little which under the circumstances can be called undemocratic in its *methods*.

The question may be asked whether the Communists would have been so democratic in method if they had been faced with stronger opposition. The question is hard to answer because there has never been a strong opposition willing to cooperate on a democratic basis. In the one area where the Kuomintang has an organization, it has been allowed its own newspaper and other democratic freedoms. But this opposition was weak. In areas where the Kuomintang came in with military force to oust the Communists, the Communists won out because they had the democratic support of the people. The Kuomintang did not have this support and was unable to obtain it. This fact, together with difficulties connected with the war, forced the Kuomintang to withdraw.[36]

---

[36] Appendix A, Part 1, report no. 26. Another report, covering the same general

After two and a half months of intensive observation, interrogation, and checking the findings and opinions of the many other observers of the Communist areas, I felt prepared to offer a conclusion and forecast.

Reports of two American officers, several correspondents, and twenty-odd foreign travelers regarding conditions in the areas of North China under Communist control are in striking agreement. This unanimity, based on actual observation, is significant. It forces us to accept certain facts, and to draw from those facts an important conclusion.

The Japanese are being actively opposed—in spite of the constant warfare and cruel retaliation this imposes on the population. This opposition is gaining in strength. The Japanese can temporarily crush it in a limited area by the concentration of overwhelming force. But it is impossible for them to do this simultaneously over the huge territory the Communists now influence.

This opposition is possible and successful because it is total guerrilla warfare aggressively waged by a totally mobilized population. In this total mobilization, the regular forces of the Communists, though leaders and organizers, have become subordinate to the vastly more numerous forces of the people themselves. They exist because the people permit, support and whole-heartedly fight with them. There is complete solidarity of Army and people.

This total mobilization is based upon and has been made possible by what amounts to an economic, political and social revolution. This revolution has been moderate and democratic. It has improved the economic condition of the peasants by rent and interest reduction, tax reform and good government. It has given them democratic self-government, political consciousness and a sense of their rights. It has freed them from feudalistic bonds and given them self-respect, self-reliance and a strong feeling of cooperative group interest. *The common people, for the first time, have been given something to fight for.*

The Japanese are being fought now not merely because they are foreign invaders but because they deny this revolution. *The people will continue to fight any government which limits or deprives them of these newly won gains.*

Just as the Japanese Army cannot crush these militant people now, so also will Kuomintang force fail in the future. With their new arms and organization, knowledge of their own strength, and determination to keep what they have been fighting for, these people— now some 90 million and certain to be many more before the Kuomintang can reach them—will resist oppression. They are not Communists. They do not want separation or independence. But at present they regard the Kuomintang—from their own experience—as oppressors; and the Communists as their leaders and benefactors.

With this great popular base, the Communists likewise cannot be eliminated. Kuomintang attempts to do so by force must mean a complete denial of democracy. This will strengthen the ties of the Communists with the people: a Communist victory will be inevi-

subject but of possible interest, is Appendix A, Part 1, report no. 37: "The Communist Success in Eliminating Banditry."

table. If, as the Communists hope, the Kuomintang turns to democracy, this established popular support will ensure influential Communist participation in national affairs. If the Kuomintang continues its present policy of quarantine without itself instituting thoroughgoing democracy, the better condition of the common people in the Communist areas will be an example constantly working in Communist favor.

From the basic fact that the Communists have built up popular support of a magnitude and depth which makes their elimination impossible, *we must draw the conclusion that the Communists will have a certain and important share in China's future.*

I suggest the further conclusion that unless the Kuomintang goes as far as the Communists in political and economic reform, and otherwise proves itself able to contest this leadership of the people (none of which it yet shows signs of being willing or able to do), the Communists will be the dominant force in China within a comparatively few years.[37]

A month later, after John Davies had taken my place in Yenan, he formed the same conclusion but found better language: "The Communists are in China to stay. And China's destiny is not Chiang's but theirs."[38]

DOES REALISM HAVE A PLACE IN FOREIGN POLICY?

Realism in foreign policy can probably be defined in various ways. But surely none of them include persisting, with eyes open, on a clear road to disaster by excessive (and unnecessary) commitment to a foreign political party whose decline is certain because it has lost the support of its own people. In early 1945 most Americans in China and in Washington who were concerned with China affairs saw this danger in the situation developing in China. This was, of course, the rationale behind the long line of policy papers drafted in Washington during 1944 and 1945 (and examined above in Chapter VI) stating that American policy in China "favored no faction," was aware of "possible disintegration of the authority of the existing Government," and sought to "maintain a degree of flexibility to permit cooperation with any other leadership in China which may give greater promise of achieving unity and contributing to peace and security in east Asia."[39]

These were careful diplomatic words. Discussion in the field was likely to be more unbuttoned. One of my early recollections of Ambassador Gauss—who cherished few illusions about the Chinese or anyone else—was a conversational statement to the effect that American policy could have no purpose except to serve American national interests, and he was

---

[37] Appendix A, Part 1, report no. 39.

[38] *Foreign Relations 1944,* pp. 670–671.

[39] The quotations are from State Department memorandum of April 18, 1945, to President Truman (*Foreign Relations 1945,* pp. 93–95). A list of other, generally similar, policy statements appears in Chapter IV, note 84.

"damn tired of having foreigners tell us what those interests are." An admirable man, Gauss would have been happy with George Washington's Farewell Address. Stilwell was more a positivist: "Nothing can be done in China until we get rid of Chiang Kai-shek"—which, of course, implied that something could be done.[40] I seem to have been prone to triteness: we should keep the policy initiative in our own hands; to be swayed by Chiang would be to "let the tail wag the dog."[41] The language of the racetrack was surprisingly popular. If we stuck with the Kuomintang, we would be "backing the losing horse," or find ourselves "riding the wrong horse." There was even much talk of the "loss of China" if we remained committed to the support of Chiang Kai-shek—which proves at least that the phrase was not original with Senator McCarthy and the China Lobby.

There was, then, a clearly seen dilemma for American policy. The State Department papers on the need for flexibility were realistic, but in a remote way. Except for those written during the period January to March 1945, they spoke generally of flexibility as something for the long-range, post-war period, thus seeming to slight the need for constructive action in the interim before the war ended. But it was precisely the immediate future, before the war ended, that was critical. By early 1945, both sides were actively and openly girding themselves for civil war.[42] And it was also apparent—to all, it seems, but Hurley—that the starting signal for open civil war was likely to be the Japanese defeat itself.[43] The end of the Japanese war could be expected, however, to reduce the American presence in China. Simultaneously, it would terminate the wartime possibility of influencing events by American military policy. A "flexible" policy thus could mean a laudable neutrality, but amount in effect to little more than passively standing by to award the prize of American recognition to whichever side proved the eventual winner—though by that stage the winner might not care about our recognition.

For many reasons, civil war—which, in my view, all the evidence indicated that the Communists would eventually win—would not be in American interests. Aside from the terrible human and physical costs to China,

---

[40] Stimson diary, December 13, 1944, cited by Tuchman, *Stilwell*, p. 511.

[41] Appendix A, Part 3, (c). The use of a part of this memorandum by the Internal Security Subcommittee in its investigation of the IPR is an illustrative example of investigative techniques. By questioning an uninformed witness (General Wedemeyer) only on three isolated and unrelated sentences, the memorandum was made to appear to have a meaning the precise opposite of what it actually said (see my article, "Pertinent Excerpts," *Foreign Service Journal*, October 1951, p. 22).

[42] See, for example, Appendix A, Part 2, reports 8 and 22.

[43] For instance, Appendix A, Part 1, report no. 2 ("the greatest danger [of civil war] will be soon after the cessation of hostilities against Japan"); and report no. 20 ("The crisis will increase as the defeat of Japan is approached"). For a report from the Kuomintang side, Edward E. Rice in Sian: ". . . full-scale civil war may be expected to follow the defeat of the Japanese. . . ." (*Foreign Relations 1945*, p. 397). Tang Tsou concludes that Chiang "placed his hopes exclusively on a successful military campaign. . . ." (*America's Failure*, p. 170).

it would divide the country for a prolonged period, postpone its recovery, and delay the possibility of peace and stability in east Asia. There would be great pressures on us to give aid and support to the losing side (the Kuomintang). And the Communists, who would start out by holding north China and Manchuria, would be forced to turn to the Soviet Union. Furthermore, a civil war could be expected, by its bitter nature and probable long duration, to result in the elimination of moderates on both sides (both in and out of the two contending parties), the ending of the liberal United Front economic and political policies then being followed by the Communists, and the final consolidation of a more orthodox Communist regime closely linked to the Soviet Union and strongly antagonistic to the United States. The first and most urgent priority for American policy, therefore, should be to find means, if possible, to prevent the civil war from starting. This meant that our initiative could not be long delayed. In early 1945 we did not know that the Japanese war would end so soon. But tension in China was steadily growing. To those of us on the spot, the threat of the impending civil war was like a time bomb ticking steadily toward detonation.[44]

There were three chief impediments to our breaking out of the straight chute to swift catastrophe in China: Hurley, the American fixation on Chiang as the embodiment of China, and the fact that the only viable al-

---

[44] Feis, *China Tangle*, pp. 90–91, seems to suggest that this concern over civil war reflected, in large part at least, an emotional astigmatism of "the State Department and its representatives in China."

> They also were moved by a longing that since China was their cause, and it *was* their cause, it should be a worthy cause. They did not think or write solely as American officials who wanted to win a war, indifferent to the plight of the people of China.

The extent of our emotional attachment to China is probably best left to outside judgment. It is, of course, a fact that a number of us had spent most of our lives in China, primarily because—another frequent cause of raised eyebrows—our parents were missionaries. It is also a fact that many shared this view about civil war who did not share our background. I can only suggest that "the plight of the people of China" was indeed a matter of realistic concern to American policy, especially—but not only—because Mao Tse-tung had found a highly effective formula for using it to build political power—while Chiang Kai-shek was still oblivious. It is hard to conceive of a more graphic illustration of Chiang's "fundamentally erroneous appraisal of the factors contributing to the spread of Communist influence" than a passage from his diary (on October 21, 1944) cited by Tang Tsou (*America's Failure*, p. 169):

> The essentials of the organization of the Communist Party are: (1) violence (i.e., oppression) and ruthless killing; (2) special agents (i.e., control and surveillance) and repression. The purposes of its training are: (1) elimination of nationalistic spirit and development of internationalist spirit (destruction of the nation's history and ethics), (2) elimination of human nature and development of animal nature (arbitrarily dividing the society into classes and causing hatred and struggle)....

ternative was a communist party.[45] Much has already been said concerning Hurley. The American attachment to Chiang Kai-shek is beyond my subject here. What, then, of the problem of working with a Chinese communist party?

Nothing was gained, it seemed to me, by fuzzing the issue with such currently popular locutions as "so-called Communists" or "agrarian reformers." Mao and his men steadfastly insisted that their communism was bona fide. I made several attempts to summarize their application of Marxism to China. Here is a quotation, noted down at the time, of some conversational statements by Po Ku (Ch'in Pang-hsien).

> We regard Marxism not as a dogma but as a guide. We accept its historical materialism and its ideological method. It furnishes us with the conclusions and the objectives toward which we strive. This objective is the classless society built on socialism—in other words, the good of the individual and the interests of all the people.

> But to try to transplant to China all of Marx's description of the society in which he found himself (the Industrial Revolution of Europe in the 19th Century) and the steps (class struggle and violent revolution) which he saw would be necessary for the people to escape from these conditions, would not only be ridiculous, it would also be a violation of our basic principles of realistic objectivism and the avoidance of doctrinaire dogmatism.

> China at present is not even capitalistic. Its economy is still that of semi-feudalism. We cannot advance at one jump to socialism. In fact, because we are at least 200 years behind most of the rest of the world, we probably cannot hope to reach socialism until after most of the rest of the world has reached that state.

> First we must rid ourselves of this semi-feudalism. Then we must raise our economic level by a long stage of democracy and free enterprise.

> What we Communists hope to do is to keep China moving smoothly and steadily toward this goal. By orderly, gradual and progressive development we will avoid the conditions which forced Marx to draw his conclusions of the necessity (in his society) for class struggle: we will *prevent* the need for a violent revolution by a peaceful planned revolution.

> It is impossible to predict how long this process will take. But we

---

[45] I have already mentioned my talk with Harry Hopkins in November 1944 (Chapter V, note 5). He had asked that I come; had read some of my reports from Yenan (see, for instance, Feis, *China Tangle,* p. 258, note 4); suggested that I summarize my impressions; and asked a number of pertinent questions. His White House office, as I remember it, was a plain, small room not much larger than the cluttered desk. There was just enough space on the floor to unroll the Yenan map (note 25, above) between two chairs. His final comment, after a talk that had lasted some forty-five minutes, was laconic and, in effect, a dismissal. "Very interesting. I have no doubt that the picture you give is largely correct. But the only Chinese that most Americans have ever heard of is Chiang Kai-shek. And they call themselves Communists." He was concerned, of course, with realism of a different, but also important, kind: the realities of American public opinion.

can be sure that it will be more than 30 or 40 years, and probably more than 100 years.[46]

Washington had, of course, its experts on communism to analyze and evaluate such statements, and also the books and publications of the Chinese Communists which I and others collected and forwarded. While I was in Washington, in 1944 and again in 1945, I had discussions with some of the experts. One problem was the disparity in our experience. I was convinced that I had seen one version of reality in China. Their intensive study and long experience had been solely of the Communist Party in the Soviet Union and its manipulation of the Communist parties in Europe and the United States. My suggestions that China might be different usually brought a knowing—and, it seemed to me, slightly condescending—smile, but no meeting of minds.[47]

It is common to criticize China specialists for a contention that China and its civilization are unique. Certainly, I did not follow this to its logical extreme of thinking that no real change was possible. We were, after all, witnessing a successful revolution that was in the process of changing Chinese society. But to me it seemed obvious—so much so that I hardly bothered to debate it—that China was not going to be a carbon copy of either the Soviet Union (if it turned toward communism), or of the United States (if it turned, as we had hoped, toward liberal democracy under the Kuomintang).[48] The revolution could not be entirely unrelated to the country's history, the long social and cultural conditioning of its people, and the background of the political, social, and economic circumstances existing there. Other factors, too, were bound to influence the character of a Communist regime in China. One of these was the nature of its leadership. This impressed me as being strong, independent, pragmatic, and unified under a leader of great intellect, charisma, and populist conviction.[49] Also important was their nationalism, which they had been so suc-

---

[46] Appendix A, Part 1, report no. 34.

[47] One Kremlinologist (who shall remain nameless) insisted that I was completely wrong about Mao Tse-tung "having no love for the Russians." There was "reliable evidence," he said, that Mao had been trained in Moscow; and, in any event, it would never be possible for him to oppose the Russians. Unfortunately, he did not have the evidence with him. Kremlinology, I recognize, is a useful science. But it became necessary mainly because of the need to probe a closed society. Certainly there has never been a Communist society that has been so open to Americans as the Chinese Communists for the eight-month period from July 1944 to March 1945. Large numbers of Americans were traveling in almost every part of their territories, engaging in various forms of cooperation and exploring others, and living in close and friendly daily association with leaders and rank and file both in Yenan and in the field.

[48] My missionary father had also assumed (and welcomed the prospect) that a native Chinese Christian church would develop which would be different (if only in a lack of sectarianism) from the Protestant churches in the West.

[49] Appendix A, Part 1, report no. 21.

cessfully using in their competition with the Kuomintang during the war against Japanese aggression.

Another factor that would reflect, if not influence, the character of the regime was their attitude in foreign relations. Here it seemed indicative that they sought American cooperation, both as an aid in the war and in the eventual postwar period when they hoped to be the dominant party in China. This was a constant theme in Mao Tse-tung's several extended conversations with me. The first of these was on August 23, 1944, and, being his first statement, I recorded it more fully than on following occasions. The speaker here is Mao: my few contributions are parenthesized.

American policy in China therefore becomes not merely a matter of concern to Americans alone; it is also a question of the most vital interest to the democratic people of China. The Chinese people, accordingly, are interested in three general questions.

First, is there a chance of an American swing back toward isolationism and a resultant lack of interest in China? Are Americans going to close their eyes to foreign problems and let China "stew in her own juice"? We Communists feel that this problem will not arise if Roosevelt is re-elected.

(This and other questions about the United States were addressed directly to me. I therefore made it clear, in the most explicit terms, that I had no official authority and that my replies were only my purely private and completely unofficial opinions.

On the above points, I mentioned America's long and special interest in China; the fact that we would have no internal reconstruction problem as a result of war destruction; that on the contrary our greatly expanded economy and our more international outlook would impel us to seek trade and investment beyond our borders; that it was therefore unlikely that we would become isolationist or unconcerned about China; and that I doubted whether administration of the country by either Republicans or Democrats would fundamentally affect our China policy.)

Second, is the American Government really interested in democracy—in its world future? Does it, for instance, consider democracy in China—one-fourth of the world's population—important? Does it want to have the government of China really representative of the people of China? Is it concerned that the present government of China, which it recognizes, has no legal status by any law and is in no way representative of the people of China? Chiang Kai-shek was elected President by only 90 members of a single political party, the Kuomintang, who themselves cannot validly claim to represent even the limited membership of that party. Even Hitler has a better claim to democratic power. He was selected by the people. And he has a Reichstag. Does the United States realize the obvious fact that the present Kuomintang has lost the confidence and support of the Chinese masses? The important question, however, is not whether the American Government realizes this fact, but whether it is willing to try to improve the situation by helping to bring about democracy in China.

(I referred to the numerous official American statements regarding unity in China and our general hope for democratic development in all countries. I mentioned the apparent trend of at least an important part of American opinion as shown in recent critical articles in the American press.)

It is obvious that the Kuomintang must reform itself and reorganize its government. On its present basis it cannot hope to fight an effective war. And even if the war is won for it by the United States, subsequent chaos is certain.

The government must broaden its base to take in all important groups of the people. We do not call for full and immediate representative democracy: it would be impractical. And, under Kuomintang sponsorship and control, it would be an empty fraud. But what can and should be done—at once—is to convene a provisional (or transitional) national congress. To this all groups should be invited to send delegates. These delegates must not be selected and appointed by the Kuomintang, as in the past. They must be genuine representatives—the best qualified leaders. They should include the Communist Party, all minor parties, the intellectual groups, newspaper interests, students, professional groups, central organizations of cooperative societies, labor and other mass organizations.

A workable compromise for the distribution of strength might be that the Kuomintang would have one-half of the members, all others together the other half. It would have to be agreed beforehand, for reasons of practical politics, that the Generalissimo would be confirmed as temporary president.

This provisional congress must have full power to reorganize the government and make new laws—to remain in effect until the passage of the constitution. The Government should be directly responsible to the congress. Its functions and powers might be somewhat like those of the British House of Commons.

The provisional congress would also have full charge of the preparations for full democracy and constitutionalism. It would supervise the elections and then convene the national congress. It would then turn over its powers and pass out of existence.

Is the American Government willing to use its influence to force the Kuomintang to carry out such a proposal? Is the American Government willing to make the proposal and actively support it?

(Chairman Mao made the suggestion that this matter was of such importance that it would warrant my making a trip to Chungking to present it to the Ambassador. I said that the Ambassador would be fully informed. I also suggested that we had already heard this general proposal from other quarters in Chungking.

Subsequently on August 26 I learned in a conversation with Chou En-lai that the Politbureau of the Communist Party was considering the making of this proposal to the Kuomintang. They would base it on the Kuomintang's refusal to discuss the Communist demands for democracy in their present negotiations on the ground that they are "too abstract.")

Third, what is the attitude and policy of the American Government toward the Chinese Communist Party? Does it recognize the Communist Party as an active fighting force against Japan? Does it recognize the Communists as an influence for democracy in China?

Is there any chance of American support of the Chinese Communist Party? What will be the American attitude—toward the Kuomintang and toward the Communists—if there is a civil war in China? What is being done to ensure that the Kuomintang will not use its new American arms to fight a civil war?

(These questions, especially the points raised in the second and third, formed the framework of our further conversation. I returned to a number of points for further amplification and discussion.

Regarding the question of "support" of the Communist Party, I pointed out that the question was obscure and, in any case, premature inasmuch as the Communists themselves publicly supported the Central Government and Chiang Kai-shek.)

We Communists accepted KMT terms in 1936-7 to form the United Front because the foreign menace of Japan threatened the country. We are, first of all, Chinese. The 10 years of inconclusive, mutually destructive civil war had to be stopped in order to fight Japan. Even though we had not started the civil war, we took the lead in stopping it. Also, the foreign countries recognized the KMT and Chiang; they did not support us. But the United Front was not all one-sided: The KMT also promised political reforms—which they have not carried out.

Our support of Chiang does not mean support of despotism: we support him to fight Japan.

We could not raise this question of recognition before. In a formal sense it is still premature. We only ask now that American policy try to induce the Kuomintang to reform itself. This would be a first stage. It may be the only one necessary: if it is successful there will be no threat of civil war.

But suppose that the KMT does not reform. Then there must be a second stage of American policy. Then this question of American policy toward the Communists must be raised. We can risk no conflict with the United States.

We can ignore the question of the supply of American arms now which can be used by the KMT in a future civil war. But must we expect a repetition of past history. In the early days of the Republic, the Powers recognized only Peking—long after it was apparent that the only government that could claim to represent the people of China was that in Canton. Nanking was not recognized until after the success and completion of the Northern Expedition. Now the internal situation in China is changing. The lines are not yet clearly drawn. But a somewhat similar situation may develop. Will the United States continue to give recognition and support to a government that in ineffectiveness and lack of popular support can only be compared to the old Peking government?

(I suggested the diplomatic impossibility of withdrawing recognition from a government that had not committed a directly unfriendly act, the obvious undesirability of working behind a recognized government to support an opposition party, and finally the delicacy of the whole problem of interference in the domestic affairs of another country.)

America has intervened in every country where her troops and supplies have gone. This intervention may not have been intended, and may not have been direct. But it has been nonetheless real—

merely by the presence of that American influence. For America to insist that arms be given to all forces who fight Japan, which will include the Communists, is not interference. For America to give arms only to the Kuomintang will in its effect be interference because it will enable the Kuomintang to continue to oppose the will of the people of China. "Interference" (Mao noted his objection to the term because of its having no meaning in this situation) to further the true interests of the people of China is not interference. It will be welcomed by the great mass of the people of China because they want democracy. Only the Kuomintang is against it.

We do not ask the stopping of all aid to the KMT forces. The effect would not be good on the war. The KMT would collapse and the American landing in China will be more difficult.

(I raised the question of how American influence could be exerted effectively, expressing skepticism about "dictation" to Chiang. Mao vigorously rejected my suggestion.)

Chiang is in a position where he must listen to the United States. Look at what happened in Honan, is happening now in Hunan, and shows every sign of happening in Kwangsi! Perhaps it will be Yunnan next. Look at the economic situation! Chiang is in a corner.

Chiang is stubborn. But fundamentally he is a gangster. That fact must be understood in order to deal with him. We have had to learn it by experience. The only way to handle him is to be hardboiled. You must not give way to his threats and bullying. Do not let him think you are afraid: then he will press his advantage. The United States has handled Chiang very badly. They have let him get away with blackmail—for instance, talk of being unable to keep up resistance, of having to make peace, his tactics in getting the 500 million dollar loan, and now Kung's mission to the U.S. and the plea for cloth. Cloth! Are we or are we not fighting the Japanese! Is cloth more important than bullets? We had no cotton here in the Border region and the KMT blockade kept us from getting any from the parts of China that did have it. But we got busy and soon we are going to be self-sufficient. It would be 100 times easier for the KMT, and if they were a government that had an economic policy they would have done it themselves.

With Chiang you can be friendly only on your own terms. He must give in to constant, strong and unified pressure. Never relax on your objectives: keep hammering at him.

The position of the United States now is entirely different from what it was just after Pearl Harbor. There is no longer any need or any reason to cultivate, baby or placate Chiang. The United States can tell Chiang what he should do—in the interest of the war. American help to Chiang can be made conditional on his meeting American desires. Another way for American influence to be exerted is for Americans to talk American ideals. Every American official meeting any Chinese official, in China or in the United States, can talk democracy. Visits like Wallace's give good opportunities; there should be more of them. Kung's presence in the United States should not be wasted.

Every American soldier in China should be a walking and talking advertisement for democracy. He ought to talk it to every Chinese he meets. American officers ought to talk it to Chinese officers. After all, we Chinese consider you Americans the ideal of democracy.

(I suggested that the use of our Army as a political propaganda force was alien—and that we had nothing corresponding to the Communist Political Department to indoctrinate the troops and direct such work.)

But even if your American soldiers do not actively propagandize, their mere presence and contact with Chinese has a good effect. We welcome them in China for this reason. The Kuomintang does not. It wants to segregate them and keep them from knowing what conditions really are. How many American observers do you have now in the front lines? We are happy to take your men anywhere. The KMT is worried about the effect of a lot of Americans in China. They fear an American landing only second to their fear of Russian participation.

The presence of Americans is good in another negative way. If Americans are scattered widely they will have a restraining effect on the Kuomintang. It will be more difficult for the KMT to start trouble. An example is Kunming. It has become a center of liberal thought and student freedom because the KMT doesn't dare to arrest and throw the students into concentration camps under the eyes of so many Americans. Compare this with Sian, where Americans are very few and the Secret Police unrestrained.

Criticism of the Kuomintang in American periodicals is good. Its effect may not be immediately apparent. Sometimes it may even seem temporarily to have a bad reaction. But if it is fair (the KMT will know if it is) it causes the KMT to hesitate and think—because they need American support.

Finally any contact you Americans have with us Communists is good. Of course we are glad to have the Observer Section here because it will help to beat Japan. But there is no use in pretending that—up to now at least—the chief importance of your coming is its political effect on the Kuomintang.

(I noted his emphasis on American landing in China and suggested that the war might be won in other ways and a landing not necessary.)

We think the Americans must land in China. It depends, of course, on Japanese strength and the developments of the war. But the main Japanese strength is in the Yangtze valley and North China—not to speak of Manchuria.

If the Americans do not land in China, it will be most unfortunate for China. The Kuomintang will continue as the government—without being able to be the government.

If there is a landing, there will have to be American cooperation with both Chinese forces—KMT and Communist. Our forces now surround Hankow, Shanghai, Nanking and other large cities. We are the inner ring: The KMT is further back.

If there is to be this cooperation with both Communist and KMT forces, it is important that we be allowed to work in separate sectors. The KMT is too afraid of us to work with us. Their only concern will be to checkmate us. When we are in separate sectors, the U.S. Army can see the difference: That we have popular support and can fight.

(I questioned whether open civil war was, as he had suggested, inevitable if the KMT was not restrained or induced to reform.)

We can say that civil war is "inevitable but not quite certain." Subjectively, the present KMT leaders are determined on the elimination of the Communists. They are afraid of us just as, and for the same reason as, they are afraid of the people. Objectively, there are factors—the five mentioned at the beginning of the talk—which restrain the KMT. The strongest of these—the Japanese—will be out of the picture. Another—strong because outside and independent of the KMT—is foreign opinion. But it is now unpredictable. The KMT still hopes that foreign influence may be on its side.

The KMT is already busy preparing pretexts for civil war. The more you know of us and conditions in our areas, the less value these pretexts will have.

So the KMT may resort to indirect methods of attack. It will be hard to define or set a line to its aggression.

But if the KMT undoes the progress that has been accomplished in our areas, if they take away the new democratic rights of the people, the people will resist and will demand our help.

Another line of KMT action will be through the puppets. The puppets will turn back to the KMT—claiming to have been "patriotic" all the time. The KMT will then use the puppets to hold the cities and areas from which the Japanese withdraw. They will incite the puppets to attack us and to create friction.

(Chou En-lai carries this line further by suggesting that this may be a part of the possible fraudulent Japanese surrender to Chiang: The Japanese will turn over their arms to the puppets [or the KMT] on the condition that the Communists will be liquidated.

This may seem at first a little far-fetched. The only possible comment is that the forces involved in this situation are so complicated and their hatred so intense, that almost anything is possible.)

The fact is clear, even to the Kuomintang, that China's political tendency is toward us. We hold to the Manifesto of the First Kuomintang Congress. This is a truly great and democratic document. Sun Yat-sen was no Communist. The Manifesto is still valid. It will not quickly pass out of date. We will hold to it even if the KMT should collapse because its general policies are good and suited to China. Everything we have done, every article of our program, is found in that document.

Of course, we do not pretend that we are perfect. We still face problems of bureaucracy and corruption. But we do face them. And we are beating them. We welcome observation and criticism—by Americans, by the KMT or by anyone else. We are constantly criticizing ourselves and revising our policies toward greater efficiency and effectiveness.

Our experience proves that the Chinese people understand democracy and want it. It does not take long experience or education or "tutelage." The Chinese peasant is not stupid; he is shrewd and, like everyone else, concerned over his rights and interests. You can see the difference in our areas—the people are alive, interested, friendly. They have a human outlet. They are free from deadening repression.

(I queried his emphasis on the importance of the United States and his neglect to consider Russia.)

Soviet participation either in the Far Eastern War or in China's post-war reconstruction depends entirely on the circumstances of the Soviet Union. The Russians have suffered greatly in the war and will have their hands full with their own job of rebuilding. We do not expect Russian help.

Furthermore, the KMT because of its anti-Communist phobia is anti-Russian. Therefore KMT-Soviet cooperation is impossible. And for us to seek it would only make the situation in China worse. China is dis-unified enough already! In any case Soviet help is not likely even if the KMT wanted it.

But Russia will not oppose American interests in China if they are constructive and democratic. There will be no possible point of conflict. Russia only wants a friendly and democratic China. Cooperation between America and the Chinese Communist Party will be beneficial and satisfactory to all concerned.

(I jokingly remarked that the name "Communist" might not be reassuring to some American businessmen. Mao laughed and said that they had thought of changing their name but that if people knew them they would not be frightened.)

The policies of the Chinese Communist Party are merely liberal. Our rent reduction is from the old 80–70–60% down to the legal (by unenforced Kuomintang law) 37½%. Even this we only try to accomplish gradually because we don't want to drive away the landlords. Our limit on interest is 10% a year. This is not extreme—though it is much lower than it used to be.

Even the most conservative American businessman can find nothing in our program to take exception to.

China must industrialize. This can be done—in China—only by free enterprise and with the aid of foreign capital. Chinese and American interests are correlated and similar. They fit together, economically and politically. We can and must work together.

The United States would find us more cooperative than the Kuomintang. We will not be afraid of democratic American influence—we will welcome it. We have no silly ideas of taking only Western mechanical techniques. Also we will not be interested in monopolistic, bureaucratic capitalism that stifles the economic development of the country and only enriches the officials. We will be interested in the most rapid possible development of the country on constructive and productive lines. First will be the raising of the living standard of the people (see what we have done here with our limited resources). After that we can come to the "national defense industry" that Chiang talks of in his *China's Destiny*. We will be interested in the welfare of the Chinese people.

America does not need to fear that we will not be cooperative. We must cooperate and we must have American help. This is why it is so important to us Communists to know what you Americans are thinking and planning. We cannot risk crossing you—cannot risk any conflict with you.[50]

---

[50] Appendix A, Part 1, report no. 15. The first part of the conversation, dealing with KMT-CCP relations, has been omitted. My memorandum was, necessarily, a summarization of a conversation that lasted for six hours (or almost eight if preliminary generalities and a break for dinner are included). As it was my first in-depth, "formal" talk with Mao, some background may be pertinent. Soon after my arrival in Yenan, Mao indicated that he preferred to delay our "exchange of ideas"

When I returned to Yenan in 1945, Mao resumed this subject of long-term U.S.-Communist relations during our first talk on March 13.

Mao commenced by asking a number of questions about my recent trip to the United States. He was interested in American official and public opinion toward the war in the Far East, toward China generally, and toward the Chinese Communists particularly.

He then rather mildly observed that America did not yet have a clear view of the issues involved in China, that it did not yet fully understand the Communists, and that although American policy as recently shown in China was still an enigma, he could not believe that it was fixed and unchangeable. America would eventually realize that support of the Central Government alone was not the best way to fight the war, to speed China's progress toward democracy, or to ensure post-war stability in the Far East. "A few months ago," he said, "we were told that the Kuomintang and the Communists were only this far apart." (Holding his thumb and forefinger about an inch apart.) "Now it is certainly apparent that we are this far apart." (Extending the thumb and forefinger in as broad a V as possible.)

From this introduction, Mao launched into a long discussion which may be summarized as follows.

Between the people of China and the people of the United States there are strong ties of sympathy, understanding and mutual interest. Both are essentially democratic and individualistic. Both are by nature peace-loving, non-aggressive and non-imperialistic.

China's greatest post-war need is economic development. She lacks the capitalistic foundation necessary to carry this out alone. Her own living standards are so low that they cannot be further depressed to provide the needed capital.

America and China complement each other economically: they will not compete. China does not have the requirements of a heavy industry of major size. She cannot hope to meet the United States in its highly specialized manufactures. America needs an export market

---

until I had had an opportunity to become familiar with the situation in the Communist areas (Appendix A, Part 1, report no. 2). His idea of a sufficient familiarization period turned out to be one month: I arrived in Yenan on July 22 and our talk was on August 23. In the meantime, as he knew, I had talked at length with most of the other Communist leaders—but not on questions of U.S.-CCP relations.

As was customary in my non-social talks with the Communist leaders, I took copious notes as Mao talked. This was facilitated, on this particular occasion, by the fact that we used an interpreter. Mao and I could, and often did, converse directly in Chinese. His use of an interpreter I took to be an added indication of the importance that he attached to the talk, and the desire to obviate any possibility, in this foundation-laying instance, of any mutual misunderstanding.

Since the question has been raised in Congressional hearings (*Tydings Transcript*, p. 1279), I might add that neither the memorandum of this conversation, nor any other reports of conversations I had with Communist leaders, were shown to any of the Communists—for censorship, approval, clearance, or any other purpose. Furthermore, both the Communists and I proceeded on the basis that I would report everything I saw, heard, or was told. There was never any suggestion that statements were being made to me personally, or that I should treat anything as "off the record."

for her heavy industry and these specialized manufactures. She also needs an outlet for capital investment.

China needs to build up light industries to supply her own market and raise the living standards of her own people. Eventually she can supply these goods to other countries in the Far East. To help pay for this foreign trade and investment, she has raw materials and agricultural products.

America is not only the most suitable country to assist this economic development of China: she is also the only country fully able to participate.

For all these reasons there must not and cannot be any conflict, estrangement or misunderstanding between the Chinese people and America.[51]

And, not surprisingly, it was again an important subject in his parting conversation with me on April 1 (when I had received unexplained orders, later learned to have been arranged by Hurley in Washington, to depart "soonest").

I was invited to Mao Tse-tung's residence at 4 P.M. Chou En-lai and Chu Teh were already there. There was about half an hour of general conversation.

All showed interest in the reason for my return to Chungking, particularly whether it might be for return to the United States—which presumably might indicate consultation regarding China (I had received no indication of the reason for my return.)

Mao repeated previous hopes that American political observation and contact with Yenan would be maintained. He expressed that the developments in China during the coming months would be important and that the Communists hoped for American understanding from on the spot contact.

Chou twice made pointed remarks to the effect that it was unfortunate that I could not stay in Yenan another ten days; that I would find the stay worthwhile and interesting. (I took this to be a hint that the Party Congress is to be convened within that time.). . . .

Mao then took control of the conversation. He was in exceptionally good spirits—getting out of his chair to act out dramatic embellishments of his talk, and diverging to recall amusing anecdotes. Chou occasionally explained or amplified Mao's points. Chu sat back, silent and smiling.

Mao skimmed over the history of the recent fruitless negotiations with the Kuomintang. He felt that foreigners in general did not yet understand that the Kuomintang-Communist issue was far more than the usual bickering and jockeying between two ordinary political parties. The issues here were basic and vital to China's future.

. . .

Repeating the unchangeableness of Communist objectives, Mao emphasized that the Communists had fought for them when weak, few in numbers and entirely alone, and that they would continue to

---

[51] Appendix A, Part 2, report no. 10. This is approximately one-fifth of my report of a lengthy conversation of considerable interest.

work toward those objectives regardless of outside influence, for or against.

In one sense, Mao admitted, the Kuomintang's complaints are justified. "Our objectives are unchanged but our voice gets louder as the situation in China becomes more desperate and more urgent and as more and more of the people see that we are right. Such complaints by the Kuomintang show that it is feeling the pressure. Delay, however, will not help it."

Mao then proposed to give a brief statement of Communist policies toward the United States and toward the Kuomintang, from which it could be seen that they were as consistent and unchanging as the Communist main objectives.

Communist policy toward the United States is, and will remain, to seek friendly American support of democracy in China and cooperation in fighting Japan. But regardless of American action, whether or not they receive a single gun or bullet, the Communists will continue to offer and practice cooperation in any manner possible to them. Anything they can do—such as intelligence, weather reporting and rescue of airmen—the Communists consider an obligation and duty because it helps the Allied war effort and brings closer the defeat of Japan. If Americans land in or enter Communist territory, they will find an army and people thoroughly organized and eager to fight the enemy.

The Communists will continue to seek American friendship and understanding because it will be needed by China in the post-war period of reconstruction. (For amplification of this argument, please refer to Mao's talk on March 13 reported in my despatch no. 10.)

Whether or not America extends cooperation to the Communists is, of course, a matter for only America to decide. But the Communists see only advantages for the United States—in winning the war as rapidly as possible, in helping the cause of unity and democracy in China, in promoting healthy economic development of China through industrialization based on solution of the agrarian problem, and in winning the undying friendship of the overwhelming majority of China's people, the peasants and liberals.[52]

I turn back now to August, 1944. I had had a good deal of contact with Communist representatives for more than three years in Chungking, and I had just spent a month in Yenan. Nonetheless, two things surprised me in my initial solid encounter with Mao Tse-tung. First, the depth and conviction of a desire for American friendship and cooperation with China. And second, Mao's strongly implied confidence that he and the Communist Party would be free agents and either in control of China or, at the very least, important participants in its government. This led, in my mind, to two important questions. First, was this avowed desire for American cooperation a short-term political tactic against the Kuomintang, or could we expect it to persist even under conditions of Communist control of China? Second, what was the place of the Soviet Union in

---

[52] Appendix A, Part 2, report no. 26.

Mao's desires for the future of China? A good deal of effort was devoted, henceforth, to trying to find convincing answers to these questions.

Concerning the first question, there was the fact of Mao's consistent repetition and amplification of the theme. Furthermore, it was repeated and supported by the other ranking members of the Politbureau—notably Chou En-lai, Po Ku, Liu Shao-ch'i, and Chu Teh—in talks which I had with them individually.[53] Mao's public statements were admittedly (and perhaps understandably in view of the lack of American indications of support) less specific. But Mao was saying, for instance in a speech on "Our Task in 1945" to the Shen-Kan-Ning Border Region Peoples Congress on December 15, 1944, that "Our sole task is to cooperate with the Allies to overthrow the Japanese invaders."[54] Actions, though, could be regarded as speaking louder than words. The cooperation we received from the Communists along many lines (such as intelligence, weather, air crew rescue, procurement of Japanese publications, prisoner interrogation, and bombing target data) was enthusiastic, prompt and, within the limits of their resources, efficient. They willingly met our requests for many kinds of information and facilities: the strength, equipment, training methods, and combat capabilities of their forces; the opportunity for American officers to visit forward guerrilla areas and to see their forces in combat; their treatment and use of Japanese prisoners; methods of psychological warfare against both Japanese and puppets; economic data, political organization, and so forth. Considering the scattered nature of their territories and forces, and the difficulties of communication, the information we were given appeared to be realistic and reliable. We were never met with a refusal, or with a suggestion that we should make any compensating commitment. It is easy to say that a return in the form of American support was nonetheless hoped for. But the same could be said on the Kuomintang side, where this eagerly cooperative attitude was conspicuous by its absence. The thing that perhaps impressed us most of all, however, was the atmosphere of open and genuine friendliness toward the United States and toward Americans as individuals. This was true wherever we went, in Yenan or in the forward areas, among the *lao pai-hsing,* 8th Route Army men, political cadres, or Party leaders. This was so widespread and so obviously popular that it could not have been staged for our benefit.[55]

---

[53] See, for instance, Appendix A, Part 1, report no. 34. None of these leaders had been present at my August 23 talk with Mao.

[54] *Chieh-fang jih-pao,* December 16, 1944. This speech was included in the 1947 edition of Mao's *Selected Works* (3:125–135), but omitted from later editions. I am indebted to Mr. Barry Burton for reminding me of this statement by Mao.

[55] The veterans of Kiangsi—which included all the principal Communist leaders—were quite conscious that this vigorously expressed friendship toward us and the United States was not without some ironies. Until 1935, missionaries falling into their hands had been treated very harshly (including execution in several cases) as "agents of foreign imperialism." At least it could be said (in contrast to a patron-

But however genuine seemed the Communist desire for American support, it was really the answer to the second question that was basic. For it was Mao's conception of the relationship which he wished China to have with the Soviet Union that would inevitably govern his long-term attitude toward the United States. If he was serious in what he was saying to me—and through me, he hoped, to the American government—then he obviously visualized China's relationship to the Soviet Union as something very different from the conventional idea of a Soviet satellite. He was, indeed, assuming that a Communist China could have considerable independence and freedom of action in international affairs.

Several lines of exploration seemed relevant. One was the internal history of the Party. It was known in general terms, for instance, that Mao had come into leadership only after a long struggle against men trained in and imposed on the Chinese Party by Moscow. The second, and related, topic was the history of the relations of the Chinese Communist Party with the Comintern—which meant Stalin. It may be useful here to remember that almost all that had been published in the West at this time about the history of the Chinese Communists was contained in two books. One was *The Tragedy of the Chinese Revolution,* which I had read many years before but was not available in Yenan.[56] This dealt primarily with the 1925–1927 period and the effects of the Stalin-Trotsky conflict on Comintern policies in China. The second was Edgar Snow's *Red Star Over China.*[57] This covered the period up to the outbreak of the Sino-Japanese War in 1937, and contained the only biography (actually an autobiography) of Mao. I had a copy of this book with me.

I soon found out, after several unproductive attempts, that there was a very definite limit to Mao's willingness to talk to me on these subjects. He was quite prepared to discuss mistaken "leftist" policies of the Kiangsi

---

izing attitude often encountered in Kuomintang circles) that they assumed that we were well informed about China and recent Chinese affairs, and wasted little time in apologies or trying to gloss things over. Out of our original contingent of sixteen, three (Stelle, Whittlesey, and myself) were sons of missionaries and had spent most of our lives in China. A fourth (Domke) had spent several years as a teacher in a missionary college and had learned Chinese. Our doctor (Casberg) had been a medical missionary in India. Colonel Barrett, the commanding officer of the Observer Group, had lived in China for twenty-three years, mostly in intelligence work for the U.S. Army, and had an unusual command of the language. Ludden was a China specialist in the Foreign Service and had spent twelve years at various posts in China. Dolan had spent several years in China, had traveled extensively, and also spoke some Chinese. We were not, therefore, without some background.

[56] Harold Isaacs, *The Tragedy of the Chinese Revolution* (London: Sacker and Warburg, 1938). (A "second revised edition" was published by Stanford University Press in 1961.)

[57] Edgar Snow, *Red Star Over China* (London: Victor Gollancz, 1937). There were, of course, a number of other accounts by British and American writers (and an American Marine officer, Evans Carlson) who had visited the Communist areas in the years from 1937 until the blockade was imposed in 1939. Their emphasis, however, was more contemporary and descriptive than historical.

period (they provided a neat contrast to the successful United Front policies of Yenan). Ch'en Tu-hsiu could be criticized; so could the "Li Li-san line" and Chang Kuo-t'ao. But, by and large, he was blandly disinclined to go beyond the few rather vague, if suggestive, comments that he had made to Snow in 1936.[58] Other leaders, such as Chou En-lai and Po Ku, were similarly circumspect. This disinclination to bring the skeletons out of the closet, or to engage in anything that might be construed (and reported) as criticism of Stalin and the USSR, was not surprising. I was, after all, a representative of a foreign, capitalist country—with which the Communists hoped to have friendly relations, but which had as yet given no inkling of any serious willingness to enter into such relations, or to abandon its longstanding commitment to the Communists' enemy. In fact, my probings might well have been considered as impertinent. There were, it turned out, other sources of enlightenment.

Before arriving in Yenan, I had heard vaguely that a party reform movement (generally referred to as the *cheng-feng yün-tung*, or simply as *cheng-feng*) had been going on since early 1942. But this was the first of Mao's great exercises in mass persuasion, exhortation, and criticism that have since become well-known as a basic tool of his political leadership. It was only in Yenan that I began to realize the scope and intensity of the movement. Many people that I talked to had been struggled with and criticized. They seemed to have come out of it with a sense of emotional uplift, purgation, and group solidarity through the process of self-criticism. This struck me as psychologically interesting and not entirely different in effect from the revivalism and public confession of sins characteristic of some Christian sects. My first reaction was that it was important mainly as a tactic of conversion and renewal of fervor and faith.

The Chinese in Yenan with whom I had the best background of acquaintance was a man a few years younger than myself who had spent most of the war in Chungking as a secretary to Chou En-lai. He still had the same job in Yenan; but, as he was also acting as one of the liaison staff with our Observer Section, we had ample opportunity to renew our informal friendship. Not long after our arrival, I asked him about *cheng-feng,* which I had been hearing so much about. He surprised me by the seriousness of his reply, which was to the effect: "This movement is absolutely basic, and not merely a propaganda technique. If you want to understand our Party's policy and where we actually stand, you must study and truly understand the *cheng-feng* documents." He promptly got

---

[58] One can find quite a number of these remarks in *Red Star:* "Roy had been a fool, Borodin a blunderer" (p. 161); "the Central Committee now definitely repudiated me" (p. 165); "the fifth point at that time was opposed by the Comintern" (p. 163). But when Snow made statements such as ". . . the Comintern may be held responsible for serious reverses suffered by the Chinese Communists in the anguish of their growth" (p. 382) he seemed to be expressing his own view rather than clearly reflecting anything directly said by Mao.

me a copy (in Chinese, since most had not been translated) and I commenced reading.[59]

The problem, I soon discovered, was that they were often allusive and not specific. They were addressed to Party members; and, in order for an outsider like myself to "truly understand" them, one needed precisely the knowledge of Party history which I lacked. Few names appeared, and never that of Wang Ming (Ch'en Shao-yü) who was in Yenan but never seen and obviously in disgrace.[60] Similarly, properly respectful things were said about the Russian Communist Party (and pieces by Lenin, Stalin, and Dimitrov were included), but a consistent theme—particularly in the many articles by Mao Tse-tung—was along the line that "a Communist Party member living in China who divorces himself from the practical necessities of the Chinese situation in speaking of Marxism is a false Marxist, even though he reads ten thousand Marxist books a thousand times."[61] I turned to my friend and he became a helpful interpreter and guide.

In the course of many conversations, sporadically as I read, I received an exegesis of the *cheng-feng* documents that was certainly neither complete nor systematic. Still, I was given inklings of much party history that has since become better known. My friend realized, of course, that I was interested in CCP relations with the USSR, and it was this aspect that received most emphasis. His unfolding of internal party history was understandably more frank and detailed about figures who had fallen (such as Wang Ming) than about those who had made their peace with Mao and were still in seats of power (such, for instance, as Chou En-lai and Po Ku). In any event, much that I was told about *cheng-feng* was supported by our observations and by what could be gathered from other sources. Several conclusions seemed valid.

The *cheng-feng* movement had been an effective means of indoctrinating, unifying, and imposing discipline on the huge mass of new members, with diverse backgrounds and political experience, who had been admitted into the Party since the beginning of the Anti-Japanese War. An important content of the campaign, even though stated in Marxist terms, was nationalistic: the steady insistence that the Party's thinking must be Chinese; the rejection of foreign (i.e., Soviet) influence and models. The campaign reflected Mao's final victory over the "Twenty-eight Bolshe-

---

[59] The Chinese documents have been translated, with a useful introduction, by Boyd Compton, *Mao's China: Party Reform Documents, 1942–44* (Seattle: University of Washington Press, 1952).

[60] When I inquired about an interview with Wang Ming, I was told that it could be arranged but that he "probably would not say much to me." Not being sure that a great deal would be gained in pressing an obviously unwelcome request, I dropped the matter. I thus never met him.

[61] Mao Tse-tung, "In Opposition to Party Formalism," translated in Compton, *Mao's China*, p. 52.

viks" and other rivals within the Party. This was significant for several reasons. The fact that Mao had achieved undisputed leadership of a unified Party strengthened his hand for the coming contest for power (political or military) with the Kuomintang. It also increased his freedom of action in other directions—even in ways that might not conventionally be expected of an "orthodox" Communist, such as genuinely wishing Chinese independence, not relishing a role of reliance on "big brother" in the form of Stalin, and being quite honest in seeking American cooperation into the postwar period.[62]

Some additional clues on Chinese Communist attitudes toward the Soviet Union were revealed when I sought information on their policies toward areas that would involve contact with the Soviet Union. For instance: "Outer and Inner Mongolia are parts of China. . . . Given fair treatment, active assistance in improvement of their social, economic and cultural conditions, and autonomy on a federative basis, the peoples of Outer and Inner Mongolia will join together and remain a part of China."[63] Or in regard to Manchuria. The Communists openly anticipated that the USSR would enter the war against Japan (though they apparently did not expect this to happen until the spring of 1946), and they correctly assumed that the Soviet action would be in the form of an invasion of Manchuria. To meet and collaborate with this, they were talking freely (to me, at least) of their plans, already in preparation, to move quickly into Manchuria from the south.[64] However:

> Regarding the possibility of Russian demands of territory or special rights in Manchuria, the Communists are most emphatic. They insist that because "the days of Russian imperialism are over" there will be no such demands. But Russia does want, they believe, a China which will have cordial and friendly relations with Russia, and which will permit normal use, on a commercial basis and without any infringement of Chinese sovereignty, of Manchurian transport and port facilities. This would mean absence of unreasonable or onerous impediments to trade between the two countries or in transit. Such conditions, the Communists maintain, would be of advantage to both countries.
>
> It does not need to be pointed out that such a course of development will leave the Chinese Communists in control of Manchuria.

---

[62] These conclusions were not pulled together in any single report that I wrote from Yenan. Perhaps the closest to a summarization is Appendix A, Part 1, report no. 34.

[63] Appendix A, Part 2, report no. 14. When I reported these views of Yenan, Roosevelt had already agreed to Stalin's demand at Yalta for China's formal recognition of Outer Mongolia's independent status. For a sequel see Harrison E. Salisbury, "Image and Reality in Indochina," *Foreign Affairs,* 49:3 (April 1971), pp. 387–388: "Premier Tsedenbal of Outer Mongolia has told me that one of Mao's first acts on coming to power was a request to Stalin for the return to Chinese suzerainty of Outer Mongolia. Stalin refused this request and tightened his control of this strategic area with its 1,500-mile frontier on China. . . ."

[64] Appendix A, Part 2, report no. 11.

> That the Communists are confident of gaining this control . . . is obvious. The Communists are fully aware—as is the Kuomintang—of the importance of Manchuria as China's major and only well developed heavy industrial base.[65]

At the risk of some repetition, it may be useful to summarize my impressions of Mao's objectives. First, the short-term future. Confident of Communist strength, and of the popular support on which it was based, he did not want and would not initiate civil war. At the same time, force would be met with force: the Communists would fight if necessary to hold their gains.[66] His immediate goal was a coalition government. But this would have to be one which recognized the Communist local governments in areas which they actually controlled; and which permitted their army to remain in being and under their control.[67] Since such a coalition government would involve some cooperation with the Kuomintang, and a resurrected United Front, American support was desirable and close involvement with the Soviet Union a practical liability. This represented, as Mao continually insisted, no conflict with American interests. In fact, it coincided with what we said we were trying to accomplish. We could assume that the coalition would be perhaps little more than a loose mantle to preserve the fiction of unity between what would in effect be two Chinas. The Communists, at this time, were likely to draw parallels with a federal system.[68] Those of us who had experience in China were more likely to remember that China had not, in reality, been unified since 1911. Genuine unity was certainly a desirable goal; but two

---

[65] *Ibid.* Again, these statements by the Chinese Communists were being made after Stalin had already shown at Yalta that he had quite different intentions. Even at Yalta, however, Stalin gave no hint of the Russians' later looting the heavy industrial base which his fellow Communists in Yenan so clearly counted on controlling.

[66] The Communist leaders never wavered in their insistence that they would fight if attacked. This determination was stated to me on numerous occasions by Mao, Chou En-lai and Chu Teh. I have been told by officers serving at the time with the Observer Group in Yenan that, when Japan surrendered, the Group was asked for its estimate of Communist intentions if it was required that Japanese forces in Communist-controlled areas surrender only to Kuomintang forces. The Observer Group reply was that the Communists would fight. At almost the same time I had a conversation with Tung Pi-wu, then in the United States as a member of the Chinese delegation at the United Nations Conference in San Francisco. He unhesitatingly made the same reply.

[67] Although Chiang had refused an American commander for his own armies, he (and Hurley, and at times Washington) hoped that the problem of the Communist armies could be solved by putting them under American command. Mao was not impressed: "We are glad to accept American command, as the British have in Europe. But it must be of all Chinese armies" (Appendix A, Part 2, report no. 10).

[68] Chou En-lai was apt to try out a line such as: "After all, you have a Democratic government in Washington, but Republicans can govern and carry out their own policies in important states such as California and New York." Chou did not, however, press the parallel very seriously.

Chinas, neither an enemy, were at least better than a civil war, with one China an enemy and the U.S. committed to the losing side.

For the long-term, Mao of course sought, like the leader of any political party, the position of control. It was hard to know just in what manner and how rapidly he expected (or hoped) that this could be accomplished.[69] Certainly he counted on the deep and very widespread desire for national unity shared by most articulate Chinese. Also he clearly believed that his Communist Party had become a far more dynamic, effective, and popular political force than the moribund Kuomintang under the backward-looking leadership of Chiang Kai-shek. With the chance for political activity which should be made possible by a coalition government, he seemed to expect that this transfer of leadership could be accomplished without a major civil war. Be that as it may, Mao was convincing that he preferred to acquire the "mandate" by nonviolent rather than violent means. Obviously, in these circumstances a benign American attitude—if not actual cooperation—was much to be desired. And quite beyond the argument for the need of American economic aid in China's postwar development (which also was a stock theme heard in Moscow), I thought that Mao was sincere in hoping to avoid a close and isolated dependence on the USSR. One could argue that Mao was unrealistic and inexperienced in international affairs.[70] But he had had twenty years of experience with the Soviet Union and Stalin. Or one could suggest that he was thinking of the old Chinese game of playing off one barbarian against another. Essentially, it seemed to me that Mao was treating foreign relations as basically non-ideological. He was thinking in nationalistic Chinese terms; and assuming that most countries (including the Soviet Union *and* the United States) base their foreign policy on national interest. With the overwhelming Russian presence so oppressively close, it was reasonable to wish for American friendship. And of course, Mao must also have thought, it should be reasonable for the United States to wish to have friendly relations with China rather than see the continent of Asia dominated by Sino-Soviet unity brought about by China's enforced reliance on Russia.

---

[69] I did, though, go on record (in a way) with my personal opinion of the likely time span. As should be expected, not all Americans in China agreed with my view of the strength of the Chinese Communists. In February 1945, a lunch-time discussion in the headquarters mess was finally ended by my proposing a bet that "the Communists would be the dominant force in China within five years." My friendly adversary, who had also spent much time in China, accepted. The payoff was to be a dinner in a Washington restaurant of the winner's choice. My friend acknowledged the debt but we never got together for the dinner: by that time it hardly seemed a cause for convivial observance.

[70] It may be of interest, for instance, to note the Communist views on the postwar treatment of Japan (Appendix A, Part 1, report no. 31).

The denouement of this lengthy tale has already been related. I made several rather general and tentative policy proposals from Yenan.[71] But the most specific, and probably the most thoroughly developed proposal was the lengthy telegram of February 28, 1945, in which I joined with the Embassy staff in Chungking.[72]

The setting may be worth recalling. By this time we had had seven months of close contact and widespread observation of the Chinese Communists. Ludden had just returned to Chungking after his four-month trek into the forward guerrilla areas bringing reports that confirmed and strengthened our findings in Yenan and Shansi.[73] The deterioration in Kuomintang-controlled China continued; despite a few personnel shifts to meet American criticism, the situation was still essentially as described in my report of June 20, 1944.[74] Hurley's attempt to negotiate an agreement between the Kuomintang and Communists had come to an obvious impasse. Hurley and Wedemeyer were returning to the United States for consultations. It was, we all assumed, a time to take stock.

There was vigorous discussion among Americans in China about all kinds of policy alternatives. One occasionally heard the exasperated complaint that China was "such a mess" that the best course was to disentangle and get out. But few took this seriously. The war was not yet won. And even though it was now generally assumed that China's military role would not be great, the American interest in China's future was not diminished. We could not abandon China because we had a mission and special responsibility there—or so it seemed to almost everyone.

There were also some, but a minority, who thought that the problem could be solved by putting pressure on the Communists. It was never clearly explained how this pressure was effectively to be exerted. The Communists were doing very well—in fact, they were expanding their forces and territory very rapidly—without any American aid or support. There was no need for them to heed our admonitions to sacrifice what they considered their own vital interests. Hurley, as I have mentioned, thought that he could mobilize Stalin to bring pressure to bear on the Communists. But this did not impress us as realistic.

There were a few who would go beyond "pressure" and urged direct

---

[71] For example, Appendix A, Part 1, reports 16, 20, and 40.

[72] The text of the telegram is printed above in Chapter VI in the section "No Dictation to the Generalissimo." See also Appendix A, Part 3, (f).

[73] "For the first time in modern Chinese history a purely Chinese administration extending over wide areas has positive popular support and popular participation is developing"; R. P. Ludden, "Popular Support of Communists as Evidenced by People's Militia Organization in Shansi-Chahar-Hopei Communist Base Area" (*Foreign Relations 1945,* pp. 200–204).

[74] Appendix B.

184

American intervention against the Communists. For instance, Captain Joseph Alsop, then an aide to General Chennault, suggested:

> We are childish to assume that the Chinese Communists are anything but an appendage of the Soviet Union, that they are really willing to accept any compromise or coalition short of complete control of China, or that they can be swung into cooperation with our interests. Attempts to arrange a reconciliation in China, or to utilize Communist military forces, are therefore dangerous and "idiotic."
> Our only correct policy, accordingly, is to support the Central Government, giving it all the aid possible (on a much larger scale than at present), helping it to create a strong army, and then assisting (by our own forces if necessary) in unifying the country, liquidating the Communists, and establishing a strong government.[75]

I know of no one, however, who made a reasoned estimate of the American forces that would be required for an American military suppression of the Communists; or who seriously thought the American public at the end of a long war would willingly support a massive effort of this kind and almost certainly of indefinite duration.[76] At any rate, none of us who had seen the Communists thought that this would be an easy task; or a successful way of winning a friendly, united China.

A much larger group continued to cling to the hope that Chiang could be persuaded, in the interests of himself if not the United States, to reform his government. For instance, Chennault urged "thorough reconstruction at Chungking, followed by true unification between Chungking and Yenan."[77] Alsop also thought that " 'really capable American statesmanship,' which we have not yet had applied to China, would be able to persuade the Central Government of the advantages of progressive liberalism."[78] The trouble with the persuasion tactic was that we had already

---

[75] Appendix A, Part 2, report no. 7. This is not a direct quotation, but my attempt to reproduce the gist of remarks made by Alsop in a conversation with me. Alsop went on: "To back up China, we must adopt a strong policy toward Russia ... 'tell the Russians that they must stay out of China.' " Alsop was correct, though, in arguing that the important issue was not the war against Japan but the future balance of power in Asia: our difference was that we had opposite views of the most realistic way of achieving it.

[76] For an inexpert (pre-Korea) opinion, note a statement of Secretary of War Patterson in November 1945: "He thought that the 60,000 Marines who are there could walk from one end of China to the other without serious hindrance. Such incidents as there have been are merely comic opera fighting" (*Foreign Relations 1945*, p. 646). The Chinese in Korea were fighting in a foreign country, without the backing of their own people in guerrilla warfare.

[77] Chennault to Roosevelt, September 21, 1944; cited by Tuchman, *Stilwell*, p. 486.

[78] See note 75, above. Alsop, it might be noted, was speaking some six months after Hurley had taken over American affairs in China. Alsop's solution thus combined American military intervention against the Communists with persuasion directed at Chiang. This, if I understand him correctly, is also roughly the policy that Tang Tsou believes that the United States should have adopted. He does not, however, seem to estimate the magnitude of the American military commitment that

rung all the changes, and had mobilized all the voices of exhortation from the President on down, without budging Chiang one iota. The President had tried to get Chiang to agree to American command. Gauss and the State Department had been eloquent about a first step toward unity by a "war cabinet." Hurley had jawboned earnestly for months. The State Department had talked discreetly of flexibility—though it may be doubtful whether this was ever clear to the Chinese through Hurley's counterbarrage. It was time, it seemed to me and many others, for a more positive and realistic step.

That Hurley's particular brand of "realism" might be a problem was, by this time, well understood. We were encouraged, though, by the continuing desire of the U.S. Army to be able to utilize the military potential of the Communist forces and their strategic positions in North China.[79] This interest also had the support of the State Department in its policy guidance memorandum of January 29, 1945, which had been approved and forwarded to Chungking by Secretary of War Stimson.[80] All the various plans and proposals had been thwarted, however, by Hurley's insistence that there could be no military cooperation with the Communists—nor any planning for it—without Chiang's prior approval. Not surprisingly, Chiang consistently declined such approval; nor was there even a pretense of considering the possible military merits of the actual proposals.

When Ludden returned to Chungking in early February from his 1200-mile tour of the Communist area, he had called on General Wedemeyer—who, as General Stilwell's replacement, had now become his commanding officer—to make a personal report. Wedemeyer had seemed much impressed by Ludden's conclusions regarding popular support of the Communist forces, their possible usefulness in guerrilla operations against the Japanese if American aid could be gotten to them, and the consequent

---

would be required. Nor is he specific on the degree of persuasion vis-à-vis the Kuomintang that would be necessary: "The basic fact in China was that there could not have been any genuine reform without a change of leadership at the very top" (Tang Tsou, *America's Failure,* p. 456).

[79] "In the month preceding Stilwell's recall, the President and the Joint Chiefs had desired to see Stilwell, under the Generalissimo, command both Chinese Nationalist and Chinese Communist forces in the war against Japan. The War Department had contemplated giving lend-lease to a Chinese Army that might include Communist forces. Stilwell's recall had not changed these views. . . . Wedemeyer had sought and obtained as his chief of staff General McClure. . . . He very soon took an active part in formulating plans and proposals to arm and use the Chinese Communists against the Japanese. . . . From the discussions in Wedemeyer's headquarters, three projects for using the Chinese Communists finally evolved" (Romanus and Sunderland, *Time Runs Out in CBI,* pp. 72–75). There was also a plan for large-scale OSS cooperation with the Communist forces, though this may have been considered as a part of the third of the three projects mentioned above (*ibid.,* pp. 249–254; and Barrett, *Dixie Mission,* pp. 76–78).

[80] See Chapter VI, footnote 18, above.

need for greater flexibility in American military policy to make this possible. Mentioning that he was about to return to Washington, where overall policy matters would be discussed, he requested a written summary of the views that Ludden had expressed orally. He also issued orders for Ludden's prompt return to Washington so that he could be available for consultation.[81]

Time was short, and Ludden suggested my collaboration.[82] Together and in some haste, we prepared our memorandum of February 14 to General Wedemeyer. The following may be sufficient to indicate the gist:

> At present there exists in China a situation closely paralleling that which existed in Yugoslavia prior to Prime Minister Churchill's declaration of support for Marshal Tito. That statement was as follows: "The sanest and safest course for us to follow is to judge all parties and factions dispassionately by the test of their readiness to fight the Germans and thus lighten the burden of Allied troops. This is not a time for ideological preferences for one side or the other." A similar public statement issued by the Commander in Chief with regard to China would not mean the withdrawal of recognition or the cessation of military aid to the Central Government; that would be both unnecessary and unwise. It would serve notice, however, of our preparation to make full use of all available means to achieve our primary objective. It would supply for all Chinese a firm rallying point which has thus far been lacking. The internal effect in China would be so profound that the Generalissimo would be forced to make concessions of power and permit united front coalition. The present opposition groups, no longer under the prime necessity of safeguarding themselves, would be won wholeheartedly to our side and we would have in China, for the first time, a united ally.[83]

This, then, was the background a few days later when George Atcheson took over charge of the Embassy in the absence of Hurley and courageously decided that he had a responsibility to give the State Department a more realistic report of the situation in China than it had been possible to render under Hurley. It was this background, and what we understood

---

[81] I am thoroughly aware that Wedemeyer's statements in later years give a somewhat different impression of his attitude during this period (see, for instance, his testimony in *Institute of Pacific Relations,* Hearings, pp. 775–841). Apart from the personal recollections of myself and others, the official record is, however, copious and clear (see footnote 79, above).

[82] Ludden and I were both assigned to the staff of the Theater commander, and I had accompanied him for this conversation with General Wedemeyer.

[83] Appendix A, Part 3, (e). The text in *Foreign Relations 1945* makes the usual omission of some harsh comments about Chiang Kai-shek. This memorandum had a brief notoriety as proposing a "Tito policy." Actually, we were not being wholly original. The potential parallel had been noted for some time in Chungking discussions; it had been mentioned by me, for instance, as long ago as October 10, 1944 (Appendix A, Part 1, report no. 40). Nor was the parallel with Yugoslavia very precise—inasmuch as we were specifically stating that recognition and aid of Chiang and his government should not be withdrawn.

to be the active American Army interest, that was at least partially responsible for the military cast of both the February 14 memorandum of Ludden and myself, and the shortly subsequent February 28 telegram and recommendations of the Embassy staff.

The key element in the Embassy telegram of February 28 was the proposal "that the President inform the Generalissimo in definite terms that military necessity requires that we supply and cooperate with the Communists and other suitable groups who can assist the war against Japan . . . and that we are taking direct steps to accomplish this end."

The telegram itself was a committee effort. As I recall, there were five officers, including Atcheson, who signed it. All of us participated in the preliminary discussions, and in the consideration and modifications of the several drafts. Atcheson had the final word; but his minor revisions were then approved by the rest of us. My recollection is that there was very broad unanimity from the start on the general content of the message and the nature of the recommendations we wished to make. What discussion there was chiefly concerned phraseology and manner of presentation. I believe the message is clear, and that it stands by itself. However, there is always the possibility that it had a different meaning, however slight, to the individual signers. What follows, then, is my own view of the significance of what we were recommending.

We were recommending, first of all, that the veto power over American policy in China be taken out of the hands of Chiang Kai-shek. Our action would relate to the use of American aid and American forces, matters which should rightfully be within our own control.[84] Unlike earlier proposals for American command, or for the use of Kuomintang troops in the Burma campaigns, no approval, action, or the provision of facilities by Chiang was required. No approval, therefore, would be asked.

The significance of our action would, however, go far beyond this in its effect within China. It would be clear notice to all groups concerned (Chiang and the Kuomintang, the Communists, liberal groups, Chinese

---

[84] Despite the fact that we were allies fighting a common enemy, this would admittedly be an unusual diplomatic step. For State Department arguments supporting our recommendation see the memorandum of March 1 from the Chief of CA: ". . . there should be no question of our prerogative dictated by military necessity, to utilize all forces in China. . . ." (*Foreign Relations 1945*, p. 248); and also the FE memorandum of March 7, 1945, to Assistant Secretary Dunn (*ibid.*, pp. 262–264). Some facts generally overlooked: there was no civil war in China and the Communists were not in rebellion against the Central Government; the Communists officially recognized the authority of the Central Government and the leadership of Chiang Kai-shek; the Central Government had granted legal status to the two principal Communist local governments; the Communist 18th Group Army, and the three (much inflated) divisions comprising it, were officially a part of the armed forces of the Central Government; and Chu Teh and the other commanders of that Army still held valid commissions issued to them by the Central Government. We were not, therefore, recommending cooperation with an unrecognized, rebel force.

public opinion—and the USSR) that American policy in China was in fact neutral and not committed to the unconditional support of Chiang or any faction. We would, in other words, simply be demonstrating that American policy was what we had consistently been saying it was.

So far as the war in China was concerned, we would no longer be wholly dependent on frustrating and laborious efforts to prod, mold, change, and stimulate the flabby, inert, and resistant Kuomintang. If Chiang and the Kuomintang chose to sulk and sit on their hands, there would be no great change there from the situation already existing. But we would gain an active ally who clearly recognized that his strength grew through warfare which, as incidental to gains in territory, gave access to the minds and loyalties of people and thus the creation of wider popular support.

There was as yet no need for a choice between the Kuomintang and Communists. No one, as a matter of fact, was suggesting that such a choice should be made.[85] But by this assertion of an independent, uncommitted American policy, we would be in a position to adjust to and move with, rather than be standing against, the tidal development of events in China. Whether Mao's revolution would be successful, and the final shape that it would take, were still in the future. But at least we would not be foreclosing an opportunity to see whether the preview in Yenan was indicative, and whether Mao's statements and reiterated invitation to friendly cooperation could be taken seriously.

What would have happened if our recommendation had been accepted and acted upon? The usual assertion is that things could not have been worse for American interests and relations with China than they turned out to be. It is hard to argue with this resigned but uninformative conclusion. The attempt to reconstruct history is a speculative and slippery game. But perhaps the footing is firmer the closer one remains to the take-off point.

Had the recommendation of our February 28 telegram been approved, the U.S. Army in China would have started promptly to implement at least some of the plans for active military cooperation with the Communists that had been prepared but put on ice because Hurley had supported Chiang's veto. The full details of these plans have never been published. But they envisaged some thousands of American personnel, and consid-

---

[85] It does not seem to require much detective work to determine the inspiration for Hurley's constant cry that this recommendation, and every other suggestion contrary to the approval and wishes of Chiang Kai-shek, was actually an either-or choice because it would cause the overthrow, downfall, or collapse of Chiang's government. It was a view held only by Hurley and the group around Chiang. Our recommendation could be expected to lead to a change in the form of Chiang's government in the direction of a coalition government of some sort, but that is precisely what Hurley was supposed to be trying to bring about.

erable quantities of supporting equipment for guerrilla warfare.[86] Logistically, the means were available. The Burma Road and pipeline were completed. The Hump was carrying far greater tonnage than ever before. The war in Europe was winding down; OSS and other trained personnel were becoming available. From the end of April, the American position in Okinawa was secure and a huge base was being built up. Okinawa was only about 700 miles from Communist areas in north Kiangsu; air supply by this route would quickly have become easier than the long line through India and across the Hump.

Confronted with proof that the United States was no longer willing to debate this matter endlessly, Chiang Kai-shek would have permitted the formation of a coalition government. This would have been a practical political necessity; it would be the only way that Chiang could save prestige and maintain even the fiction of national leadership. The precise form of this coalition government was not important. It might be very loose (no more, perhaps, than the vague "war council" that Gauss had originally proposed); but there would be an organ having the name of a national government and giving legitimation to Communist as well as Kuomintang armies.

By August, it could be expected that Americans (instructors, intelligence officers, demolition experts, and radio teams) would be well dispersed through the Communist base areas and working with the Communist military units. The Japanese surrender in China, one must then assume, would have been handled very differently. There would have been no basis or arguable need for ordering that the Japanese surrender (in North China areas which the Communists had fought for and held for eight years) be made only to Chiang's forces; nor for the strange orders for the Japanese to stand fast and resist the Communists until the Nationalists could find some way to reach them. Nor would it have been necessary for the U.S. to land 60,000 Marines to hold North China ports as proxy for the Nationalists.

With American assistance, the Communists would have taken the surrender of the Japanese in North China, disarmed or absorbed the puppet armies, and in the process accumulated arms and supplies. With the railways and communications intact, they would have been able to move the Japanese expeditiously to embarkation ports for repatriation to Japan. With American mediation, there would have to be a division of zones between the Kuomintang and Communists. But any reasonable drawing of the line would leave the Communists in control of substantially all of North China, while the Kuomintang would hold the Yangtze valley and South China. Without American logistical support to move their armies

---

[86] See footnote 79, above.

by air and sea beyond these areas, it would have been difficult and clearly suicidal for the Kuomintang to commence civil war.

From this point, everyone can improvise his own scenario. What would have happened, for instance, when the Communist units, accompanied by cooperating American liaison and communications teams, moved rapidly into Manchuria? The fact that the Communists were part of the armed forces of the national, coalition government of China would have deprived the Russians of an excuse for a protracted occupation. Would it also have changed their intention to remove most of Manchuria's heavy industrial equipment? The Russians, one may assume, would not have welcomed the Americans. But under these circumstances, one wonders what the Chinese Communist reaction would have been. Russians, for a number of historical reasons, had never been popular in Manchuria; and their army, from all reports, behaved much as most foreign occupying forces do—only perhaps more so. Liaison teams, who are normally small groups of specialized, highly trained personnel, are usually more successful than multi-division mass armies in maintaining good relations with the native population and the army they are cooperating with.

Whatever fanciful games one constructs, it seems clear that the implementation of an independent, uncommitted American policy in China, and the initiation of military cooperation with the Communists during the spring of 1945 before the Japanese surrender, would have placed our relations with China at the beginning of the postwar period on an entirely different, and much more realistically favorable basis. There probably would have been no civil war. But if there had been one, it would likely have been short and far less destructive. And we would not carry the onus—contrary to our intention but hard to refute—of having prolonged it by aid and support of the losing side. We could have maintained our contact and relations with China. And while we would certainly have had to give up our paternalistic, missionary attitude of wishing to shape China to our wishes, we might have found co-existence with a stoutly independent, nationalistic Mao Tse-tung not wholly impossible—and the world as a result considerably less complicated.

Toward the close of his brief excursion into the history of U.S.-China relations, Dr. Kubek makes the statement: "When the United States unwittingly assisted the wrong side in gaining control of China proper, Korea and Vietnam became inevitable. . . ."[87] I would suggest a revision: "If the United States had been able in 1945 to shed some of its illusions about China, to understand what was happening in that country, and to adopt a realistic policy in America's own interests, Korea and Vietnam would probably never have happened." I would even add a few dividends. We would not still be confronted with an unsolvable Taiwan problem. Indeed,

---

[87] *Papers*, p. 113.

there never would have been a Taiwan problem, because we would not have "lost" China. And Mao's China, having come to power in a different way and not thrust into isolation by a hostile West, might be quite a different place. It might be one, for instance, where Chinese-American ping-pong matches were normal occurrences instead of being a world-shaking event, unprecedented for more than twenty-one years.

APPENDIX A

PART 1—1944 YENAN REPORTS

ABBREVIATIONS

* CWP: State Department, *China White Paper*
  PJH: Lohbeck, *Patrick J. Hurley*
  TYT: Foreign Relations Committee, *Tydings Transcript*
  IPR: Internal Security Subcommittee, *Institute of Pacific Relations*
** (I) : Incomplete
  (S): Summary only
  (E): Excerpt(s)
  (P): Paraphrase

Absence of symbol indicates that text is complete—though enclosures referred to in the text may, in some cases, be missing.

Rpt. No.	Date		Amer. Papers	USFR 1944	Other Sources*
1	7–28–44	First Informal Impressions of North Shensi Communist Base	681	517	
2	7–28–44	Communist Desire Continued American Representation at Yenan *(Interview with Mao Tse-tung)*	684	522	
3	7–30–44	Views of Communist Military and Political Leaders *(Mao interviews with Stein, Votaw; Chou En-lai with Service; Chu Teh with Stein, Votaw, Epstein; Lin Piao with Service)*	690	536(S)**	
4	7–31–44	Kuomintang and Japanese Views of Effectiveness of Communist Forces *(Ho Ying-chin interview with Guenther Stein in Chungking)*	718	534	
5	8– 3–44	Communist Policy Toward the Kuomintang	723	562	CWP: 565(E)**
6	8– 3–44	Economic Situation in North Shensi	728	525(S)	

194

195

45	10–15–44	Censorship of Escape Stories Should Not Regard CCP Bases as Enemy Occupied	1081	—
46	10–16–44	Communist Comment on Chiang's October 10 Speech	1083	—
47	10–17–44	Policies and Administrative Program of the CCP	1109	—
48	10–18–44	Communist Propaganda Use of Statements by Foreign Correspondents	1114	—
49	—	*(No record: Presumably routine transmittal)*	—	—
50	10–21–44	Transmitting Chieh Fang Jih Pao	1117	—
51	10–21–44	Texts of English Broadcasts	1118	—

PART 2—1945 YENAN REPORTS

Rpt. No.	Date		Amer. Papers	USFR 1945	Other Sources*
1	2–14–45	Failure of Kuomintang-Communist Negotiations *(interview with Chou En-lai)*	1337	—	
2	2–16–45	Russian Concern Over American Support of Central Government	1338	—	
3	2–17–45	The Kuomintang Hopes to Make a Deal With Russia	1345	—	
4	2–17–45	Views of Sun Fo	1347	—	
5	—	Chinese Feelers Regarding Formosa	—	—	
6	2–23–45	Proposal to Make Shanghai an Open City	1355	52	
7	2–28–45	Views of Captain Alsop	1372	—	
8	3–11–45	Present Communist Attitude Toward the Central Government	1390	—	

197

24	—	*(No record: presumably routine)*	—	—
25	—	*(No record: presumably routine)*	—	—
26	4- 1-45	Policy to be Adopted by Communist Congress: Conversation with Mao Tse-tung and Other Communist Leaders	1572	310

PART 3—OTHER PAPERS

Rpt. No.	Date		Amer. Papers	USFR	Other Sources*
a)	1-23-43	Kuomintang - Communist Situation	—	(43)193	TYT: 1975 CWP: 570(E)
b)	3-20-44	(Need for Quid Pro Quo Policy)	404	(44) 37	
c)	4- 7-44	Situation in Sinkiang	—	(44)777(I)	TYT: 1978(I) CWP: 564(E)
d)	6-20-44	The Situation in China and Suggestions Regarding American Policy *(for full text see Appendix B)*	575(I)	—	TYT: 2035(I) IPR: 816(I) CWP: 567(E)
e)	2-14-45	Military Weakness of Our Far Eastern Policy *(with R. P. Ludden)*	—	(45)216(I)	TYT: 1980 CWP: 575(I)
f)	2-28-45	(The Situation in China) *(Telegram by Embassy staff)*	—	(45)242(I)	TYT: 2086 CWP: 87(P)**

APPENDIX B

THE SITUATION IN CHINA AND SUGGESTIONS
REGARDING AMERICAN POLICY

June 20, 1944

I. THE SITUATION IN CHINA IS RAPIDLY BECOMING CRITICAL.

.A. The Japanese strategy in China, which has been as much political as military, has so far been eminently successful.

Japan has had the choice of two alternatives.

1) It could beat China to its knees. But this would have required large military operations and a large and continuing army of occupation. And there was the danger that it might have driven the Kuomintang to carry out a real mobilization of the people, thus making possible effective resistance and perhaps rendering the Japanese task as long and costly as it has been in North China.

2) Or Japan could maintain just enough pressure on China to cause slow strangulation. Based on the astute use of puppets, the understanding of the continuing struggle for power within China (including the Kuomintang-Communist conflict), and the knowledge that Chiang expects to have the war won for him outside of China by his allies, this policy had the advantage that as long as the Kuomintang leaders saw a chance for survival they would not take the steps necessary to energize an effective war. It would thus remove any active or immediate threat to Japan's flank, and permit the accomplishment of these aims at a relatively small cost.

Japan chose the second alternative, accepting the gamble that the Kuomintang would behave exactly as it has. Like many other Japanese gambles, it has so far proved to have been nicely calculated. China *is* dying a lingering death by slow strangulation. China *does not* now constitute any threat to Japan. And China *cannot,* if the present situation continues, successfully resist a determined Japanese drive to seize our offensive bases in East China.

B. The position of the Kuomintang and the Generalissimo is weaker than it has been for the past ten years.

China faces economic collapse. This is causing disintegration of the army and the government's administrative apparatus. It is one of the chief causes of growing political unrest. The Generalissimo is losing the support of a China which, by unity in the face of violent aggression, found a new and unexpected strength during the first two years of the war with Japan. Internal weaknesses are become accentuated and there is taking place a reversal of the process of unification.

1) Morale is low and discouragement widespread. There is a general feeling of hopelessnes.

2) The authority of the Central Government is weakening in the areas away from the larger cities. Government mandates and measures of control cannot be enforced and remain ineffective. It is becoming difficult for the Government to collect enough food for its huge army and bureaucracy.

3) The governmental and military structure is being permeated and demoralized from top to bottom by corruption, unprecedented in scale and openness.

4) The intellectual and salaried classes, who have suffered the most heavi-

ly from inflation, are in danger of liquidation. The academic groups suffer not only the attrition and demoralization of economic stress: the weight of years of political control and repression is robbing them of the intellectual vigor and leadership they once had.

5) Peasant resentment of the abuses of conscription, tax collection, and other arbitrary impositions has been widespread and is growing. The danger is ever-increasing that past sporadic outbreaks of banditry and agrarian unrest may increase in scale and find political motivation.

6) The provincial groups are making common cause with one another and with other dissident groups, and are actively consolidating their positions. Their continuing strength in the face of the growing weakness of the Central Government is forcing new measures of political appeasement in their favor.

7) Unrest within the Kuomintang armies is increasing, as shown in one important instance by the "Young Generals conspiracy" late in 1943. On a higher plane, the war zone commanders are building up their own spheres of influence and are thus creating a "new warlordism."

8) The break between the Kuomintang and the Communists not only shows no signs of being closed, but grows more critical with the passage of time: the inevitability of civil war is now generally accepted.

9) The Kuomintang is losing the respect and support of the people by its selfish policies and its refusal to heed progressive criticism. It seems unable to revivify itself with fresh blood, and its unchanging leadership shows a growing ossification and loss of a sense of reality. To combat the dissensions and cliquism within the Party, which grow more rather than less acute, the leadership is turning toward the reactionary and unpopular Chen brothers clique.

10) The Generalissimo shows a similar loss of realistic flexibility and a hardening of narrowly conservative views. His growing megalomania and his unfortunate attempts to be "sage" as well as leader—shown, for instance, by "China's Destiny" and his book on economics—have forfeited the respect of many intellectuals, who enjoy in China a position of unique influence. Criticism of his dictatorship is becoming more outspoken.

These symptoms of deterioration and internal stress have been increased by the defeat in Honan and will be further accelerated if, as seems likely, the Japanese succeed in partially or wholly depriving the Central Government of east China south of the Yangtze.

In the face of the grave crisis with which it is confronted, the Kuomintang is ceasing to be the unifying and progressive force in Chinese society, the role in which it made its greatest contribution to modern China.

C. The Kuomintang is not only proving itself incapable of averting a debacle by its own initiative; on the contrary, its policies are precipitating the crisis.

Some war-weariness in China must be expected. But the policies of the Kuomintang under the impact of hyper-inflation and in the presence of obvious signs of internal and external weakness must be described as bankrupt. This truth is emphasized by the failure of the Kuomintang to come to grips with the situation during the recently concluded plenary session of the Central Executive Committee.

1. On the internal political front the desire of the Kuomintang leaders to perpetuate their own power overrides all other considerations: the result is the enthronement of reaction.

The Kuomintang continues to ignore the great political drive within the country for democratic reform. The writings of the Generalissimo and the Party press show that they have no real understanding of that term. Constitutionalism remains an empty promise for which the only "preparation" is a half-hearted attempt to establish an unpopular and undemocratic system of local self-government based on collective responsibility and given odium by Japanese utilization in Manchuria and other areas under their control.

Questions basic to the future of democracy, such as the form of the Constitution and the composition and election of the National Congress, remain the dictation of the Kuomintang. There is no progress toward the fundamental conditions of freedom of expression and recognition of non-Kuomintang groups. Even the educational and political advantages of giving power and democratic character to the existing but impotent Peoples Political Council are ignored.

On the contrary, the trend is still in the other direction. Through such means as compulsory political training for government posts, emphasis on the political nature of the Army, thought control, and increasing identification of the Party and Government, the Kuomintang intensifies its drive for "Ein Volk, Ein Reich, Ein Führer"—even though such a policy in China is inevitably doomed to failure.

The Kuomintang shows no intention of relaxing the authoritarian controls on which its present power depends. Far from discarding or reducing the paraphernalia of a police state—the multiple and omnipresent secret police organizations, the Gendarmerie, and so forth—it continues to strengthen them as its last resort for internal security. (For the reenforcement of the most important of these German-inspired and Gestapo-like organizations we must, unfortunately, bear some responsibility.)

Obsessed by the growing and potential threat of the Communists, who it fears may attract the popular support its own nature makes impossible, the Kuomintang, despite the pretext—to meet foreign and Chinese criticism—of conducting negotiations with the Communists, continues to adhere to policies and plans which can only result in civil war. In so doing it shows itself blind to the facts: that its internal political and military situation is so weak that success without outside assistance is most problematic; that such a civil war would hasten the process of disintegration and the spread of chaos; that it would prevent the prosecution of any effective war against Japan; and that the only parties to benefit would be Japan immediately and Russia eventually. Preparations for this civil war include an alliance with the present Chinese puppets which augurs ill for future unity and democracy in China.

2. *On the economic front the Kuomintang is unwilling to take any effective steps to check inflation which would injure the landlord-capitalist class.*

It is directly responsible for the increase of official corruption which is one of the main obstacles to any rational attempt to ameliorate the financial situation. It does nothing to stop large-scale profiteering, hoarding and speculation—all of which are carried on by people either powerful in the Party or with intimate political connections.

It fails to carry out effective mobilization of resources. Such measures of war-time control as it has promulgated have remained a dead letter or have intensified the problems they were supposedly designed to remedy—as for instance ill-advised and poorly executed attempts at price regulation.

It passively allows both industrial and the more important handicraft production to run down, as they of course must when it is more profitable for speculators to hold raw materials than to have them go through the normal productive process.

It fails to carry out rationing except in a very limited way, or to regulate the manufacture and trade in luxury goods, many of which come from areas under Japanese control. It shows little concern that these imports are largely paid for with strategic commodities of value to the enemy.

It fails to make an effective attempt to reduce the budgetary deficit and increase revenue by tapping such resources as excess profits and incomes of landlords and merchants. It allows its tax-collecting apparatus to bog down in corruption and inefficiency—to the point that possibly not more than one-third of revenues collected reach the government. It continues to spend huge government funds on an idle and useless Party bureaucracy.

At best, it passively watches inflation gather momentum without even attempting palliative measures available to it, such as the aggressive sale of gold and foreign currency.

It refuses to attack the fundamental economic problems of China such as the growing concentration of land holdings, extortionate rents and ruinous interest rates, and the impact of inflation.

3. *On the external front the Kuomintang is showing itself inept and selfishly short-sighted by progressive estrangement of its allies.*

By persistence in tactics of bargaining, bluff, and blackmail—most inappropriate to its circumstances—and its continuing failure to deal openly and frankly and to extend whole-hearted cooperation—which its own interests demand—the Kuomintang is alienating China's most important ally, the United States. It has already alienated its other major potential ally, Soviet Russia, toward which its attitude is as irrational and short-sighted as it is toward the Communists. The latest example of this is the irresponsible circulation of the report that Soviet Russia and Japan have signed a secret military agreement permitting Japanese troop withdrawals from Manchuria.

It is allowing this situation to develop at a time when its survival is dependent as never before upon foreign support. But the Kuomintang is endangering not only itself by its rash foreign policy: there are indications that it is anxious to create friction between the United States and Great Britain and Russia. When speedy victory—and any victory at all—demands maximizing of agreements and the minimizing of frictions, such maneuvers amount to sabotage of the war effort of the United Nations.

4. *On the military front the Kuomintang appears to have decided to let America win the war and to have withdrawn for all practical purposes from active participation.*

Its most important present contribution is to allow us—at our own and fantastic cost—to build and use air bases in China.

It delayed, perhaps too long for success, to allow forces designated for the purpose and trained and equipped by us to take the offensive in West Yunnan, even though needed to support the American-Chinese campaign in North Burma, the purpose of which is to open a "life-line" into China and facilitate the eventual landing on the China coast. It agreed to this action only after long months of obstruction.

It fails to make effective use of American equipment given to it as it also failed with earlier Russian supplies. Equipment brought into China has often not been transported to the fighting fronts. In other cases it has been known to have been hoarded or diverted to non-military purposes. China has displayed a "dog-in-the-manger" attitude in regard to equipment consigned to China and deteriorating in India for lack of transportation. It has concealed and refused to make available to our forces hoards of supplies, such as gasoline, known to exist in China, even when the emergency was great and China's own interests directly served.

It has consistently refused to consolidate and efficiently administer transportation. In the past this resulted in great losses of supplies in the Japanese capture of Burma and West Yunnan; now it is crippling Chinese internal transportation on which military activity must depend.

It has allowed military cooperation to be tied up with irrelevant financial demands which can only be described as a form of blackmail. It has made these excessive demands in spite of the fact that American expenditures in China (against which there are almost no balancing Chinese payments) continually add to the large Chinese "nest egg" of foreign exchange, which cannot be used in China at present and thus constitutes in effect a "kitty" being hoarded for post-war use.

It has failed to implement military requisitioning laws to assist us in obtaining supplies in China and has left us at the mercy of conscienceless profiteers, some of whom have been known to have official connections. It has permitted the imposition on us of fantastic prices, made more so by a wholly unrealistic exchange rate, for articles in some cases originally supplied to China through American credits. It seemingly has ignored the fact that the more supplies that can be obtained in China, the greater the tonnage from India that can be devoted to other essential military items.

It remains uncooperative and at times obstructive in American efforts to collect vital intelligence regarding the enemy in China. This attitude is exemplified by the disappointing fruits of promised cooperation by Chinese espionage organizations (toward which we have expended great effort and large sums); by the continued obstruction, in the face of agreement, to visits by American observers to the actual fighting fronts; and by the steadfast refusal to permit any contact with the Communist areas. It apparently remains oblivious to the urgent military need, both in China and in other related theaters, for this intelligence regarding our common enemy, and it seemingly cares little for the fact that exclusion from Communist controlled territory hampers our long-range bombing of Japan and may cost needless loss of American lives.

In its own war effort a pernicious and corrupt conscription system works to ensure the selection and retention of the unfit—since the ablest and strongest can either evade conscription, buy their way out, or desert. It starves and maltreats most of its troops to the degree that their military effectiveness is greatly impaired and military service is regarded in the minds of the people as a sentence of death. At the same time it refuses to follow the suggestion that the army should be reduced to the size that could be adequately fed, medically cared for, trained, and armed. It bases this refusal on mercenary political considerations—the concentration on the continuing struggle for power in China, and the ultimate measurement of power in terms of armies.

For the same reason it refuses to mobilize its soldiers and people for the only kind of war which China is in a position to wage effectively—a people's guerrilla war. Perhaps our entry into the war has simplified the problems of the Kuomintang. As afraid of the forces within the country—its own people—as it is of the Japanese, it now seeks to avoid conflict with the Japanese in order to concentrate on the perpetuation of its own power.

The condition to which it has permitted its armies to deteriorate is shown most recently by the defeat in Honan, which is due not only to lack of heavy armament but also to poor morale and miserable condition of the soldiers, absence of support by the people—who have been consistently mistreated—lack of leadership, and prevalent corruption among the officers through such practices as trade with the occupied areas.

If we accept the obvious indications that the present Kuomintang leadership does not want to fight the Japanese any more than it can help, we must go further and recognize that it may even seek to prevent China from becoming the battleground for large-scale campaigns against the Japanese land forces. This helps to explain the Kuomintang's continued dealings with the Japanese and puppets. Thus the Kuomintang may hope to avert determined Japanese attack, maintain its own position and power, save the east China homes of practically all of its officials, and preserve its old economic-industrial base in the coastal cities.

If this analysis is valid it reveals on the part of the Kuomintang leadership—which means the Generalissimo—a cynical disregard of the added cost of the inevitable prolongation of the war in American lives and resources.

D. These apparently suicidal policies of the Kuomintang have their roots in the composition and nature of the Party.

In view of the above it becomes pertinent to ask *why* the Kuomintang has lost its power of leadership; *why* it neither wishes actively to wage war against Japan itself nor to cooperate wholeheartedly with the American Army in China; and *why* it has ceased to be capable of unifying the country.

The answer to all these questions is to be found in the present composition and nature of the Party. Politically, a classical and definitive American description becomes ever more true: the Kuomintang is a congerie of conservative political cliques interested primarily in the preservation of their own power against all outsiders and in jockeying for position among themselves. Economically, the Kuomintang rests on the narrow base of the rural gentry-landlords, the militarists, the higher ranks of the government bureaucracy, and merchant-bankers having intimate connections with the government bureaucrats. This base has actually contracted during the war. The Kuomintang no longer commands, as it once did, the unequivocal support of China's industrialists, who as a group have been much weakened economically, and hence politically, by the Japanese seizure of the coastal cities.

The relation of this description of the Kuomintang to the questions propounded above is clear.

The Kuomintang has lost its leadership because it has lost touch with and is no longer representative of a nation which, through the practical experience of the war, is becoming both more politically conscious and more aware of the Party's selfish shortcomings.

It cannot fight an effective war because this is impossible without greater reliance upon and support by the people. There must be a release of the national energy such as occurred during the early period of the war. Under present conditions, this can be brought about only by reform of the Party and greater political democracy. What form this democracy takes is not as important as the genuine adoption of a democratic philosophy and attitude; the threat of foreign invasion is no longer enough to stimulate the Chinese people and only real reform can now regain their enthusiasm. But the growth of democracy, though basic to China's continuing war effort, would, to the mind of the Kuomintang's present leaders, imperil the foundations of the Party's power because it would mean that the conservative cliques would have to give up their closely guarded monopoly. Rather than do this, they prefer to see the war remain in its present state of passive inertia. They are thus sacrificing China's national interests to their own selfish ends.

For similar reasons, the Kuomintang is unwilling to give wholehearted cooperation to the American Army's effort in China. Full cooperation necessarily requires the broad Chinese military effort which the Kuomintang is unable to carry out or make possible. In addition, the Kuomintang fears that large-scale widespread and direct contact by Americans with the Chinese war effort will expose its own inactivity and, by example and personal contacts, be a liberalizing influence.

The Kuomintang cannot unify the country because it derives its support from the economically most conservative groups, who wish the retention of China's economically and socially backward agrarian society. These groups are incapable of bringing about China's industrialization, although they pay this objective elaborate lip service. They are also committed to the maintenance of an order which by its very nature fosters particularism and resists modern centralization. Countless examples can be given to show the line-up of the Party with the groups that oppose modernization and industrialization—such as connection with Szechwan warlords and militarists. The Kuomintang sees no objection to maintaining the economic interests of some of its component groups in occupied China or in preserving trade with occupied China, the criterion of which is not the national interest but its profitability to the engaging groups. This explains why Free China's imports from occupied China consist largely of luxuries, against exports of food and strategic raw materials. It is therefore not surprising that there are many links, both political and economic, between the Kuomintang and the puppet regimes.

E. The present policies of the Kuomintang seem certain of failure: if that failure results in a collapse of China it will have consequences disastrous both to our immediate military plans and our long-term interests in the Far East.

The foregoing analysis has shown that the Kuomintang under its present leadership has neither the ability nor desire to undertake a program which could energize the war and check the process of internal disintegration. Its preoccupation with the maintenance and consolidation of its power must result, to the contrary, in acceleration rather than retardation of the rate of this disintegration. Unless it widens its base and changes its character, it must be expected to continue its present policies. It will not of its own volition take steps to bring about this broadening and reform. The opposite will be the case: precisely because it has lost popular support, it is redoubling its efforts to maintain and monopolize control.

The present policies of the Kuomintang seem certain to fail because they run counter to strong forces within the country and are forcing China into ruin. Since these policies are not favorable to us, nor of assistance in the prosecution of an effective war by China, their failure would not of itself be disastrous to American interests. For many reasons mentioned above we might welcome the fall of the Kuomintang if it could immediately be followed by a progressive government able to unify the country and help us fight Japan.

But the danger is that the present drifting and deterioration under the Kuomintang may end in a collapse. The result would be the creation in China of a vacuum. This would eliminate any possibility in the near future of utilizing China's potential military strength. Because the Japanese and their puppets might be able to occupy this vacuum—at much less cost than by a major military campaign—it might also become impossible for us to exploit China's flank position and to continue operating from Chinese bases. The war would thus be prolonged and made more difficult.

Such a collapse would also initiate a period of internal chaos in China which would defer the emergence of a strong and stable government—an indispensable pre-condition for stability and order in the Far East.

China, which might be a minor asset to us now, would become a major liability.

F. There are, however, active and constructive forces in China opposed to the present trends of the Kuomintang leadership which, if given a chance, might avert the threatened collapse.

These groups, all increasingly dissatisfied with the Government and the Party responsible for it, include:

the patriotic younger Army officers,

the small merchants,

large sections of the lower ranks of the Government bureaucracy,

most of the foreign-returned students,

the intelligentsia, including professors, students and the professional classes,

the liberal elements of the Kuomintang, who make up a sizable minority under the leadership of such men as Sun Fo,

the minor parties and groups, some of which like the National Salvationists enjoy great prestige,

the Chinese Communist Party, and

the inarticulate but increasingly restless rural population.

The collective numbers and influence of these groups could be tremendous. A Kuomintang official recently admitted that resentment against the present Kuomintang government is so widespread that if there were free, universal elections 80 per cent of the votes might be cast against it. But most of these groups are nebulous and unorganized, feeling—like the farmers—perhaps only a blind dislike of conditions as they are. They represent different classes and varying political beliefs—where they have any at all. They are tending, however, to draw together in the consciousness of their common interest in the change of the *status quo*. This awakening and fusion is, of course, opposed by the Kuomintang with every means at its disposal.

The danger, as conditions grow worse, is that some of these groups may act independently and blindly. The effect may be to make confusion worse. Such might be the case in a military *putsch*—a possibility that cannot be disregarded. The result might be something analogous to the Sian incident of 1936. But the greater delicacy and precariousness of the present situation would lend itself more easily to exploitation by the most reactionary elements of the Kuomintang, the Japanese, or the puppets. Another possibility is the outbreak, on a much larger scale than heretofore, of unorganized and disruptive farmers revolts. A disturbing phenomenon is the apparent attempt now being made by some of the minority parties to effect a marriage of convenience with the provincial warlords, among the most reactionary and unscrupulous figures in Chinese politics and hardly crusaders for a new democracy.

The hopeful sign is that all of these groups are agreed that the basic problem in China today is political reform toward democracy. This point requires emphasis. It is only through political reform that the restoration of the will to fight, the unification of the country, the elimination of provincial warlordism, the solution of the Communist problem, the institution of economic policies which can avoid collapse, and the emergence of a government actually supported by the people can be achieved. *Democratic reform is the crux of all important Chinese problems, military, economic and political.*

It is clear beyond doubt that China's hope for internal peace and effective unity—certainly in the immediate future (which for the sake of the war must be our prior consideration) and probably in the long-term as well—lies neither with the present Kuomintang nor with the Communists, but in a democratic combination of the liberal elements within the country, including those within the Kuomintang, and the probably large section of the Communists who would be willing, by their own statements and past actions, to collaborate in the resurrection of a united front.

Given the known interest and attitudes of the Chinese people, we can be sure that measures to accomplish the solution of these problems will be undertaken in earnest by a broadly-based government. Such a government—and only such a government—will galvanize China out of its military inertia by restoring national morale through such means as the reduction of the evils of conscription and stopping the maltreatment and starvation of the troops. Such a government—and only such a government—will undertake the economic measures necessary to increase production, establish effective price controls, mobilize national resources, and end corruption, hoarding, speculation and profiteering.

It is of course unrealistic to assume that such a broadly-based democratic government can be established at one stroke, or that it can immediately achieve the accomplishment of these broad objectives. But progress will be made as, and only as, the government moves toward democracy.

II. In the Light of This Developing Crisis, What Should Be the American Attitude Toward China?

It is impossible to predict exactly how far the present disintegration in China can continue without spectacular change in the internal situation and drastic effect on the war against Japan. But we must face the question whether we can afford passively to stand by and allow the process to continue to an almost certainly disastrous collapse, or whether we wish to do what we legitimately and practically can to arrest it. We need to formulate a realistic policy toward China.

A. The Kuomintang and Chiang are acutely conscious of their dependence on us and will be forced to appeal for our support.

We must realize that when the process of disintegration gets out of hand it will be to us that the Kuomintang will turn for financial, political, and military salvation. The awareness of this dependence is the obvious and correct explanation of the Kuomintang's hypersensitivity to American opinion and criticism. The Kuomintang—and particularly the Generalissimo—know that we are the only disinterested, yet powerful ally to whom China can turn.

The appeal will be made to us on many grounds besides the obvious, well-worn, but still effective one of pure sentiment. They have said in the past and will say in the future that they could long ago have made peace with Japan—on what are falsely stated would have been favorable terms. They have claimed and will claim again that their resistance and refusal to compromise with Japan saved Russia, Great Britain and ourselves—ignoring the truth that our own refusal to compromise with Japan to China's disadvantage brought on Pearl Harbor and our involvement before we were ready. They have complained and will continue to complain that they have received less support in the form of materials than any other major ally—forgetting that they have done less fighting, have not used the materials given, and would not have had the ability to use what they asked for. Finally, they have tried and will continue to try to lay the blame on us for their difficulties—distorting the effect of American Army expenditures in China and ignoring the fact that these expenditures are only a minor factor in the whole sorry picture of the mismanagement of the Chinese economy.

But however far-fetched these appeals, our flat refusal of them might have several embarrassing effects.

1) We would probably see China enter a period of internal chaos. Our war effort in this theater would be disrupted, instability in the Far East prolonged, and possible Russian intervention attracted.

2) We would be blamed by large sections of both Chinese and American public opinion for "abandoning" China after having been at least partly responsible for its collapse. (In a measure we would have brought such blame upon ourselves because we have tended to allow ourselves to become identified not merely with China but also with the Kuomintang and its policies. Henceforth it may be the better part of valor to avoid too close identification with the Kuomintang.)

3) By an apparent abandonment of China in its hour of need, we would lose international prestige, especially in the Far East.

On the other hand, if we come to the rescue of the Kuomintang on its own terms, we would be buttressing—but only temporarily—a decadent regime which by its existing composition and program is incapable of solving China's problems. Both China and we ourselves would be gaining only a brief respite from the ultimate day of reckoning.

It is clear, therefore, that it is to our advantage to avoid a situation arising in which we would be presented with a Hobson's choice between two such unpalatable alternatives.

B. The Kuomintang's dependence can give us great influence.

Circumstances are rapidly developing so that the Generalissimo will have to ask for the continuance and increase of our support. Weak as he is, he is in no position—and the weaker he becomes, the less he will be able—to turn down or render nugatory any coordinated and positive policy we may adopt toward China. The cards are all in our favor. Our influence, intelligently used, can be tremendous.

C. There are three general alternatives open to us.

1) We may give up China as hopeless and wash our hands of it altogether.

2) We may continue to give support to the Generalissimo, when and as he asks for it.

3) We may formulate a coordinated and positive policy toward China and take the necessary steps for its implementation.

D. Our choice between these alternatives must be determined by our objectives in China.

The United States, if it so desired and if it had a coherent policy, could play an important and perhaps decisive role in:

1) Stimulating China to an active part in the war in the Far East, thus hastening the defeat of Japan.

2) Staving off economic collapse in China and bringing about basic political and economic reforms, thus enabling China to carry on the war and enhancing the chances of its orderly post-war recovery.

3) Enabling China to emerge from the war as a major and stabilizing factor in post-war East Asia.

4) Winning a permanent and valuable ally in a progressive, independent, and democratic China.

E. We should adopt the third alternative—a coordinated and positive policy. This is clear from an examination of the background of the present situation in China and the proper objectives of our policy there.

The first alternative must be rejected on immediate military grounds—but also for obvious long-range considerations. It would deprive us of valuable air bases and a position on Japan's flank. Its adoption would prolong the war. We cannot afford to wash our hands of China.

The results of the second alternative—which, insofar as we have a China policy, has been the one we have been and are pursuing—speak for themselves. The substantial financial assistance we have given China has been frittered away with negligible if any effect in slowing inflation and retarding economic collapse. The military help we have given has certainly not been used to increase China's war effort against Japan. Our political support has been used for the Kuomintang's own selfish purposes and to bolster its short-sighted and ruinous policies.

The third, therefore, is the only real alternative left to us. Granted the rejection of the first alternative, there is no longer a question of helping and advising China. China itself must request this help and advice. The only question is whether we give this help within a framework which makes sense, or whether we continue to give it in our present disjointed and absent-minded manner. In the past it has sometimes seemed that our right hand did not know what the left was doing. To continue without a coherent and coordinated policy will be dissipating our effort without either China or ourselves deriving any appreciable benefit. It can only continue to create new problems, in addition to those already troubling us, without any compensating advantages beyond those of indolent short-term expediency. But most important is the possibility that this haphazard giving, this serving of short-term expediency, may not be enough to save the situation: even with it, China may continue toward collapse.

F. This positive policy should be political.

The problem confronting us is whether we are to continue as in the past to ignore political considerations of direct military significance, or whether we are to take a leaf out of the Japanese book and invoke even stronger existing political forces in China to achieve our military and long-term political objectives.

We must seek to contribute toward the reversal of the present movement toward collapse and to the rousing of China from its military inactivity. This can be brought about only by an accelerated movement toward democratic political reform within China. Our part must be that of a catalytic agent in this process of China's democratization. It can be carried out by the careful exertion of our influence, which has so far not been consciously and systematically used.

This democratic reform does not necessarily mean the overthrow of the Generalissimo or the Kuomintang. On the contrary—if they have the vision to see it—their position will be improved and the stability of the Central Government increased. The democratic forces already existing in China will be strengthened, the reactionary authoritarian trends in the Kuomintang will be modified, and a multiparty United Front government will probably emerge. It is almost certain that the Generalissimo and the Kuomintang would continue to play a dominant part in such a government.

It goes without saying that this democratization of China must be brought about by, and depend on, forces within the country. It cannot be enforced by us—or by any foreign nation. For us to dictate "democracy" would not only be paradoxical, it would also open us to the charge, which the Japanese and reactionary elements would exploit, of being "imperialistic." Our task therefore is to find means of exerting our political influence in indirect and sometimes unassuming ways and of showing to the Kuomintang and the people of China our benevolent and serious interest in democracy.

The popular desire for democracy in China is already strong. We can be sure that as our attitude becomes clear, and as our desire that China itself should be the prime mover in bringing about reform becomes apparent, steady progress will be made.

Doubts as to the success of such a policy of political persuasion can be allayed by the considerations that:

the Kuomintang has already shown itself vulnerable and sensitive to foreign criticism,

the liberal groups in China welcome foreign criticism and regard it as one of the strongest forces now impelling the Kuomintang toward reform, and

the politically influential groups in China do not number more than a few hundred thousand and can be easily reached.

III. THE IMPLEMENTATION OF THIS POLITICAL POLICY, THOUGH DIFFICULT IN SOME RESPECTS, IS PRACTICAL AND CAN BE CARRIED OUT BY MANY MEANS.

A. Diplomatic finesse will be required in the execution of this policy in such a way as not to offend the strong current of genuine nationalism (as distinguished from the chauvinism of the Kuomintang) which characterizes almost all sections of the Chinese people. There must be a sensitivity to the situation in China and the political changes there so that there can be an appropriate and immediate stiffening or softening of the measures which we undertake. This tact and sensitivity will be required not only of the top policy directing agency but of all other agencies actually implementing that policy and concerned in direct relations with China.

B. There must be effective coordination of the policies and actions of all American Government agencies concerned in these dealings with China.

The present lack of effective cooperation between the various Government agencies—State, War and some of the newer autonomous organizations—detracts from the efficient functioning of each, and weakens American influence when it is most needed.

It must be recognized—and it will be even more the case under the policy proposed—that *all our dealings with, and all our activities in, China have political implication.* Coordination is absolutely essential for the achievement of unity of policy and synchronization of action. Its attainment will require intelligent and forceful direction both in Washington and in Chungking.

The logical person to coordinate activities in Chungking is obviously, because of the broad issues involved, the Ambassador. Similarly the corresponding person in Washington might be the Chief of the China Section of the State Department, who would watch the whole field for the President or a responsible Cabinet member. Positive action, of course, would depend on constant and close consultation, both in Washington and in the field, between the representatives of the State, War, Navy, and Treasury departments and the other agencies operating in China.

C. Since all measures open to us should not be applied simultaneously, there should be careful selection and timing.

Some measures will be simple and immediately useful. Others should be deferred until primary steps have been taken. Still others will be more forceful or direct, and their use will depend on the Kuomintang's recalcitrance to change its ways. We must avoid overplaying or underplaying our hand.

D. Specific measures which might be adopted in the carrying out of this positive policy include the following:

1. *Negative:*

a) Stop our present "mollycoddling" of China:
by restricting lend-lease,
cutting down training of Chinese military cadets,
discontinuing training of the Chinese army,
taking a firmer stand in the financial negotiations, or
stopping the shipment of gold.

Any or all of these restrictive measures can be reversed as the Generalissimo and the Kuomintang become more cooperative in carrying on military operations, using equipment and training supplies, being reasonable on financial questions, or allowing us freedom in such military requirements as establishing contact with the Communist areas.

b) Stop building up the Generalissimo's and the Kuomintang's prestige internationally and in the United States. Such "face" serves only to bolster the regime internally and to harden it in its present policies. Our inclusion of China as one of the "Big Four" served a useful purpose in the early stage of the war and as a counter to Japanese racial propaganda but has now lost its justification.

We make fools of ourselves by such actions as the attention given to the meaningless utterances of Chu Hsueh-fan as a spokesman of Chinese labor, and the prominence accorded to China in the International Labor Office Conference. Our tendency toward overlavish praise is regarded by the Chinese as a sign of either stupidity or weakness.

Abandonment of glib generalities for hard-headed realism in our attitude toward China will be quickly understood—without the resentment that would probably be felt against the British. We can make it clear that praise will be given when praise is due.

c) Stop making unconditional and grandiose promises of help along such lines as UNRRA, post-war economic aid, and political support. We can make it clear without having to be very explicit that we stand ready to help China when China shows itself deserving. This ties into the more positive phase of publicity and propaganda to the effect, for instance, that American post-war economic aid will not be extended to build up monopolistic enterprise or support the landlord-gentry class but in the interests of a democratic people.

d) Discontinue our present active collaboration with Chinese secret police organizations, which support the forces of reaction and stand for the opposite of our American democratic aims and ideals. This collaboration, which results in the effective strengthening of a Gestapo-like organization, is becoming increasingly known in China. It confuses and disillusions Chinese liberals, who look to us as their hope, and it weakens our position with the Kuomintang leaders in pressuring for democratic reform.

2. *Positive:*

a) High Government officials in conversations with Chinese leaders in Washington and in China can make known our interest in democracy and unity in China and our dissatisfaction with present Kuomintang military, financial, and other policies. Such suggestions will bear great weight if they come from the President, and advantage can be taken of opportunities such as the visits of Vice President Wallace to China and H. H. Kung to the United States. A progressive stage can be questions or statements by members of Congress regarding affairs in China.

b) We should take up the repeated—but usually insincere—requests of the Kuomintang for advice. If advisers are asked for, we should see that they are provided, that good men are selected, and that they get all possible aid and support from us. While the Kuomintang will be reluctant to accept the advice we may give, its mere reiteration will have some effect.

c) We should seek to extend our influence on Chinese opinion by every practical means available.

The Office of War Information should go beyond its present function of reporting American war news to pointing up the values of democracy as a permanent political system and as an aid in the waging of war against totalitarianism. We should attempt to increase the dissemination in China, by radio or other direct means, of constructive American criticism. This should include recognition and implied encouragement to liberal and progressive forces within China. Care should be taken to keep this criticism on a helpful, constructive and objective plane, and to avoid derogatory attacks which may injure Chinese nationalistic sensitivities. To do this work, there may have to be some expansion of the OWI in China and of our propaganda directed toward this country.

A second line is the active expansion of our cultural relations program. The present diversion—by Kuomintang wishes—to technical subjects should be rectified and greater emphasis laid on social sciences, cultural and practical political subjects such as American government administration. We should increase our aid and support to intellectuals in China by the many means already explored, such as aid to research in China, translation of articles, and opportunities for study or lecturing in the United States.

Other, more indirect lines, are the expansion of our American Foreign Service representation in China to new localities (since each office is in some measure a center of American influence and contact with Chinese liberals and returned students from the United States); and the careful indoctrination of the American Army personnel in China to create, by example and their attitude toward Chinese, favorable impressions of America and the things that America stands for. Where contact between American and Chinese military personnel has been close, as in Burma, the result has apparently been a democratizing influence.

d) We should assist the education of public opinion in the United States toward a realistic but constructively sympathetic attitude toward China. The most obvious means would be making background information available, in an unofficial way, to responsible political commentators, writers and research workers. Without action on our part, their writings will become known to Chinese Government circles and from them to other politically minded groups. We should, however, coordinate this with the activity described in the section above to promote dissemination in China.

e) We should maintain friendly relations with the liberal elements in the Kuomintang, the minor parties, and the Communists. This can—and should for its maximum effect—be done in an open, aboveboard manner. The recognition which it implies will be quickly understood by the Chinese.

Further steps in this direction could be publicity to liberals, such as distinguished intellectuals. When possible they may be included in consideration for special honors or awards, given recognition by being asked to participate in international commissions or other bodies, and invited to travel or lecture in the United States. A very effective action of this type would be an invitation to Madame Sun Yat-sen from the White House.

We should select men of known liberal views to represent us in OWI, cultural relations, and other lines of work in China.

f) We should continue to show an interest in the Chinese Communists. This includes contact with the Communist representatives in Chungking, publicity on the blockade and the situation between the two parties, and continued pressure for the dispatch of observers to North China. At the same time we should stress the importance of North China militarily—for intelligence regarding Japanese battle order, Japanese air strength, weather reporting, bombing data and damage assessment, and air crew evasion and rescue work. We should consider the eventual advance of active operations against the Japanese to North China, and the question of assistance to or cooperation with Communist and guerrilla forces. If our reasonable requests based on urgent military grounds do not receive a favorable response, we should send our military observers anyway.

g) We should consider the training and equipping of provincial or other armies in China in cases where we can be satisfied that they will fight the Japanese.

h) We should continue to press—and if necessary insist—on getting American observers to the actual fighting fronts. We should urge, and when possible assist, the improvement of the condition of the Chinese soldier, especially his treatment, clothing, feeding, and medical care.

i) We should publicize statements by responsible government officials indicating our interest in Chinese unity and our attitude toward such questions as the use of American lend-lease supplies by the Kuomintang in a civil war. It is interesting, for instance, that Under-Secretary Welles' letter to Browder regarding American interest in Chinese unity was considered so important by the Kuomintang that publication in China was prohibited.

This program is, of course, far from complete. Other measures will occur to the policy agency and will suggest themselves as the situation in China develops.

E. Most of these measures can be applied progressively.

This is true, for instance, of the various negative actions suggested, and of the conversations, statements, and other lines of endeavor to influence public opinion in China. A planned activity of encouragement and attention to liberals, Minor Party leaders, and the Communists can advance naturally from stage to stage.

F. The program suggested contains little that is not already being done in an uncoordinated and only partially effective manner.

What is needed chiefly is an integration, systematic motivation, and planned expansion of activities in which we are already, perhaps in some cases unconsciously, engaged. We *do*, for instance, try to maintain contact with liberal groups; we *have* expressed the desire to send observers to the Communist area; we *have* a weak cultural relations program; and the OWI *has* made some attempts to propagandize American democratic ideals.

G. The program constitutes only very modified and indirect intervention in Chinese affairs.

It must be admitted that some of the measures proposed would involve taking more than normal interest in the affairs of another sovereign nation. But they do not go so far as to infringe on Chinese sovereignty. If we choose to make lend-lease conditional on a better war effort by China, it is also China's freedom to refuse to accept it on those conditions. We do not go nearly as far as imperialistic countries have often done in the past. We obviously do not, for instance, suggest active assistance or subsidizing of rival parties to the Kuomintang—as the Russians did in the case of the Communists.

Furthermore, the Chinese Government would find it difficult to object. The Chinese have abused their freedom to propagandize in the United States by the statements and writings of such men as Lin Yu-tang. They have also, and through Lin Yu-tang, who carries an official passport as a representative of the Chinese Government, engaged in "cultural relations" work. They have freely criticized American policies and American leaders. And they have attempted to dabble in American politics—through Madame Chiang, Luce, Willkie, and Republican congressmen. They have had, and will continue to have, freedom to try to influence public opinion in the United States in the same way that we will try to do it in China.

Bibliography

A number of brief or informal titles have been used in the text and footnotes. They may be identified by reference to the numbered items of the Bibliography as noted below.

* * *

1) Barrett, David D. *Dixie Mission: The United States Army Observer Group in Yenan 1944.* Berkeley: Center for Chinese Studies, 1970. 92 pp.

2) Chang, Carsun. *The Third Force in China.* New York: Bookman Associates, 1952. 345 pp.

3) Cohen, Warren I. "Who Fought the Japanese in Hunan? Some Views of China's War Effort." *Journal of Asian Studies* 18:1 (November 1967), pp. 111–115.

4) Compton, Boyd. *Mao's China: Party Reform Documents, 1942–44.* Seattle: University of Washington Press, 1952. 278 pp.

5) Feis, Herbert. *The China Tangle.* Princeton: Princeton University Press, 1953. 445 pp.

6) Forman, Harrison. *Report From Red China.* New York: Henry Holt, 1945. 250 pp.

7) Isaacs, Harold. *The Tragedy of the Chinese Revolution.* London: Sacker and Warburg, 1938. 501 pp.

8) Johnson, Chalmers A. *Peasant Nationalism and Communist Power: The Emergence of Revolutionary China, 1937–1945.* Stanford: Stanford University Press, 1962. 256 pp.

9) Kerr, George H. *Formosa Betrayed.* Boston: Houghton, Mifflin, 1965. 514 pp.

10) Latham, Earl. *The Communist Controversy in Washington: From the New Deal to McCarthy.* Cambridge: Harvard University Press, 1966. 446 pp.

11) Leahy, William D. *I Was There.* New York: McGraw-Hill, 1950. 527 pp.

12) Liu, F. F. *A Military History of Modern China.* Princeton: Princeton University Press, 1956. 312 pp.

13) Loh, Pichon P. Y. *The Kuomintang Debacle of 1949: Conquest or Collapse?* Boston: Heath, 1965. 114 pp.

14) Lohbeck, Don. *Patrick J. Hurley.* Chicago: Regnery, 1956. 513 pp.

15) Miles, Milton E. *A Different Kind of War.* New York: Doubleday, 1967. 629 pp.

16) Peck, Graham. *Two Kinds of Time.* Boston: Houghton, Mifflin, 1950. 725 pp.

17) Romanus, Charles F., and Sunderland, Riley. *Stilwell's Mission to China.* Washington: Department of the Army, Historical Division, 1953, 441 pp.

18) ———. *Stilwell's Command Problems.* Washington: Department of the Army, Historical Division, 1956. 518 pp.

19) ———. *Time Runs Out in CBI.* Washington: Department of the Army, Historical Division, 1959. 428 pp.

20) Rosinger, Lawrence K. "The White Paper in Brief." *Far Eastern Survey* 18:18 (September 7, 1949), pp. 205–208.

21) Salisbury, Harrison E. "Image and Reality in Indochina." *Foreign Affairs* 49:3 (April 1971), pp. 381–394.

22) Service, John S. "Pertinent Excerpts." *Foreign Service Journal,* October 1951, p. 22.

23) Snow, Edgar. *Red Star Over China.* London: Victor Gollancz, 1937. 464 pp.

24) ———. *Journey to the Beginning.* New York: Random House, 1958. 434 pp.

25) Tsou, Tang. *America's Failure in China, 1941–50.* Chicago: University of Chicago Press, 1963. 614 pp.

26) Tuchman, Barbara. *Stilwell and the American Experience in China, 1911–1945.* New York: Macmillan Co., 1971. 621 pp.

27) U.S. Congress. Senate. Committee on Armed Services and Committee on Foreign Relations. *Military Situation in the Far East.* Hearings. 82d Cong., 1st sess. Washington: Government Printing Office, 1951. 5 vols. 3691 pp.

28) U.S. Congress. Senate. Committee on Foreign Relations. *Investigation of Far Eastern Policy.* 79th Cong., 1st sess. Mimeograph transcript: December 5, 6, 7 and 10, 1945.

29) ———. *State Department Employee Loyalty Investigation.* Hearings before a subcommittee of the Committee on Foreign Relations pursuant to S. Res. 231. 81st Cong., 2d sess. Washington: Government Printing Office, 1950. 2 vols. 2509 pp.

30) ———. *State Department Employee Loyalty Investigation.* Report of the Committee on Foreign Relations pursuant to S. Res. 231.

81st Cong., 2d sess. Report no. 2108. Washington: Government Printing Office, 1950. 347 pp.

31) U.S. Congress. Senate. Committee on the Judiciary. Internal Security Subcommittee. *Institute of Pacific Relations.* Hearings. 82d Cong., 2d sess. Washington: Government Printing Office, 1951, 1952. 15 parts. 5964 pp.

32) ———. *The Amerasia Papers: A Clue to the Catastrophe of China.* [Edited and Introduction by Anthony Kubek.] 91st Cong., 1st sess. Washington: Government Printing Office, 1970. 2 vols. 1819 pp.

33) U.S. Department of State. *United States Relations with China with Special Reference to the Period 1944–1949.* Washington: Government Printing Office, 1949. 1079 pp. Reprinted under title *The China White Paper.* Introduction by Lyman P. Van Slyke. Index. Stanford: Stanford University Press, 1967.

34) ———. *Foreign Relations of the United States, 1945, The Conferences at Malta and Yalta.* Washington: Government Printing Office, 1955. 1032 pp.

35) ———. *Foreign Relations of the United States, 1943, China.* Washington: Government Printing Office, 1957. 908 pp.

36) ———. *Foreign Relations of the United States, 1944, vol. 6, China.* Washington: Government Printing Office, 1967. 1206 pp.

37) ———. *Foreign Relations of the United States, 1945, vol. 7, The Far East, China.* Washington: Government Printing Office, 1969. 1506 pp.

38) Van Slyke, Lyman P., ed. *The Chinese Communist Movement: A Report of the United States War Department, July 1945.* Stanford: Stanford University Press, 1968. 274 pp.

39) Wedemeyer, Albert C. *Wedemeyer Reports!* New York: Henry Holt, 1958. 497 pp.

40) White, Theodore H., and Jacoby, Annalee. *Thunder Out of China.* New York: William Sloane Associates, 1946. 331 pp.

RECENT PUBLICATIONS OF THE
CENTER FOR CHINESE STUDIES

CHINA RESEARCH MONOGRAPHS

(available from the Center for Chinese Studies, 2168 Shattuck Avenue, Berkeley, California 94704):

1. Townsend, James R. *The Revolutionization of Chinese Youth: A Study of Chung-Kuo Ch'ing-Nien.* 1967. ($2.50)

2. Baum, Richard and Teiwes, Frederick C. *Ssu-Ch'ing: The Socialist Education Movement of 1962–1966.* 1968. ($4.00)

3. Rinden, Robert and Witke, Roxane. *The Red Flag Waves: A Guide to the Hung-ch'i p'iao-p'iao Collection.* 1968. ($4.00)

4. Mehnert, Klaus. *Peking and the New Left: At Home and Abroad.* 1969. ($4.00)

5. Yu, George T. *China and Tanzania: A Study in Cooperative Interaction.* 1970. ($4.00)

6. Barrett, David D. *Dixie Mission: The United States Army Observer Group in Yenan, 1944.* 1970. ($4.00)

STUDIES IN CHINESE COMMUNIST TERMINOLOGY

(available from the Center for Chinese Studies):

*11. The Commune in Retreat as Evidenced in Terminology and Semantics, by T. A. Hsia.

*12. The Great Proletarian Cultural Revolution, by H. C. Chuang.

13. The Little Red Book and Current Chinese Language, by H. C. Chuang. ($1.50)

14. Evening Chats at Yenshan, Or, The Case of Teng T'o, by H. C. Chuang. ($1.00)

* Out of print: These and earlier issues may be purchased on microfilm or xerox from University Microfilms, Inc., 313 North First Street, Ann Arbor, Michigan 48106. Please write directly.

(For other recent publications
sponsored by the Center for
Chinese Studies please see next page.)

RECENT PUBLICATIONS SPONSORED BY THE CENTER FOR CHINESE STUDIES

CALIFORNIA BOOKS ON MODERN CHINA

(Published by and available from the University of California Press):

Schurmann, Franz. *Ideology and Organization in Communist China.* Revised ed. 1968. (also in paperback)

Wakeman, Frederic, Jr. *Strangers at the Gate: Social Disorder in South China, 1839–1861.* 1966.

Townsend, James R. *Political Participation in Communist China.* 1967. (also in paperback)

Potter, Jack M. *Capitalism and the Chinese Peasant.* 1968.

Schiffrin, Harold Z. *Sun Yat-sen and the Origins of the Chinese Revolution.* 1968. (also in paperback)

Van Ness, Peter. *Revolution and Chinese Foreign Policy: Peking's Support for Wars of National Liberation.* 1970.

Larkin, Bruce D. *China and Africa, 1949–1970: The Foreign Policy of the People's Republic.* 1971.

CENTER LANGUAGE PUBLICATIONS (by University of California Press):

Chi, Wen-shun, *Reading in Chinese Communist Documents.* 1963.

————, *Readings in Chinese Communist Ideology.* 1968.

————, *Readings in the Chinese Communist Cultural Revolution.* 1971.

(For other recent publications of the Center for Chinese Studies please see page 219.)

PB-37516

5-25